The Consumer Insights Handbook

The Consumer Insights Handbook

Unlocking Audience Research Methods

Danielle Sarver Coombs
Kent State University

ROWMAN & LITTLEFIELD
Lanham • Boulder • New York • London

Executive Editor: Natalie Mandziuk
Assistant Editor: Sylvia Landis
Sales and Marketing Inquiries: textbooks@rowman.com

Credits and acknowledgments for material borrowed from other sources, and reproduced with permission, appear on the appropriate page within the text.

Published by Rowman & Littlefield
An imprint of The Rowman & Littlefield Publishing Group, Inc.
4501 Forbes Boulevard, Suite 200, Lanham, Maryland 20706
www.rowman.com

86-90 Paul Street, London EC2A 4NE, United Kingdom

British Library Cataloguing in Publication Information Available

Library of Congress Cataloging-in-Publication Data

Names: Coombs, Danielle Sarver, author.
Title: The consumer insights handbook : unlocking audience research methods / Danielle Sarver Coombs.
Description: Lanham : Rowman & Littlefield, [2022] | Includes bibliographical references and index. | Summary: "This practical introduction to audience research shows students that conducting consumer research is not only a necessary skill for any future media professional but that it can also be a creative and fun experience. Students learn how to plan for and complete a research projects from the initial RFP to the final presentation of findings"— Provided by publisher.
Identifiers: LCCN 2021010688 (print) | LCCN 2021010689 (ebook) | ISBN 9781538145517 (cloth ; alk. paper) | ISBN 9781538145524 (paperback ; alk. paper) | ISBN 9781538145531 (epub)
Subjects: LCSH: Consumers—Research. | Consumer behavior. | Marketing research.
Classification: LCC HF5415.32 .C665 2022 (print) | LCC HF5415.32 (ebook) | DDC 658.8/34—dc23
LC record available at https://lccn.loc.gov/2021010688
LC ebook record available at https://lccn.loc.gov/2021010689

This book is dedicated to Linda J. Lawrie

You convinced me I'd be a good researcher
You read every word of this book
And you've been my best friend for most of my life.

Thank you.

And to all of my past, present, and future consumer insights research students:
Thank you for filling my heart with joy (and laughing at my jokes).
I hope the wonder of discovery keeps inspiring you throughout your lives.

Contents

List of Figures and Tables   xiii

Preface   xvii

Acknowledgments   xix

1   Introduction and Overview   1
  What Is Research?   2
    How We See the World   3
      Academic versus Applied Research   3
    Planning for Research Design   4
      Who Is Your Target Audience? And How Many People Do You Need?   5
      What Do You Need to Learn? And How Long Do You Have?   6
      What Does This Look Like?   6
  Working on Teams   7
  How to Use This Book   8
  Key Terms   10

2   Working with Clients   13
  General Best Practices   14
    Looking Good (and by Good, I Mean Professional)   14
    Confidence Is Key; So Is Humility   14
  Getting Work Started   16
    Responding to RFPs   16
      What Does an RFP Look Like?   16
      What Do You Do Once You Get the RFP?   18
    Pitching New Business   18
    Understanding and Assessing Needs   19
    Business Objectives and Research Objectives   20
    Developing Actionable Research Questions   20
      Remain Open to Possibility   21
      Stay Focused on the Big Picture   21

    Scope Appropriately   21
    Establishing and Working with Budgets   22
  Best Practices and Key Takeaways   24
  Key Terms   25

3 Secondary Research and Analysis   27
  Conducting Secondary Research   28
    What Are You Looking For?   28
  Secondary Research Sources   29
    Nonpublic Sources   30
      Internal Client Materials   30
      Academic Resources   30
      Proprietary Resources   31
      Centralized Information and Data   31
      Trend Analysis   32
      Audience/Market Analytics   32
    Public Sources   32
      Government Resources   33
      Other Publicly Available Datasets and Reports 35
      Media Coverage and Content   36
  Best Practices and Key Takeaways   37
  Notes   37
  Key Terms   38

4 Applied Research Ethics   39
  Why This Matters   40
  Key Ethical Principles   42
  Applied Research Ethics   44
    Gaining Consent   45
    Anonymity versus Confidentiality   47
    Privacy Laws and Legal Implications   48
    Conducting Research Online   49
    Accurate Representation of Ideas, or How to Avoid Plagiarism 49
  Best Practices and Key Takeaways   50
  Notes   50
  Key Terms   52

5 Qualitative Research Design and Considerations   53
  Why Do Qualitative Research?   54
    Benefits and Limitations   54
      Benefits   54
      Limitations   55
  Qualitative Methods   56
    Interviews   56
    Ethnographies   57
    Participant Observation   59
    Focus Groups   60
    Online Communities   61
  Ensuring Rigor   62

Ways to Ensure Rigor 62
Best Practices and Key Takeaways 63
Key Terms 64

6 Qualitative Data Collection 65
Writing an Effective Instrument 66
Guide Structure 67
Tips for Writing 68
General Best Practices 69
Record, Record, Record 70
Data Collection: In the Field 71
Conducting Interviews 72
Conducting Ethnographies 73
Conducting Focus Groups 74
Starting the Group 74
Maintaining Good Discussion 76
Managing Difficult Participants 77
Wrapping Up 79
Conducting Qualitative Research Online 79
Best Practices and Key Takeaways 80
Key Terms 82

7 Using Creative Exercises for Deeper Insights 83
General Best Practices 84
Generating Good Data 84
Process 86
"Selling" Creative Exercises 86
Types of Creative Exercises 87
Collage 87
Drawings and Storytelling 88
Bring Brands to Life 89
Fill-in-the-Blank 89
"Magic Wand" 90
Creating Lists and Organizing Data 91
Card Sorts 92
Marketing Exec 92
Best Practices and Key Takeaways 93
Key Terms 94

8 Qualitative Data Analysis and Reporting 95
General Best Practices: During Fielding 96
General Best Practices: Post-Collection Data Analysis 97
In the Debrief 98
Debrief Roles 99
Physical Space 100
Debriefing 100
Topline Research Reports 101
Best Practices and Key Takeaways 103
Key Terms 104

9 Quantitative Research Design and Considerations   105
 Why Do Quantitative Research?   106
  Benefits   107
  Limitations   108
 Basic Principles and Characteristics   109
  Correlation Is Not Causation   109
  Standardization   110
  Hypotheses versus Research Questions   110
 Sampling and Samples   111
  Probability Sampling   112
   Cluster Sampling   114
  Nonprobability Sampling   114
 Error, Margin of Error, and Confidence Level   116
  Margin of Error and Confidence Level   116
 Quantitative Research for Academics   119
 Best Practices and Key Takeaways   120
 Key Terms   121

10 Quantitative Data Collection   123
 General Best Practices   124
 Preparing to Write Your Survey   125
 Structuring Your Survey   126
  Screener   126
  The Body   128
  Demographics   130
  Editing Your Survey   133
 Writing Good Questions   133
  Different Types of Questions   134
  Basic Rules for Writing Questions   137
  Writing Good Responses   139
 Trend Studies   140
 Best Practices and Key Takeaways   140
 Note   140
 Key Terms   141

11 Quantitative Data Analysis and Reporting   143
 Good Preparation, Good Data   144
 Ensuring Data Accuracy   144
  Descriptive Statistics   145
  Weighting   147
  Checking on What Happens in the "Black Box"   147
 Statistical Models for the Non-Statistician   148
  Conjoint Analysis   149
  Maximum-Difference Scaling (MaxDiff)   150
  Discrete Choice Modeling   150
  Factor Analysis   151
  Cluster Analysis   152
 Data Reports and Banners   153

Debriefing and Data Analysis   155
  Preparing for Your Debrief   156
  Debriefing   156
Reporting Quantitative Research   157
Best Practices and Key Takeaways   158
Notes   159
Key Terms   160

12 Writing Your Report   161
Goal and Purpose   162
Develop Your "Elevator Pitch"   163
Organizing Your Thoughts   164
  Preparing Your Outline   164
  Integrate and Synthesize Insights into Themes   165
  Plan Your Signposting   166
  Bake in Transitions   166
  Flesh Out Your Recommendations   166
  Always Come Back to Your Story   167
Telling a Story   167
  Keep the Story Moving   168
  Share Data Strategically   169
  Focus on Your Flow   169
  Stay Focused   170
Report Sections   170
Report Formats   171
Best Practices and Key Takeaways   173
Note   173
Key Terms   174

13 Developing (and Designing) Your Deliverable   175
Designing Your Deliverable   176
  Make Sure Your Story Is Clear   176
    Text-Based Programs   176
    Design Programs   177
  Make Signposts Clear   178
    Headlines   178
    Consistency   179
  Metaphors Matter   179
Deliverable Formats   180
Design Basics (Very, Very Basics)   183
  Designing Your Deliverable   183
    Readability   184
    Hierarchy   184
    Consistency   185
    Effective Use of Color and Contrast   186
Presenting Data   188
  Forms of Data Presentation   188
    Charts and Graphs   188

        Axis Mapping   189
        Qualitative Quotes   190
            Creative Exercises   191
        Guidelines for Presenting Data   191
    Best Practices and Key Takeaways   192
    Notes   192
    Key Terms   193

14 The Client Presentation   195
    Goal and Purpose   196
    Preparation   197
        Know Your Audience   197
        Know Your Material   198
        Internalizing   198
    During the Presentation   199
    Wrapping Up the Project   200
        Back in the Office   200
    Best Practices and Key Takeaways   201
    Final Thoughts   201

Glossary   203

References   209

Index   211

About the Author   221

Thank you for your order, Matthew McElwain!

Thank you for shopping with Half Price Books! Please contact Support@hpb.com. if you have any questions, comments or concerns about your order (687401157)

Visit our stores to sell your books, music, movies games for cash.

Half Price Books
1835 Forms Drive
Carrollton, TX 75006
OFS OrderID   30109494

SKU	ISBN/UPC	Title & Author/Artist	Shelf ID	Qty	OrderSKU
S390908854	9781538145524	The Consumer Insights Handbook: Unlocking Coombs, Danielle	DB 20.15.3	1	

ORDER# **687401157**
Abebooks

SHIPPED STANDARD TO:
Matthew McElwain
594 Prestwick Path
Painesville OH 44077
matthew.mcelwain@gmail.com

List of Figures and Tables

FIGURES

Figure 1.1   Consumer insights mantra   2
Figure 1.2   Consumer insights researchers use every available surface during
              analysis in order to translate their data into insights and insights into
              meaningful recommendations   3
Figure 2.1   Example of a request for proposal (RFP)   17
Figure 2.2   Example of a project fee proposal showing a range of deliverables/
              task package options   24
Figure 3.1   The WARC website offers a robust explanation of what the company
              does and the benefits it offers customers   32
Figure 3.2   The Pew Research Center is a leading public research organization,
              covering a range of topics and issues in the United States   35
Figure 3.3   A Google Trends graph showing interest in the Cleveland Browns and
              Pittsburgh Steelers over a one-year period   36
Figure 4.1   The Belmont Report established the ethical principles we follow as
              research practitioners   43
Figure 4.2   Example of an informed consent form used in applied research   46
Figure 4.3   The Georgetown Law Library is an outstanding resource for
              researching laws related to privacy and information   48
Figure 5.1   During an in-home ethnography on moms and fitness, a participant
              talks to the researcher through her collection of finishing medals   58
Figure 5.2   During an in situ ethnography on moms and fitness, a participant talks
              through the appeal of a display window at the starting point for a
              number of rigorous hikes   59
Figure 5.3   During her first appearance as host on *Saturday Night Live*, a
              bewigged Melissa McCarthy played an overeager focus group
              participant as part of a now-classic sketch   60
Figure 6.1   Example of a focus group timetable and cover sheet   67
Figure 6.2   Moderators will use a whiteboard to record ideas and information
              from participants   71
Figure 6.3   Online focus groups are increasingly common in today's research
              environment   80

Figure 7.1   An image from the OK Go video for "Here It Goes Again," used as
              part of a collage exercise   84

Figure 7.2   Example of collage created based on the prompt "Imagine you've
              now succeeded in [goal]. What would your life look like?"   88

Figure 7.3   Example of a "fill-in-the-blank" love letter exercise   90

Figure 7.4   Example of a "plus/minus list" created to generate ideas around how
              to create a successful group culture   92

Figure 7.5   Focus group members work together to develop ideas and shared
              understandings   93

Figure 9.1   Example of a sample size calculator used to determine the sample
              size needed for the approximate population of the United States with
              95 percent confidence and a +/−4 percent margin of error   118

Figure 9.2   Example of a sample size calculator used to determine the sample
              size needed for a much smaller population (330,000) with 95 percent
              confidence and a +/−4 percent margin of error   118

Figure 10.1   Example of a survey screener   127

Figure 10.2   In this example of a screener, the question is written to measure
              frequency of viewership for the client without letting the participant
              know which channel is the client   128

Figure 10.3   An example of survey questions written to measure the association of
              characteristics with certain networks   130

Figure 10.4   Example of how demographics can be asked in a client-driven survey 131

Figure 10.5   The U.S. Census's race question used in the 2020 Census   133

Figure 10.6   Example of a matrix question   135

Figure 10.7   Example of a rank-order question   135

Figure 10.8   Example of a rating slider   136

Figure 10.9   Example of a constant-sum question   136

Figure 10.10 Example of a semantic differential scale   137

Figure 11.1   Example of a bell curve   146

Figure 11.2   Example of a banner-processing request, used to request specific data
              reports ("banners") from the data processing team   154

Figure 11.3   Example of how data categories would be weighted after data
              collection to better represent the characteristics of the target population 154

Figure 11.4   Example of the types of custom tables that can be requested to aid in
              data analysis   155

Figure 12.1   Example of a methods slide in a PowerPoint deck   165

Figure 12.2   From the outline through to the final presentation, remember that
              recommendations must be relevant and actionable   167

Figure 12.3   As this slide shows, the headline makes clear the theme to advance
              the story; the remainder of the slide supports that headline   168

Figure 12.4   The secondary sources covered in chapter 3 often offer white papers
              for free downloads on their sites, which provide fabulous examples
              for what these can (and should) look like   169

Figure 12.5   Companies and organizations are often incentivized to offer white
              papers for free download because they can collect contact information
              for future customer leads   172

Figure 13.1   Example of a text box in Word to summarize the story   177

Figure 13.2   When properly utilized, visually oriented programs like PowerPoint
              provide a powerful platform for creating compelling and effective
              presentations   177
Figure 13.3   A good headline communicates the main theme or insight; the body
              of the slide includes an illustrative data point   178
Figure 13.4   Example of an infographic   181
Figure 13.5   Example of a dashboard used to manage a range of relevant data   182
Figure 13.6   Example of the effective use of white space in a presentation   185
Figure 13.7   As these two websites show, color can be used as cues for who the
              target audience is   186
Figure 13.8   Color contrast chart by Canva.com   187
Figure 13.9   This slide shows a range of data visualization approaches, including
              bar charts and pie charts   188
Figure 13.10 As this slide shows, relevant axes can be used to differentiate among
              competitive brands on key criteria   189
Figure 13.11 Examples of qualitative data presentation in a PowerPoint deck   190

TABLES

Table 9.1   Stratified Random Sample (One Variable)   113
Table 9.2   Stratified Random Sample (Two Variables)   113
Table 9.3   Proportionate Stratified Sample   114
Table 11.1   Frequency Distributions   145
Table 11.2   Maximum-Difference Scaling (MaxDiff)   150

Preface

I know my students well enough to acknowledge that many of you will not read this preface. I get it. These usually are quite dry and boring, and I make no promises that this one will be any different. But! For those of you who *do* want a little extra insight and background about how this book was created: This is for you.

After working in and teaching consumer insights research for the better part of two decades, I finally decided it was time to craft my dream textbook—the one I always wished I had. To make sure this text includes the best possible information, I interviewed experts and professionals in consumer insights generally as well as specialists working in relevant areas (ethics, quant analysis, research design, etc.). These interviews, combined with my own personal experiences as a researcher, are the foundation for the concepts and techniques included in this volume. Once written, each chapter was reviewed by a team of consumer insights researchers and academics to ensure all material contained was comprehensive, accurate, and representative of industry best practices. While this is not exhaustive—all companies and clients have their own ways of doing things—the strategies and techniques included here will give you an excellent foundation for understanding both the "hows" and the "whys" of consumer insights research (with a good bit of "why does this matter" thrown in as well!). And while this volume has been thoroughly vetted by both general and specialty experts, I am 100 percent sure mistakes have wormed their way through. Those are all on me.

Finally, when you are reading this text, I hope my serious love of this work comes through and inspires you to give consumer insights research a try. Being able to better understand and connect with people is one of the great joys of life, and what you learn in here will help you do that well. Enjoy!

Acknowledgments

Pulling together a textbook on something like consumer insights research methods requires the time and investment of way more people than I had ever anticipated when I started this endeavor. Enormous barrels of thanks go to the troopers who read, commented, critiqued, fact checked, occasionally tried to edit out my hilarious jokes (cough Linda cough), and offered their own experiences and examples to really make this book sing. Stephanie Danes Smith, David Lawson, Linda Lawrie (Dunbar), thank you for reading every chapter and offering your feedback, suggestions, and commentary. This book is much stronger due to your intellectual generosity. Evan Bailey, Wendy Wardell, Cheryl Ann Lambert, Jan Leach, Mark Goodman, Norman Mallard, Kathryn Coduto, Mark Turner, and all others: Thank you for helping me make this textbook real. I am so grateful for your time, efforts, and friendship.

This book collects the thinking and recommendations of a wide range of consumer insights researchers, and I could not have done this without their insights and kindness. Thank you to all, particularly Tracey Jewell Gibb and Elizabeth Falke. I'm also grateful to the team at Rowman & Littlefield for their support during this process: Elizabeth Swayze, Natalie Mandziuk, and Sylvia Landis. And to my graduate assistants who were involved in this process from the original proposal research to the final push—David Cassilo, Jake Kucek, and Harrison LeJeune—thank you!

My time as a professional consumer insights researcher was incredible, in large part because of the ridiculously amazing team I got to work with back in my day. You all blew me away with your intelligence, kindness, senses of humor, mad karaoke skills, and outrageous dance moves, and I am so grateful to have been part of your team. Particular thanks to those who helped build this book: Rachel Cooper, Sarah Chumsky, Sarah Gardiner, Sarah Huffman, Erica Rutt, Amelia Sandell, Boaz Mourad, Stacey Matthias, and Supriya Sanyal. Thank you then, now, and always!

As always, I must acknowledge that I am indescribably grateful (#blessed) to have the most incredible support network around. To my friends and family, I love you and am grateful for you every single day. Thank you. And especially to my parents, Bill and Pat Sarver, for nagging me when needed; to my ever-patient husband, Lindsey, for dealing with my penchant for procrastination; to my future PA and always-cheerleader/boss, Heather Seifert, for subtle encouragement and gentle reminders, often in GIF form; and *especially* to my two darling girls, Genevieve and Avie. You are the best part of my life, and I love you with all my heart.

Finally, to all of the students I have taught over the years: This book exists because you made me want to create something worthy of you. Your hard work, trust, dedication, willingness to be vulnerable and uncomfortable as you learned new things, and patience with my inability to grade in a timely fashion have meant more to me than you could ever imagine. I am so lucky to have had the two greatest jobs in the world, but my students win out every time—I still can't believe I get to do this every day. Thank you.

1

Introduction and Overview

You're sitting at home, trying to work on an assignment while you listen to Spotify. Suddenly, an advertisement comes on for Doritos, your favorite snack. This ad speaks to you—it's funny, irreverent, and just a little bit outrageous. You're now paying attention. The ad breaks through the clutter. Despite the fact it might have been the third or fourth—or tenth or twentieth—commercial to play during your listening period, this particular one managed to grab your attention and get you to listen. It worked for you. The ad did its job.

The question is: Why? What made this particular advertisement the one that could get you to stop and listen? What made it appeal to you, a busy listener who was in the middle of doing other things? Sure, maybe some of it was circumstantial—you were starting to feel a little hungry, or maybe you were getting bored and food sounded like a good distraction. But ultimately, there was something about that particular advertisement that caught your ear and then kept you listening. Most likely, that was the result of creative thinking directed by sophisticated consumer insights research. As we see in figure 1.1, rather than simply presenting data and results, consumer insights research is focused **on translating data into insight** and **insight into meaningful recommendations**. The brand gets you, so you get the brand.

By focusing on **insight**—a deeper, clearer understanding that transcends individual data points—businesses are better prepared to reach their customers with compelling, engaging messages and content that will break through the clutter.

While we often default to thinking of audience research—or, more specifically, consumer insights-based research—as applying almost exclusively to strategic communications like the example shared above, this type of research isn't limited to advertising and public relations. Movie producers use consumer insights at every phase of the production process, from gauging the appeal of concepts and early scenes to evaluating the final product. Television networks test actors, hosts, on-camera journalists, and their overall brand positioning to see who resonates with audiences and which are the right fit for their brand. Music companies conduct research on everything from a new artist's look and style to an established musician's efforts to expand their genre. It is no exaggeration to say consumer insights research is conducted in every single field and discipline in media and mass communication. Everything we read, watch, and listen to probably was tested to maximize impact and increase audience reception and engagement. Doing this well can make the difference between a wild success and abject failure—or, perhaps equally frustrating, making no impact at all.

> **Consumer insights research
> is focused on
> translating <u>data</u> into <u>insight</u>
> and insight into
> <u>meaningful recommendations</u>**

Figure 1.1   Consumer insights mantra. (Created by Danielle Sarver Coombs, 2021)

This book is designed to help you learn how to successfully design, conduct, and analyze consumer insights research—and do it well. Drawing from real-life examples and interviews with professionals in a range of areas, this book is designed to present information that reflects the reality of these industries. At its core, consumer insights research is *fun*. Fast-paced, creative, and exciting, working in this field means constant interaction and engagement with people, concepts, and ideas. Consumer insights researchers get to spend their days partnering with clients to solve complex and knotty problems across all mass communication industries, including film, television, digital, advertising, and public relations. They do deep dives to understand the perceptions and perspectives of target audiences using a wide range of approaches and methods. On every project, hours are spent playing with data and ideas, coming up with creative and innovative ways to approach problems and uncover the insights that will lead to effective audience engagement. This work is dynamic and intellectually challenging, celebrating innovative approaches that lead to unique explanations of—and solutions for—important problems. It also is essential to success: Whether you are working on a media product or a strategic communication campaign, successfully reaching your audience and meeting your objectives requires good research.

If you are like most students, the word "research" makes you a little bit itchy. You picture a spreadsheet full of incomprehensible numbers or spending your day in the top floors of a library, mucking through stacks of dusty books. Most research-methods textbooks don't do much to help you feel better about this, focused on how research is conducted in the academic world rather than in the media industries in which you hope to work. While this approach certainly can be useful, it unfortunately does not reflect the reality of consumer insights research—and it definitely does not reflect how creative, interesting, and exciting this work can be. This book is designed to shift the emphasis from the academic to the applied, showing you how this process actually *works*. While I certainly don't think all of you will want to go into research at the end of the semester, most of you will work with research teams throughout your career. This semester's experience will give you an appreciation for the work that research teams do and better equip you to ask questions, make suggestions, and ensure you are getting the right information from the right people as you produce media content.

WHAT IS RESEARCH?

At its most basic, **research** simply is trying to discover something. We all do research all the time, whether it's figuring out the shortest or fastest route between our classes, trying to find out information about how to get cheap flights to Europe, or adjusting the thermostat to get the optimal temperature in our home. Ultimately, we do to make the best possible decisions we can.

Figure 1.2 Consumer insights researchers use every available surface during analysis in order to translate their data into insights and insights into meaningful recommendations. (Getty: andresr)

Research isn't scary or intimidating or only for brainiacs—at least, it doesn't have to be. When you have a clear plan and basic skills to collect and analyze your data, you are positioned to do effective, efficient research, even if you don't really like math. To be clear, when we use "data" in this context, it doesn't mean what students often assume it means—big sets of numbers. Sure, data can mean complex numbers and statistics, but in consumer insights research **data** are words, images, drawings, observations. Whatever you use to uncover relevant information for your research, those are data. And when you collect and analyze data to help your client understand their consumers or audiences better, you are doing **consumer insights research**.

How We See the World

The beauty of consumer insights research—the magic, if you will—is that it focuses on how the consumer sees the world. The biggest mistake researchers can make is to think of audiences as participants in a research project, subjects who exist in order to produce data that can then be used to make good decisions. *Consumer insights research flips that perspective.* Rather than implicitly or explicitly framing audiences as a means for data collection, consumer insights research methods emphasize the ways data can help us understand people as thoughtful, deliberative actors who merit respect. As such, research should be done with the goal of better understanding target audiences in a meaningful way. With this orientation in mind, these insight-driven research projects allow media practitioners and strategic communication professionals to tap into audiences' wants, needs, and desires through messaging and products designed to resonate.

Academic versus Applied Research

I imagine most people using this book are undergraduate students in communication or mass communication programs at a college or university. Many (if not most) of you probably have professors who have built successful academic careers doing traditional **academic research**, publishing their findings in journals targeting like-minded peers or in scholarly monographs that cost the equivalent of a small car. These works are intended to be read and used by people with similar interests, skills, and educational backgrounds. They are chock full of vocabulary and techniques that non-experts all too often find, well, incomprehensible. This material typically is written for other experts and thus will include technical terms and specific jargon that have clear meaning for the intended audience but can be difficult to parse from the outside. Academics typically research and answer questions that have personal interest to them, building their reputations in one specific area, such as sports communication or political communication. This research also is **public**, meaning anyone who wants to access the data behind the findings can do so upon request. Finally, academic researchers often have *time* but little *money*, meaning you can take a year or more to do a study that eventually will be published.

In the **applied research** world, things look very different. A client has asked you to do a specific research project to address a business problem. Your job is to get the best information you can from their target audience, and then translate those data into insights and insights into recommendations. There will be times when you will work with the coolest clients and brands in the business; for this book, in fact, I interviewed pros who do research for Apple, Comedy Central, MTV, and IHeartRadio. Through their jobs, they get to meet some of the most interesting and culturally relevant people in creative industries, and their research is fast-paced and engaging. I also interviewed people who work in finance and pharmaceuticals. They don't have the same level of celebrity cachet in their work, but they still get to do important work that leads to meaningful results. The two things they have in common, however, are that the research they do is driven by specific business questions and their job is to produce relevant insights that can lead to action. Their work is **proprietary**—since a client is paying for it, they own the results and usually won't release them publicly unless it is through a white paper or press release. And finally, while applied researchers often have money, they usually have very little time: Because this is driven by business issues or concerns, research needs to move quickly to help inform answers.

An important note as we head into the discussion on how research works in the applied world: You sometimes will be asked to do an outrageous amount of work in a terrifyingly short amount of time. At one of my consumer insights jobs, we would joke about MREs—the market research emergencies that required us to change or cancel plans so we could turn something around in the wee small hours of the morning. The trade-off? We were paid a premium to offer that kind of service, and we were good enough to do smart, insightful, creative work in a tight timeframe. With this context in mind, there is an old adage I'd like you to remember: It can be good, it can be fast, or it can be cheap. Pick two. The pressures on consumer insights researchers to come in at a cut-rate cost with a quick turnaround can be overwhelming. Don't forget: You're still human. Pick two.

Planning for Research Design

As we move through this book, you will learn about different ways of understanding your target audiences. Two main methodologies are covered: **qualitative** (grounded in words and nonnumerical data, such as interviews and focus groups) and **quantitative** (centered on numbers and statistics, most commonly surveys). Each can be useful when used correctly, whether as independent projects or as part of multiphase research projects. Sections II and III of this book focus on qualitative and quantitative research, respectively, but there are some key terms and concepts you need to know early to make sense of the next few chapters. This may not make complete sense right now, and that is okay—it will all come together by the end of the book, I promise!

An applied research project typically starts with a Request for Proposals (RFP) from a client, which we will go into in much more detail in the next chapter. Other times, you'll be on the internal team and you'll need to figure out for yourself what you need to do to answer your business question. To make this happen, you will propose your **research design**. The research design is the specific plan of action for what you will do, when, and with how many participants. To build this, you'll need to know a few important things, each of which will be reviewed below.

Who Is Your Target Audience? And How Many People Do You Need?

Applied research studies typically will focus on one specific target audience. This can be defined quite broadly—for example, women between the ages of 18–55 who spend at least $300 each year on new shoes. Or your target audience can be much narrower: women between the ages of 45 and 55 who spend at least $300 yearly on shoes and are willing to spend top dollar for comfort and quality. While the methods may be the same for each of these targets, the ways you will conduct the research can be quite different. Here are some considerations:

- **Recruiting:** How are you going to find the people to participate in your research? If you are doing in-person or virtual qualitative research, you often will use **recruiters** to find people who fit your criteria. These recruiters often are associated with facilities that have spaces designed to hold focus groups, interviews, or experiments, and they will have expert knowledge of their geographic area. For survey research, most researchers partner with a company who can handle the recruiting and initial data collection.
- **Screening:** Recruiters will use **screeners** to find people who fit your defined criteria for target audience. These screeners usually will include a combination of **variables,** including **demographic, psychographic, lifestyle**, and **behavioral**, to ensure the people selected to participate in the research really are in the target audience.
  - **Variables** are the factors that we are interested in investigating that can vary across participants—in other words, the concepts or characteristics that matter most to our research.
  - **Demographics** are the characteristics of the population that often are used to break down large groups into smaller homogeneous subsets, such as race and ethnicity, sex and gender, household income, marital status, and educational achievement.
  - **Psychographics** center on psychological characteristics, such as attitudes and beliefs, preferences, and aspirations. These often are measured through longer-form attitudinal statements rather than simple checkboxes like you would use for demographics, which will be covered in much more detail in section III.
  - **Lifestyle** variables often are closely tied to psychographics. These variables are focused on shared interests or experiences that would help inform our attitudes and beliefs, such as being a parent or deeply religious.
  - **Behavioral** variables, our final category, measure what we actually *do*, such as time spent engaging with media, frequency of shopping trips or time spent in stores, and money spent on a particular category.
- **Cost per incidence (CPI):** The narrower the target audience, the harder it is to find them in the population—a broadly defined audience has a high incidence (easy to find) while a narrow definition has a low incidence (difficult to find). Recruiters often will base their

estimates on this **CPI**, charging more for low-incidence populations that will require more time, energy, and effort to find.

- **Incentives:** While it would be amazing if people just volunteered to participate in your research, this isn't usually the case, especially once you get out of school. You need to budget for and think about your incentives, or what you need to offer to get members of your target audience to come and take part in your study. This typically is a financial reward that increases with the effort the participant has to expend (coming to a facility to take part in a focus group or having researchers come to your house will have a higher incentive than taking part in a 15-minute survey). The narrower your audience is, the higher the incentive will be.

- **N:** The N is the total number of participants in your study. A general rule of thumb is that the broader your target audience is defined, the more people you will need to participate so you can get the information you need. If you are using subsets, or smaller homogeneous groups within your total population, you use a small "n" to denote that number. So, for example, you would represent ten total interviews split evenly between women 18–35 ($n = 5$) and 36–55 ($n = 5$) as $N = 10$.

- **Mortality/attrition:** We would love it if every person who agreed to participate in your research study actually saw it through, but unfortunately that is not the case. People will start taking a survey and then stop. Scheduled focus group members will no-show on the day of. People who have been participating in longer-term research will be gung-ho for the first month or so and then disappear. In the research field, this is called mortality or attrition. You need to plan for some people to not show up or finish so you aren't caught by surprise.

What Do You Need to Learn? And How Long Do You Have?

Once you've thought through the issues around who you need and how many, you will be ready to really think through the research design and budget. Remember that you will be working closely with your client in this process, so make sure you read chapter 2 carefully, and we will be introducing some budget considerations in there along with helping them determine the **research objective (RO)** and **research questions (RQs)**. The most important thing to remember here is that you need to stay focused on what the business question is: If you aren't designing research to help make sense of the business questions driving the research, you aren't going to be able to do your job well.

Timing is one of the most central concerns when doing research. As noted above, fast research generally will cost more than research with a more generous timeline. Money and time are both finite resources, and they need to be balanced accordingly. When designing your research plan, you need to think about how much you can actually get done in the available time frame. If you only have two months, it is much harder to do sixteen focus groups and a national survey with 1,500-plus respondents. If that timeline is inflexible, scope accordingly.

What Does This Look Like?

Designing a quality research project takes time to master. After you've been doing this for a while, you'll start to get a sense of how many focus groups or interviews you'll need to do, when ethnographies are needed (you'll learn about these in chapter 5), and what subgroups need to be sufficiently large for statistical deep dives required to address the business questions driving the research. That said, there are some basic commonalities that strong research designs will share. Always put the RO and RQs at the top so you stay focused on what you are trying to achieve. Separate phases of research (usually broken out by methodology, so qualitative would be Phase I and quant would be Phase II or vice versa) are presented in sequence and clearly defined. Make sure you are giving enough detail on how you are defining the audience and what you expect the N to be for each phase so there are no surprises. Finally, ensure that the timeline for key events (data collection starts and ends, presentation of findings, etc.) is clear. This will minimize the chances that your client and you are not on the same page and set you both up for success.

WORKING ON TEAMS

To really understand how consumer insights research works, I encourage you to think about ways you can apply what you are learning in real life. Ideally, this will be through a class project in this course where you have a client with whom you work. That isn't feasible for all classes, however, so you may need to look outside for opportunities. Think about the organizations of which you are a part. What are the areas where they could use some help? Where could you have a real impact on making things work a little better? Every organization has things that can be improved; this is your chance to make it happen.

This book is structured to help support a research project, so you can apply those recommendations either in your class project or on your own. If you *are* doing this for class, you likely are part of a team. This is a good thing—applied research is a collaborative endeavor, and you need to learn how to work with people to get the job done. I know that team projects are one of the most stressful things my students face at the beginning of the semester. They have all been on teams where you have nightmare situations, whether dealing with the group member who ghosts completely but tries to take credit during the final presentation or the team "leader" who refuses to recognize or value anyone else's contributions. Good research is collaborative and collegial, and that requires a functional team. So, to help make that happen, here are some basic suggestions:

- **Set clear ground rules and guidelines.** As one of their first activities, I have my teams develop and write a team constitution. They have to sign this and turn it in so I have record of what they've agreed are their rules of the road. In my experience, teams who have crystallized and clearly communicated expectations have a much better chance of everyone doing their part to make the project a success. Typically, constitutions will establish communication channels and frequency (text, GroupMe, WhatsApp, etc.; send thumbs-up emoji to show you've read the message; and respond within 24 hours are common rules), expectations for meeting deadlines and quality of work, a basic plan for in-person meetings (whether face-to-face or online), and agreed-upon best practices for managing conflict. Speaking of . . .
- **Be proactive about managing conflict.** There is no greater threat to functional group dynamics than festering irritation. Rather than sitting on your emotions and complaining to other group members, be proactive. Remind the group about the rules established in your constitution. Take time to reflect on how things are going and strategize around what is working well and where things could be improved. Be specific. And don't go on the attack—give everyone a chance to step it up.
- **Try to solve problems internally before going to your professor.** It's a cliché for a reason: No one likes a rat. Dramatic? Yes. But true. Don't complain to your professor until you've tried to solve things internally first. Going behind your team's backs and escalating to your boss—or, in this case, your instructor—is a quick way to sour group dynamics. Try to solve

problems internally first. If that doesn't work and you do need to go to your professor, make sure you are ready to help find solutions that will help your group succeed, not just complain.

- **Prioritize your clients, participants, and teammates.** This means keeping egos in check—your own and your team's. Just because you think you have all the answers going in, you need to trust that your client knows what they need and that your participants are the best source for information about where and how to proceed. Rampant egos can interfere with good research. If you think you know everything, you are sure to rub everyone the wrong way—including your team, your clients, and your participants.

- **Keep a positive attitude.** While this is not the best note to get you all psyched up for the semester, I do need to let you know early that research can start to feel overwhelming. Your participants aren't showing up, what you are hearing sounds inconsistent, you don't see a light at the end of the tunnel, and you are convinced you will disappoint your client and possibly fail the project. If (when) you hit this point, remember: Keep putting in the work and doing the best you can, and you'll come out with something of which you can be proud. Keep your chin up and a smile on your face, even if you don't really mean it. Be professional and keep the faith. It'll be worth it in the end.

With these suggestions in mind, we are ready to get started. Buckle up!

HOW TO USE THIS BOOK

This book was written because I saw a gap that absolutely needed to be filled. After the excitement of a career in consumer insights research and brand consulting, I started teaching mass communication research methods classes when I took my first job as an assistant professor. At that time, I was disappointed to find the textbooks available made this all seem, well, *awful*. Even *I* was bored reading these books—and I did this for a living! Beyond that, the books weren't written for students who were going into the "real world" where this research would happen. The emphasis was on how we do things in academia—where money often is limited but you have all the time you could want or need—rather than what the reality of research is like in the applied world. Since then, little has changed in how we teach methods, despite the overwhelming differences in the media world, including advertising and public relations. So this book was born of necessity—to offer an instruction manual on how to conceptualize and conduct high-quality, high-impact, full-scale research that focuses on understanding the consumer, rather than the data you can collect from them. In that spirit, this book is focused on that "how to," providing a road map to conducting your own semester-long research project to illustrate the concepts and techniques that are used in a full-scale research project.

As you go through the semester, I encourage you to make this book your own: Write notes in the margins (or, if this is a rental or something you need to return, use old-fashioned sticky notes!), doodle your inspirations, and dog-ear pages that are of particular importance. If you are using a digital copy, keep a notebook nearby where you can write down key ideas, definitions, and suggestions that you can refer back to in the future. I guarantee that the vast majority of you will be engaging with consumer insights research at some level in your mass communication careers, and this information will be incredibly useful down the road.

Most important, remember that conducting consumer insights research can be (and usually is) both intellectually challenging and extraordinarily rewarding. I've never known anyone who loved their job as much as I did. I got to travel around the country, meeting new people and asking questions to uncover as much as I could about them and how they saw the world. I worked with some of the most interesting media and commercial brands in the world, helping them better reach and engage with their target audiences. The best part: I got to do that while also working with the smartest, most creative people I've ever met—a pretty good gig, if I do say so myself.

There will be times in this process that you feel overwhelmed, and that's typical. The middle of a research project is messy. Things don't seem to be making sense or coming together the way you want. Recruiting is a nightmare. Your focus group guide is too short or way too long, and your data seem to be all over the place. When this happens, relax. Remember to keep your head down, stay focused on your objectives, keep following the process, and have faith that this will all come together.

And for those of you who do find yourselves falling in love with consumer insights research methods, you'll really enjoy chapter 2, where we explore how you work with clients as you earn business and launch projects.

KEY TERMS

Academic research: Research conducted in academic environments, often with little money but a lot of time; findings are public and usually published in scholarly journals or monographs

Applied research: Research intended to answer specific business questions; produce relevant insights that can lead to action

Attrition: Recruited participants drop out of study and do not complete their commitment (also called "mortality")

Behavioral variables: Measure what we actually *do*, such as time spent engaging with media, frequency of shopping trips or time spent in stores, and money spent on a particular category

Consumer insights research: Research focused on helping clients better understand their consumers or audiences

Cost per incidence (CPI): The cost to find individual participants for your research study, based on incidence in the general population

Data: Material generated through your research that you use to uncover relevant information for your research, including words, numbers, and visuals

Demographics: The characteristics of the population that often are used to break down large groups into smaller homogeneous subsets, such as race and ethnicity, sex and gender, household income, marital status, and educational achievement

Incentives: What you offer to persuade (or incentivize) someone to participate in your research

Incidence: How easy or hard it is to find qualified respondents for your study from the general population

Insight: A deeper, clearer understanding that transcends individual data points

Lifestyle variables: Often are closely tied to psychographics, these variables are focused on shared interests or experiences that would help inform our attitudes and beliefs, such as being a parent or deeply religious

Mortality: Recruited participants drop out of study and do not complete their commitment (also called "attrition")

N: The N is the total number of participants in your study; if you are using subsets, or smaller homogeneous groups within your total population, you use a small "n" to denote that number

Public: Anyone who wants to access the report and/or the data behind the findings can do upon request

Proprietary: Research that is confidential and "owned" by the paying client; usually not released publicly unless it is through a white paper or press release

Psychographics: Variables centered on psychological characteristics, such as attitudes and beliefs, preferences, and aspirations

Qualitative research: Research grounded in words and nonnumerical data, such as interviews and focus groups

Quantitative research: Research centered on numbers and statistics; in consumer insights research, most commonly through surveys

Recruiters (qualitative): Often are associated with fieldwork facilities, qualitative recruiters have expert knowledge of their geographic area and help consumer insights researchers find participants for their research projects

Recruiters (quantitative): Companies that specialize in finding respondents for survey research

Research: The act of trying to discover something

Research design: A specific plan of action for what a research team will do, when, and with how many participants

Research objective (RO): The research-specific component intended to address the overarching business goals driving a research project

Research questions (RQs): The "big picture" questions that provide a framework for your research project

Screeners: A series of close-ended questions crafted to identify people who fit your defined criteria for your research project

Variables: Factors researchers are interested in investigating that can vary across participants—in other words, the concepts or characteristics that matter most to our research

2

Working with Clients

The practice of consumer insights research is almost always driven by client needs. You are trying to answer key questions your client has, usually in order to advance a specific business goal. What we mean by "client," however, must be broadly defined. When most of us hear "client," we think of an outside organization—often involving slightly scary and very serious men and women in suits and uncomfortable shoes—that have hired us to do their bidding. And sure, sometimes that picture is true (the suits usually look nice and the shoes often are fabulous, for the record). But clients can be so much more than that. They can be small nonprofits just starting out in the research realm, not quite sure what they need to know in order to meet their fundraising needs. Or it can be the management for a newly discovered band, wanting to test their album and artwork to gauge the best way to position their launch. Often, if you are on the corporate side, your clients are your colleagues—other members of your internal team with specific questions they need research to answer to help make the best possible recommendations and decisions. All of these clients need careful management, good stewardship, and a productive, honest relationship with the expert on the consumer—*you*. They need to trust that you're going to help them manage their project and do careful, rigorous work that really will address what they need to understand. They need you to translate what you found in ways that help them tell the story that will lead to good decision-making. And they need you to help them do all of this while staying on budget, often a tricky part of the job.

In this chapter, we will be reviewing the central components of developing and maintaining a positive, productive relationship with your client during the early stages of a research project. First, we will cover how you make a good first impression to help establish buy-in for both the process and your role in it. Next, we will talk about how you get the work under contract, including responding to requests for proposals (RFPs) and pitching new business. Once you get the business, you often need to help your client decide what they need to do, so we will cover understanding and assessing needs, connecting business objectives and ROs, and developing actionable RQs. We then move to budgets, including how you establish and work with them and considerations related to travel, recruiting, and incentives. Finally, we will review best practices and key takeaways to help you succeed in this important role.

Good client management requires flexibility, patience, attention to detail, and the confidence to push back when it is in the best interest of the research, the consumers, or even the client. You need to be able to clearly articulate objectives and goals, helping your team succeed. Often, people who succeed in this role can manage both the research piece and a more traditional client services role—if you're a people person who also is a paper person (and an email person, and a phone person, and a person who maybe likes the fancy shoes and envies that client a little), this might just be the role for you. But no matter who is actually the client services person on your research team, everyone in consumer insights needs to be client savvy to ensure they do their job well and achieve their goals on budget and on time. Future chapters will address how to successfully navigate the client relationship throughout the research project, but this chapter gives you direction on how to set the right tone from the beginning.

GENERAL BEST PRACTICES

From the first interaction you have with your client, you need to make sure what you do inspires confidence. While the old cliché may be annoying, it's there for a reason: You never get a second chance to make a first impression. This means you need to think carefully about how you look and act, particularly if you are still fresh to the industry and maybe look a little younger than your colleagues and the clients. A little polish can go a long way, so spending some time planning what you will wear and what you will project can make a huge difference.

Looking Good (and by Good, I Mean Professional)

You need to look professional, wearing clothing appropriate for your client's area and position. This doesn't always mean a suit, although it could; if your client is in a more casual industry, you might wear something more on trend but still appropriate. Check out their website or social media to find internal pictures they might have posted. Use these to get a sense of the dress code at the office, and then dress a level up. Pro tip: When in doubt, overdress—you might feel a little silly, but you likely won't offend anyone with your look. The opposite definitely is not true—showing up to a financial services company in torn jeans (no matter how stylish) could easily lose you the business you're there to pursue. And even if you have the contract in hand and are there to launch the project or even present findings, you need this client to trust you. If you look sloppy or unkempt, why would they believe what you have to say? Make sure your appearance reflects your expertise, and you will be that much closer to your client seeing you as a trusted adviser.

Let me be clear: This does *not* mean you can't show your personality. Researchers often have tattoos, interesting hair, and fashionable clothes, especially researchers working in areas that require engaging with younger, hipper audiences. But you need to read the room—if you are working with a client in a conservative industry, think about whether your tattoos might be better covered while you are first meeting your client. Once you know the client better and you've bowled them over with your fantastic insights and useful recommendations, you can then reveal your own style a little bit more.

Confidence Is Key; So Is Humility

You've likely heard of imposter syndrome—a highly (not really) scientific term to explain how so many of us feel like we are in way over our heads and are going to be caught out as frauds the minute we open our mouths. Unfortunately, this isn't always something you outgrow. No matter how many times I do presentations, I always have at least a moment of panic that I am going to completely blow it. The thing is, almost no one in the room can tell that's how I feel, and certainly no one who doesn't know me would ever guess anything is amiss. Over time, I have learned to project confidence, no matter how much I am quaking on the inside. As the saying goes, fake it 'til you make it. Your clients, whether internal or external, are counting on your research to help them make decisions that really matter. Even if you question the validity of you being there in this role, you need to help *them* feel like they made the right decision when hiring you or your team.

So how do you do this? How do you project confidence? This will be covered more in the chapter on presenting findings to you client, but a quick overview:

- **Be prepared.** This cannot be stressed enough. Go over all of the information you have (and if this is a pitch or first meeting, that means diving into as much *secondary research* as you can—see the next chapter for more info!). Ask other team members questions to help each other think on your feet. Have questions prepared that you need answered and have suggestions ready for things you'll know they will ask. Practice your presentation until you know it inside and out. Go in feeling as prepared as possible, and you'll be ready for what comes. And this comes with a bonus: Showing that you've put time and energy into finding out about the client, their competitors, and their industry sets you up to make a fantastic impression.
- **Watch your body language.** Some specific techniques for projecting confidence through body language will be addressed in chapter 6: Qualitative Data Collection, but at this point focus on the ones with the biggest return on investment. Ask your colleagues what your nervous tics are (or, if you don't have anyone to ask, record yourself and look for yourself). This could be tapping your fingers or toes, swiveling in your chair, twirling hair—the list goes on. Once you know your "tell," practice controlling it. It'll be tough, but it will pay off in the long run.
- **Look good, feel good.** One time when I was a baby researcher, my boss and I were talking about how nervous we get before going to major client presentations—in this case, we were going to present the findings of a million-dollar research project to a Fortune 100 company CEO. She shared her secret trick with me: Whenever she had to really feel confident, she'd buy a new pair of shoes that made her feel powerful. She had to look buttoned up in every other way, but shoes? Shoes can be fun. Even if you can't afford new shoes (or, like me, you just aren't a shoe person), think about what you can do to feel like a million bucks when you're presenting your research. If you look good, you'll feel good—and that will come through.

Finally, while it is incredibly important to project confidence, you want to be careful that this does not come across as hubris. You don't want to make your client feel small, stupid, or unimportant. You need to respect their perspective and insights, and help manage the changes and suggestions you're presenting in order to maximize buy-in. Even if you cannot believe how very, very wrong they are with how they see their audience potential (and trust me, every shoe company sees themselves as being oh-so-close to trendy, even those making orthopedics!), you need to be respectful and collegial while helping them see reality a bit more clearly. Coming across as an arrogant know-it-all is a really good way to ensure you won't be working with that client again, so make sure your confidence doesn't stray into cockiness.

GETTING WORK STARTED

Responding to RFPs

In order to be able to work with your client, you need to be able to *get* your clients. Often, agencies and research shops will have a team dedicated to seeking out new business. If you're on the client or agency side and you don't have the internal team to do your research work for you, you'll need to find someone who can help. This happens through the RFP: Request for Proposal (see figure 2.1 for an example).

Since this textbook's focus is on the conduct of research, we will be approaching the RFP from the perspective of someone who receives it and puts together a proposal to do the work. Be aware, however, that you may find yourself on the writing end of an RFP—but you'll be much better equipped to do so once you've taken this on from the researcher side.

What Does an RFP Look Like?

RFPs come in all sorts of shapes and sizes. Often, potential clients will have a template that their business always follows, that includes all of their mandatories (the items that their work must always include, such as boilerplate language on brand, legal requirements, etc.). Most would—and should—include the following sections:

- **Client name and contact info**: Make sure you take careful note of the name listed on the RFP. You'll want to be able to personalize your response and, if possible, do some research to make sure you know this person's background. There is a chance you might have some contacts in common, particularly if you are working in a specific industry (pharmaceutical marketing, consumer packaged goods, etc.).
- **Project name/title**: The project name typically will give you a good sense of what the research broadly is trying to achieve. You will use this title in your response.
- **Relevant background**: In this section, the potential client will provide necessary background and context for the research project under consideration. This likely will include both industry- and client-specific information.
- **Business objective/question**: Usually called either the business objective or the business question, this section gives a quick summary of project's specific focus. This typically will be just a few sentences that allow you to get a sense of what needs to be achieved to meet the business goal.
- **Research objectives/questions**: The ROs and/or RQs are intended to build out the specific components needed to address the business objective. A typical research project has three to five "big picture" RQs that serve as a guide to developing your research design.
- **Methods**: The methods section tells you exactly what needs to be done to answer the RQs. This can include specific requirements for what research needs to be done—for example, a survey with 1,200 respondents consisting of U.S. citizens, ages 18+—or be much more general and open to the researcher's recommendations.
- **Timing**: Remember that applied research typically has more money and less time available than academic research (see chapter 1 for a refresh!). The timing section often will provide three dates: the proposal submission deadline; the anticipated project launch date; and expectations for when the final research will be delivered.
- **Deliverables**: In this section, the client will tell you what they expect in terms of seeing results and getting recommendations. This often will include a **topline presentation**, an

REQUEST FOR PROPOSAL
Barriers Analysis

VICTORIA WATERTON
New York, NY 10017
T: 212/555-6720
Email.@.com
August 14, 2020

BACKGROUND:

Previous research has shown why physicians use BRAND X and their main likes and dislikes regarding the product. The BRAND X DMT would like to further analyze the barriers to prescribing BRAND X. This research will be a quantitative analysis to identify the common barriers and understand how often psychiatrists do not prescribe BRAND X due to a "barrier." We would also like to estimate how much do each of the barriers contribute to a Psychs non-use of BRAND X. Finally, (if possible) we would like to use the results of our recent segmentation study to also understand how the barriers may differ by physician segment.

BUSINESS QUESTION:

1. What % of the time do Psychiatrists not choose BRAND X due to a "barrier"?
2. How much do each of these barriers contribute to a Psych's reluctance to use BRAND X?

RESEARCH OBJECTIVES:

- Identify the barriers to prescribing BRAND X (e.g. inconvenient dosing, Qtc prolongation, etc)
- Estimate how often Psychiatrists do not prescribe BRAND X due to a barrier
- Quantify how much each of these barriers contribute to the non-use of BRAND X
- Understand if the barriers are different or the same for Schizophrenia and Bipolar Mania and Mixed Episodes
- Understand how, if at all, the barriers may differ by physician segment

METHODOLOGY:

This study will be conducted with US Psychiatrists (only). Please outline your recommended analytical method and sample size for this analysis.

DELIVERABLES:

We request a final power point presentation and a copy of the data analysis.

TIMING:

We would like to receive all proposals by **August 20, 2020.** We anticipate kicking off this study by mid-September. We would like to get results as soon as possible.

PROPOSAL REQUIREMENTS:

In addition to your understanding of the elements discussed above, please include:

- A summary of relevant experience, references, bios of the specific team members (with role).
- A detailed timeline.
- A detailed cost estimate using the cost template provided. Please include additional costs to be incurred including estimated travel expenses, presentation costs, telecon, etc.
- A presentation of results to the Corporate research team may be required in person or via telecom. (Please include this in your cost estimate)
- Indicate any capacity constraints and key assumptions upon which your cost and timing estimates rest.

Figure 2.1 **Example of a request for proposal (RFP).**

interim presentation that comes midway through a research project or after each phase of research (depending on how many phases you are doing), a final presentation to your clients, and some sort of written leave-behind in the form of a PowerPoint deck or written Word document.

- **Proposal requirements/mandatories**: In this section, the client details what the "must-haves" are for your research proposal, often including expectations and formatting for your proposed budget, estimated timelines, your relevant experience and references, and any potential constraints on your end to meet the deadlines set in the timing section.
- **Budget**: Some clients may share budget guidelines with you, either giving you a range where you need to fall or specifying the upper limit on what they can spend. This is not always the case; some look to the research teams to include these estimates in the proposal. If this information *isn't* in there, it is okay to ask the client if they have a budget in mind.

What Do You Do Once You Get the RFP?

When responding to the RFP, it is essential that you read it carefully. If you don't follow the requirements detailed in the RFP, you likely are going to be dismissed before they even read through the rest of your proposal. Those requirements are there to make their job easier; why would they want to hire someone who can't make that effort at the upfront? Spoiler alert: They won't. So follow the rules, and you'll hopefully get them to read through what you're offering. This is particularly important because most companies will send the RFP to multiple research organizations. If you don't meet their basic requirements in the proposal, they will just move onto the next one.

As you develop your research proposal, it is essential that you remember the evergreen maxim: under-promise and over-deliver. Don't assume you'll be able to make an impractical schedule happen just because you want to come in faster than your competitors; recruiting participants and conducting quality research takes time, and you don't want to shortcut the analysis and writing periods just to get in faster. You also want to make sure your budget is feasible. We'll talk more about that below, but trust me—clients are never happy when you have to come back, hat in hand, to ask for more money or time finish up the job. If you want them to be repeat clients, be reasonable in your estimations and make sure you can hit the mark. To make sure you can do this, ask the client to share information you know to be critical for setting your budget and timeline, even if they did not include it in the RFP. If you need to know it to make a realistic estimate, ask.

Finally, and I cannot stress this enough, make sure this document looks utterly and absolutely professional. Proofread. Proofread. Proofread. Research is a careful business, so errors in the proposal will be an automatic reject. Make sure your proposal looks good—check for formatting errors that will make your work look less than stellar. And it's worth saying again: PROOFREAD. (It really is that important.)

Pitching New Business

If you are on the research side, there may be times you find yourself pitching new business rather than responding to RFPs. Often, this may happen with established clients, especially when your completed research opens up new lines of inquiry. Opportunities may come up other ways, however, including a potential client reaching based on word-of-mouth. Or, for particularly large-scale projects, the client may ask you to come in and present your research plan in direct competition with other research shops so they can ask questions and get a feel for your approach before making a final decision. In either of these scenarios, making sure you are polished, prepared, and professional will let you go forward with good will on your side.

As you move toward the pitch, you will want to do as much preparation as possible. Make sure you carefully listen to any information your contact has about what they are looking for or might need. Take good notes so you don't miss a key point, and make sure you ask questions to clarify. Look at any secondary research available (see chapter 3 for more on how to do this). Google the company and the client and learn about their competitors. You want to be armed with as much information you can before putting your pitch together. The format of the pitch itself will be directed by what the client requests, but it could involve an in-person, formal presentation in front of a range of decision-makers, or it could be a straightforward written submission. If you are going to be in person, they typically will be expecting you to put together a PowerPoint presentation. This means you have to get a little more creative than just rewriting what you put in your bid. These **decks** (the industry term for PowerPoint or other forms of slide presentations) are a great way to show them who you are and give them a sense of your company's personality and approach to business. Wow them. If you aren't clear on their expectations, ask, and be prepared to offer your own suggestions for how you can submit your proposal. Remember that your job is to demonstrate to your future client that working with you will make their lives easier, not harder, so you want to be proactive and engaged without being a pest. (It's a balancing act.)

Understanding and Assessing Needs

If you are working for a major client, you likely will have a clear set of objectives against which you can work. Typically, large companies have a history of conducting research, so your point person will be someone who has managing these projects as a regular part of their work portfolio. Examples of titles might include:

- Research analyst
- Consumer insights specialist
- Account planner

As you can see from these titles, research doesn't necessarily fall neatly into one category or department; each company approaches this a little bit differently. Usually, if you are working with someone whose job it is to coordinate research, they will be fully prepared to come into the project with a clear set of objectives and RQs. They will know what they need to get and have a good idea about how to get there. They will look to you as the expert in research to design a specific research plan and make recommendations for what to do where, when, and with how many people, but the *needs* already are clear.

Other times, however, you might have a potential client who knows they need to do research, but they aren't quite sure on what. They have a sense of the business problem that needs addressed but need help on figuring out what has to come next. This often is the case with smaller businesses that have grown organically. Research is not something they did in the past, or if they did, it was anecdotal at best. They might have a sense of their customer, but no clear definition around the population's demographics or psychographics. They don't know how to articulate their needs because maybe they aren't quite sure what they are. In cases like these, your job as a research expert is to help them understand and assess their needs.

This typically will start with an analysis of all the secondary material you can find (again, more on that in the next chapter!). See what you can learn about the company, their competitors, and the industry at large. Look for identifiable trends in the market and, in the case of a limited geographic area, assess what you can about the area (e.g., a local restaurant chain might need you to examine broader population and economic trends in the region). Once you have all the secondary information you can find collected and analyzed, conduct an informational interview with your potential client. Sit down with them and have them talk through their problem. Ask tons of questions, grounded in and contextualized by what you learned through the secondary research. Listen in particular for how audience connects to the business problem they are trying to solve; probe to understand their perceptions of barriers and opportunities. Through this conversation, you should be able to help them identify what the key needs are and—more important—how research can help them address those needs. You then can take the next step of helping them develop business objectives and related ROs.

Business Objectives and Research Objectives

Business objectives likely have been covered in other, non-research-specific classes you have taken, so we aren't going to spend much time on them in here. For researchers, these business objectives are relevant in that they help guide and inform what the ROs—our main focus—will be, as noted earlier in this chapter. Once you have a clear business objective, you can then work to establish the RO translating the business objective into something that specifically can be addressed through research. Here is an example:

- **Business objective:** Increase time spent reading on Brand X's website by an average of five minutes per visit within six months.
- **Research objective(RO):** Understand the ways audiences engage with our website to better meet their needs and maximize engagement to increase time spent viewing.

Like all good objectives, the business objective listed above is SMART: *specific, measurable, achievable, relevant,* and *time-bound*. We know exactly what the team needs done (increase time spent viewing) and you can measure it (how much time is spent viewing and how much it needs to increase). Furthermore, this objective is achievable (as opposed to a proposed 30-minute increase), relevant (keeping audiences engaged on the website), and time-bound (this increase needs to happen within six months). Because this is SMART, the research team knows exactly what the client is trying to achieve and can work against that goal while developing and conducting research. A SMART business objective will help ensure the RO can clearly meet the business question or challenge at hand.

When writing your RO, make sure you're really focused on how you can ensure the business objective is addressed at the end. It's essential that these two clearly are connected. Remember: The RO exists to address the business objective. A clear, concise RO allows you to bridge from the big problem that needs addressed (the business objective) to the overarching questions that will drive your research (the RQs).

Developing Actionable Research Questions

Research questions, commonly referred to as RQs, are the "big picture" questions that provide a framework for your research project. You can think of these as the buckets that you need to fill with data; the RQs establish the most important areas you need to understand by the end of your project in order to meet the business objective. Good RQs are crafted to provide insight and information on the specific topics and areas on which your research project is focused, providing scope and boundaries that ensure you keep a laser-sharp focus on addressing your RO to help your client meet their business goals. There are three criteria to remember when writing your RQs:

- Remain open to a range of possible outcomes
- Stay focused on the big picture
- Make sure your RQs are scoped to cover the RO

Remain Open to Possibility

One of the most important criteria to remember when writing RQs to keep them worded in a way that leaves you open to what you will find in terms of results. In academic research, scholars often will have hypotheses that indicate the predicted relationships among your variables—in other words, predict what they will find, based on existing knowledge. In applied consumer insights research, however, hypotheses are very rare. RQs are written to allow for the data shared by the consumer to be interpreted as usefully as possible. In other words, you should be careful to write your RQs in a way that does not indicate what you expect to find; instead, write them so that you are open to finding out what is really going on. This is the audience's chance to let their voice be heard; the RQs should be written in a way that allows that voice to speak its own perspective.

Stay Focused on the Big Picture

One of the most common difficulties when writing RQs as a newbie researcher is mistaking these for questions you would actually ask your participants. Remember: RQs are intended to help break down the RO into manageable buckets. Those buckets are still fairly broad, however, and typically written in a way that is quite closely tied to the research and/or business objectives. They are not what you would ask the consumer; instead, they provide the framework to develop audience-centric questions that will, in sum, let you answer each RQ to address the RO.

Scope Appropriately

Your RQs serve to scope the project and provide boundaries. When I was a baby researcher, my boss told me I was a "kitchen-sink" researcher: When I was writing research instruments, my instincts (bad ones) told me to add in questions that *might* wind up being interesting and important. Spoiler alert: If they were outside of the scope of the RQs, they could never wind up being useful, since the entire point was to answer the RQs to address the ROs. Well-crafted RQs will give you the space to find out whatever it is you need to learn to answer or address the business objective, but they will also save you from casting your net too far afield and wasting valuable research real estate on useless or irrelevant information.

Thinking about the scenario presented above, here are how your RQs might look:

- **Business objective:** Increase time spent reading on Brand X's website by an average of five minutes per visit within six months.

- **RO:** Understand the ways audiences engage with our website to better meet their needs and maximize engagement to increase time spent viewing.
- **RQ1:** Understand audience expectations and preferences for "best in class" websites for Brand X's category.
- **RQ2:** Assess users' overall perceptions of Brand X's current website, including both strengths and opportunities.
- **RQ3:** Gauge audience perceptions and preferences for the appropriate balance between and among relevant components (i.e., video, text, and images) on Brand X's website.

As you can see in the above examples, each RQ is written to help ensure you can ultimately get to the research (and then business) objectives. The RQs use action words—*understand*, *assess*, and *gauge*—that help direct the researcher for what must be achieved in that RQ. They also are discrete: each one sets the course to understand that component of the overall project. And finally, they are answerable—good research, which you will learn to do throughout the remainder of this book—can answer each of these RQs to give your client quality work grounded in consumer insights.

Establishing and Working with Budgets

In the years I've been teaching consumer insights research at the university level, one thing has remained consistent: My students went into a communications-related field because they don't want to do math. As such, the idea of a budget can be slightly terrifying; we may like spending money, but staying on top of spending can be a different story. Rest assured, however—budgets typically wind up being fairly easy to manage in consumer insights research, as long as you know what components must be considered and you carefully plan to make sure you have accounted for your anticipated costs when negotiating your contract with your client. Some clients may have a budget template they ask you to complete during the RFP process, while others may ask for a total cost estimate and leave the details up to you. Either way, there are some components you want to make sure you're considering when writing your proposal. Some of these were explained in the previous chapter but I'm including them again to help contextualize what they mean and why they matter:

- **Project timeline:** Bringing back the adage I shared earlier in this book: Your work can be good, fast, or cheap. Pick two. That is extremely applicable in consumer insights research; if you want to turn around research quickly, you're going to have to pay more for it. When determining your proposed budget, consider how much time you have to complete the project, since that will impact all other costs.
- **Travel:** If you are doing in-person qualitative work, you'll need to travel to get to your participants. We often would spend a week in the field for any given project, starting on the West Coast and traveling east so time zones could work to our advantage. If your client is a company based on the East Coast, however, they may prefer to launch closer to home so more people can observe the research in early stages without having to fly. If you have a team traveling, you need to plan for airplane tickets, rental cars or cabs, any extra baggage you might need, hotels, food, and other incidentals that might come up.
- **Recruiting:** As noted in chapter 1, researchers usually do not recruit their own participants; they will hire a professional organization to do so. Whether for qualitative or quantitative work, someone needs to recruit—and you usually have to pay someone to do it. When budgeting for

this, you'll need to consider the CPI (cost per incidence): How much does it cost to find each person who fits in your population? If your population is broadly defined and easy to find (e.g., adults 18+ who have home Internet access), the CPI should be quite low. A more narrowly defined population, however (women 40–49 with two children in elementary school who wear a size nine shoe), will be much harder to find and thus more expensive to recruit. A good rule of thumb: The narrower your population, the more you need to plan to spend on recruiting.

- **Fielding surveys/hosting qualitative research:** Often, the subcontractor you bring on to do your recruiting also can facilitate data collection. You'll learn more about this topic in sections II (qualitative research) and III (quantitative research), but earmark this as something to think about when putting together your budget.

- **Incentives:** How easy or hard it is to find someone in your population to participate in your research also has implications for your incentives. An incentive is what you offer to persuade (or incentivize) someone to participate in your research. These vary wildly based on a number of factors, including the aforementioned incidence as well as how much would actually motivate someone in your population to participate—a college student probably will be willing to take part in an interview for much less than a surgeon. This often is covered in something called the Fair Market Value (FMV). A recruiter usually can tell you what the FMV is for their area for different categories of respondents, but this is something you will want to look into as you prepare your budget. To estimate your incentives, you also need to think about how many participants you'll need so that you can plan accordingly.

- **Online versus in-person qualitative:** If you are trying to save money on your budget, consider proposing online qualitative research rather than entirely face-to-face. This will allow more people to observe the research while reducing travel budgets and facility fees.

- **Presenting findings:** Will your client expect you to present your findings in person? Will they want you to present topline findings at the midpoint of research? What kinds of deliverables do they want to see? You need to be clear on their expectations so you can budget appropriately, including potential printing and travel costs.

- **Bringing on additional talent:** Some projects might require a specialist who is not on your team; maybe you need to run specific statistical tests and you don't have anyone in-house with the necessary technical expertise, or you need to build a 3D model of a store for use during your qualitative work. Anticipate this early and budget appropriately.

- **Overhead:** Finally, don't forget that your budget needs to include the money your organization needs to survive. Office space, salaries, paper, printers. These all cost money, so you need to have overhead built into your budgets. Most companies have a standard overhead cost that they add to the other components, ranging from around 25 to 50 percent of the total project cost. While you don't want this to be so high that you price out your client, it does need to allow you to survive.

There can be some fluidity in budgets, but remember: If you want your client to come back again, you usually don't want to go over budget unless you are adding work at their request (and in those cases, you want to negotiate so there are clear expectations on both sides). If you know they have some uncertainty around the possible costs associated with the project, you can always offer a series of research packages, all priced differently (as seen in figure 2.2).

During the project itself, keep on top of where costs are coming in, and if you start to get nervous about cutting it too close, you hopefully will have time to adapt. This might mean sending fewer people to presentations or cutting back on other forms of travel, but it's always better to be proactive than come in over budget with no warning.

OBJECTIVES:
- Create a framework for establishing an architecture to guide the Township Leadership Center's "new business" of civic engagement programming
- Solidify positive working relationships among Civic Engagement Committee members
- Mobilize participants to create enthusiasm and shared investment

PROJECT FEE OPTIONS:

Option 1 ($500)
- Guide/agenda development
- Facilitation

Option 2 ($700)
- Guide/agenda development
- Facilitation
- Debrief with Township Leadership Center team

Option 3 ($800)
- Guide/agenda development
- Facilitation
- Written analysis and report

Option 4 ($1000)
- Guide/agenda development
- Facilitation
- Debrief with Township Leadership Center team
- Written analysis and report

Figure 2.2   Example of a project fee proposal showing a range of deliverables/task package options.

BEST PRACTICES AND KEY TAKEAWAYS

Clients are an integral part of working in consumer insights research, and it is essential that you understand how to make sure the relationship is successful. Professionalism, preparation, transparency, and a positive attitude will go a long way toward making sure that happens. When you are working with your client, you always want to go above and beyond to ensure you exceed expectations. Set reasonable deadlines and meet them. Come in at budget. Proofread everything you send. (Everything.) Project confidence but don't stray into arrogance. And most of all, remember that your job is to represent the consumer at the table. They are counting you to help them make the best decisions possible for their business. Your job is to be able to collect and make sense of complex data and share it with them in the most effective way possible—the focus of the rest of this textbook.

KEY TERMS

Business objective: The overarching business-wide goals that drives a research project; consumer insights research usually is only one of multiple approaches happening concurrently to address the business challenges

Decks: The industry term for PowerPoint or other forms of slide presentations

Deliverables: The final written product given to your client typically summarizing the research conducted, findings generated, and recommendations for moving forward

Incentives: What you offer to persuade (or incentivize) someone to participate in your research, sometimes based on FMV

Mandatories: "Must-haves" are for your research proposal, often including expectations and formatting for your proposed budget, estimated timelines, your relevant experience and references, and any potential constraints on your end

Request for proposals (RFP): A document created by a company or organization to solicit proposed research plans and establish study parameters

Research objective (RO): The research-specific component intended to address the overarching business goals driving a research project

Research questions (RQs): The "big picture" questions that provide a framework for your research project

Topline: An interim presentation that comes midway through a research project or after each phase of research

3

Secondary Research and Analysis

It is always a good idea to go into client meetings—especially in the early days—as smart and informed as you can possibly be. You need to know the client, their business, and their industry as deeply as possible, even before you are at the proverbial table with them. The more you know, the better you will be at asking the right questions and contextualizing information in a way that maximizes the value you offer to your client and sets you up for success. So how do you do that? The answer: secondary research.

Most of this book will focus on **primary research**—research that you are conducting to answer specific questions your client has, usually to inform a business decision. This includes both qualitative and quantitative work, as you will discover in the latter three-fourths of this book. With primary work, you are asking the questions *you've* written with your project's RO and RQs as guiding lights. The project is bound by your needs for that project, and you are getting exactly to the heart of what you need to know.

Secondary research, by contrast, uses work that exists outside and independent of your research project. This information can come from a huge range of sources. The client may have a treasure trove of material they've used in the past, including findings from previous research projects and all sorts of internal knowledge. You also can use public sources, including those provided by various governmental bodies and nongovernmental organizations. A wide range of companies provide searchable databases by subscription that your company or university may have access to. Media content services can help pull relevant information on coverage from both traditional and social media. And finally, academic sources—peer-reviewed journal articles, white papers, and so on—can be a valuable resource to help understand broader issues.

In this chapter, we will dig into some of the secondary sources you should consider when conducting a research project. As much as possible, you should work on collecting this information before you meet with the client for the first time. This allows you to get the best information you need to do your job and, perhaps equally important, reassures your client that they made a good choice by bringing you on board. Remember: You need to constantly manage your relationship with your client, and coming prepared with thoughtful, intelligent questions will help set an excellent tone as you move into your research project and ensure your research instruments are well crafted and on target.

CONDUCTING SECONDARY RESEARCH

Making good use of secondary research requires that you exercise equal parts creativity and persistence. There are some times (some amazing, wonderful, thrilling times) where you fall into an absolute treasure trove of information. You can find tons of quality articles in the mainstream and trade press about your company and its competitors. The business information is readily available. Everything you need is right there, and your main challenge is wading through and discerning what *really* matters versus what is interesting, but extraneous. In these instances, I encourage you to stay laser-focused on your RQs. Look at what you need to know for your study and foreground that information. The other material is still relevant and should be reviewed, but distill the essential information that is central to your questions so you can make sure that isn't lost.

Other times, you will need to rely on persistence. Your searches turn up next to nothing of value. The company has little to no internal material for you to review (this typically would be the case for smaller companies who are looking to grow but aren't quite sure how). If an industry is developing or the geographic area covered has little publicly available data, you may need to scratch a bit more to find what you need. For geographic challenges, this can mean putting actual, old-fashioned shoe leather (or, if you're more into the comfy styles, some nice canvas Chucks) to the case, going to local offices or libraries to find what you need. For industry challenges, look to trade organizations that might have relevant material. Finally, look for material relevant to competitors. And once you find something that works, treat it as a starting point: What questions does this raise that gives you new search terms to try? What crumbs of information can you follow to get to another helpful source? Keep trying to dig and eventually you'll be able to pull something together that will give you a solid starting point for your research.

The question then becomes: How much secondary research do you actually *need*? As is so often the case in these types of situations, there is no clear-cut answer. Whether you have an abundance of material or a dearth of sources, you need to make sure you are focused on pulling out what is important and synthesizing it to form as complete a picture as possible. A colleague of mine recommends that you have at least fifteen to twenty sources as a starting point, which is a workable rule of thumb. Remember, however, that your focus needs to be on pulling out what matters and not just collecting sources for sources' sake. What common threads do you see? How do these fit together? How do they connect to each other and then the RQs? Be smart and strategic in your analysis and interpretation so you have the strongest foundation possible for your research project.

What Are You Looking For?

Before we get into where you can go to find potentially relevant secondary research for your project, it's important that you have a clear vision of what you are trying to achieve—what you are looking for during this search. As always, having a clear vision of your goals and objectives will save you time, effort, and headache. Make sure you are checking back in with your RO and the RQs you developed with your client. Go over whatever materials you have that outline the project and/or set parameters. This can include the initial RFP and your response, a client brief, or even a short interview with your main point of contact. Scour those items. Look for key words, relevant concepts, and terms that need understood or clarified. Make a list of potential competitors you need to know and know about. Check out their **owned media** channels (social media accounts, websites, etc.) or other places the brand has a digital or media presence. Identify the business sectors and geographic markets of import. Use each of these to brainstorm what else you need to know—what other areas need investigated so you can be as smart and informed as possible when you start on your own primary research. The list will be different for each project, but you typically want to find as much information as you can about both consumers (including demographics, psychographics, and behaviors) and category.

While it can be tempting to just skip past this and go right to a baseline Google search (and trust me, there will be plenty of temptation to skip this and go right to a baseline Google search), it's important that you plan in advance for what you need to know. If you don't properly analyze your information needs and craft a plan for how you are going to approach this part of the project, it can be exceedingly difficult to actually get this done without missing something important. Take some time and brainstorm. Get creative. Use mind-mapping techniques or an outline to draw associations and spark ideas. Run this by someone outside of your project who might have expertise in the business sector. Spend some time mulling over ideas while you're walking around or enjoying a change of scenery. Do what you need to do to spend an hour or two just *thinking* about—and writing down—those pieces of information you need to find to give you maximum knowledge about and understanding of your client, their competition, their target audience, their industry or sector, and whatever else is relevant to doing your job well.

This might seem equal parts overwhelming and impossible. This task sounds much more daunting than it really is in practice. The remainder of this chapter focuses on the various tools available. Most of these have a fairly short learning curve, so even if it takes you some extra time during your first use, you'll get the hang of it quickly. Also, bear in mind that rarely are you working on a research project alone. You can split your to-do lists with your colleagues on the research team, each of you focusing on a different content area or type of source/resource. Spending a few days working on collecting and analyzing secondary sources ultimately will help you exceed your client's expectations by designing relevant research that has the necessary context and expertise to succeed.

SECONDARY RESEARCH SOURCES

While there are a vast number of secondary sources you can use, I'm dividing this chapter into two broad sections. The first, **nonpublic sources**, focuses on material that limits who can access it. This might include proprietary research your client or team has already completed, or it could be through a subscription to a relevant service. **Public sources**, the second category of secondary research, can be accessed by anyone who wants to find it. This typically will include governmental or nonprofit research databases that provide raw data as well as analysis. This section also will include some free tools you can use for media monitoring and trend work. Due to the nature of this book, each of these reviews will be fairly short. I encourage you to spend time looking for relevant secondary research for any topics you might be studying so that you get experience with using these sources. The more information you have going in, the smarter you will be. And the smarter you are, the better your outcomes will be—for you *and* your client. It's a win–win.

Two important cautions: First, as I will remind you throughout this chapter, you need to make sure that you are carefully vetting the secondary sources you are using. Not every source is created equal, and the last thing you want to do is bring bad data or wrong information to the table. Make sure that you are seeking out and using credible sources; if you aren't sure that the source is reliable, don't use it. Second, always cite your information. The next chapter focuses on research ethics, but this is an evergreen principle. Never claim information or insights as your own if you got them from other people. Good research is collaborative and cumulative, and that requires intellectual honesty. When in doubt, cite.

Nonpublic Sources

Internal Client Materials

There are a number of private sources you can use for your research. The first and often most helpful place to start is with what your client already knows: look for their *internal materials* that can help offer context and background for what has gone before as well as what they currently are doing. What specifically you are looking for will vary by client and project; there isn't one set or packet of information that will always have what you need, unfortunately. But if you have spent the time thinking through and planning for what you need to learn, you'll be in a good position to ask them for material that can help answer some of those questions and add context and background that will help inform your research. These materials can—and usually do—include any sort of investor materials, yearly financial summaries or sales reports, internal communications, and anything else that gives you a clear picture of the company's relevant strengths and weaknesses in relevant areas. Additionally, your secondary research always should include extensive reviews of any paid and owned media (websites, catalogs, etc.) as well as what efforts have been made on the public relations or publicity fronts.

During this internal audit, you should also ask for copies of relevant previous research the client has conducted, including both the final reports and the research instruments. Talk to your client about what worked and what didn't, as well as how the research was approached—was this internally conducted or were outsiders brought in? What methods were used? What drove the research and what findings were shared? How did these findings lead to recommendations, and were those recommendations followed? If they were, what were the outcomes? And if not, why not? Knowing what happened before—in terms of both the research itself and the perceived usefulness and practical application after it was completed—will help you determine the best ways to move forward with your own work. Ultimately, this will position you to do the best possible job crafting an effective research project that will maximize client buy-in.

While we talked about client relations in the previous chapter, it is worth reiterating here: The best applied research in the world won't be successful if the client doesn't buy in enough to actually use the findings and recommendations to address their business problem. This part of the secondary research process is one that will help ensure they are on board with your team and your approach. Gauging client buy-in during the secondary research process is one of the most important ancillary benefits of this phase of research: Not only are you getting the information you need to do your job really well, but you also have an opportunity to do a temperature check with both your direct point of contact and the broader team. It's incredibly helpful to know going in where the potential stumbling blocks or pressure points will be down the road, and this is fantastic chance to uncover those potential issues.

Academic Resources

In addition to internal materials, you should consider looking at *academic research* that has been done on relevant topics. While certainly not private in the proprietary sense of the word, academic research often (unfortunately) is behind paywalls and thus most of the public does not have access to it. While at your university, you likely will be able to access academic research through your library. Academic research is a vastly underutilized resource in the consumer insights world. There is an abundance of information out there about how communication works and why, which marketing techniques are the most effective, and the psychology of persuasion—yet applied researchers almost never tap into this massive pool of knowledge. It may not be the most user-friendly of materials—some of the writing is challenging at best, and the methods and results sections at times require high levels of expertise to evaluate—but there usually are a few key pieces that will give you some indication of what has been tested and demonstrated in nonproprietary contexts. As a general resource, this can be invaluable. So while this might not be the most fun you've ever had, it often can be time well spent. Finding rigorous academic work to help contextualize and make sense of your business problems—and solutions—can help elevate your work and ensure you stand out from the crowd.

Proprietary Resources

A final category of private research is the vast range of proprietary resources available. There are countless resources available, although most require a subscription. For now, you may have access through your university—it's worth calling the library or another relevant department to find out. These are resources that your future employer may utilize as well, so it's worth knowing the names and basic information about what they do. These companies also often issue white papers on both foundational and emerging topics, so their websites can be fruitful even without paid subscription plans.

Note that this list is nowhere near exhaustive, nor is it intended to be. These sources are ones that are commonly used and you likely are to encounter in your professional life, and they are useful for students working in disciplines related to media, business, and branding to know. You should always keep your eyes peeled for additional sources that can help you do secondary research well; just make sure you vet for accuracy and rigor before trusting what you learn. And with those disclaimers, here is a partial "best of" list of proprietary resources you should look over and familiarize yourself:

Centralized Information and Data

- **Mintel** (www.mintel.com): Billing themselves as the "world's leading market intelligence agency,"[1] Mintel offers research on products and people across multiple markets. Their products focus on market intelligence, market research, product intelligence, and competitive intelligence across a wide range of categories and sectors.
- **MRI-Simmons** (www.mrisimmons.com): Two of the most well-known and robust consumer survey companies—MRI and Simmons—combined forces in 2019. This partnership of industry giants has led to a behemoth that uses ongoing surveys and passive measurement to "empower advertisers, agencies, and media companies with deeper insights into the 'why' behind consumer behavior."[2]
- **WARC** (www.warc.com): Offering a powerful combination of research, case studies, and best practices (as seen in figure 3.1), WARC can "help you untangle marketing complexity by collecting, analyzing, and summarizing key takeaways from the most trusted marketing evidence."[3] Their case studies can be particularly effective as a secondary research source. Organized by objective, budget, or category, these cases give excellent insight into what has worked to help inspire and advise.

Warc is largely used at TCU for case studies "what worked vs. what didn't" in terms of advertising and PR

Figure 3.1 **The WARC website offers a robust explanation of what the company does and the benefits it offers customers.**

Trend Analysis

- **Stylus** (www.stylus.com): Focused on cross-industry trends, Stylus offers reports, webinars, workshops, and events to help companies look outside of their own areas of expertise to identify and leverage broader movements.
- **Trendwatching** (trendwatching.com): With in-house teams in Amsterdam, Berlin, Singapore, and New York—along with trendspotters in eighty-plus countries—this company specializes in identifying what is coming up next.
- **Wunderman Thompson Intelligence** (intelligence.wundermanthompson.com): Branding itself as "a center for provocative thinking that focuses on identifying shifts in the global zeitgeist,"[4] Wunderman Thompson offers trend reports and insights in areas such as tech, lifestyle, health, culture, retail, and food and drink.

Audience/Market Analytics

- **Claritas PRIZM** (claritas.com/prizm-premier): PRIZM Premier segments are built using online and offline data sources—including purchase and media behaviors—to develop an "actionable portrait of today's customers."[5]
- **Nielsen** (www.nielsen.com): Best known for their broadcast ratings services, Nielsen now offers a wide range of consumer data products for markets around the world. They also offer specific ways to target relevant segments and build insight-driven work.

Public Sources

Even when you don't have access to the proprietary information listed above, there still are a ton of resources you can use for free. These range from general Internet searching to accessing publicly available databases and information centers, including those maintained by the U.S. government and private entities. Each of these can be gold mines of information across a number of fronts. As was the case with proprietary sources, it's important to spend time learning about what is available in each of these places so you can quickly and easily find what you need to know when prepping for a new project. Side note: This also can be a surefire way to impress your new boss during an internship or your first job. A surprising number of recent grads are not aware of the vast amounts of information just waiting out there to be found, let alone how to distill those data into meaningful intel. Practice using some or all of these resources on projects you do for your classes or your job; you'll be surprised at how often this can help make your life easier and your end product stronger.

Government Resources

The U.S. federal and state governments and agencies offers a wide range of useful resources for researchers to access, ranging from information about the population and geography to lifestyles and retail. You can look for specific datapoints or broader trends, defining your population as the entirety of the American public or adults in one metropolitan area. This is a remarkable resource and one that every researcher should know. And the best part: It's all free, so there is nothing stopping you from working with these sites whenever you like. Pretty cool, right?

The grandaddy, so to speak, is the U.S. Census (www.census.gov). Conducted every ten years since 1790, the Census offers an extraordinarily rich resource for learning about the nation's population both as a cross-section (one moment in time) and longitudinally (across multiple time periods). The site is set up so you can do as deep a dive as you're comfortable doing. You can browse across a wide range of subjects, including:

- Age and sex
- Business and economy
- Education
- Emergency management
- Employment
- Families and living arrangements
- Geographic mobility/migration
- Geography
- Health
- Hispanic origin
- Housing
- Income and poverty
- International trade
- Population
- Population estimates
- Public sector
- Race
- Research
- Voting and registration

Within each of these subsites, you can read material about the topic, access data, and get more information about how the data are collected. This spectacular collection is chock full of relevant data that can give you an excellent starting point for any research project.

Beyond the data collected specifically for the census (officially called the Decennial Census), this site also features data collected from a number of surveys and programs. While there are too many to list here, it's worth noting some of the programs that likely will prove relevant for your work. These include:

- The **American Community Survey (ACS),** a central source for information about changes in the population, housing, and workforce.
- The **Annual Business Survey (ABS)** and **Annual Survey of Manufacturers (ASM)** offer estimates of economic and demographic characteristics of employers.
- The **Current Population Survey (CPS),** a monthly survey sponsored by the Bureau of Labor Statistics, offers statistics about the U.S. labor force.
  - Once a year, the CPS issues the Annual Social and Economic Supplement (ASEC) with detailed information on health insurance.
- **Population Estimates Program (PEP)** provides estimates of the population for the United States, individual states and subunits (counties, cities, and towns) as well as for Puerto Rico. This dataset includes demographic components of population change such as births, deaths, and migration.
- **Quarterly Services Survey Overview (QSS)** offers estimates of revenue and expenses for selected service-focused industries, including information, transportation, utilities, and arts, entertainment, and recreation.[6]

For those of you interested in running data and doing your own analysis, the census website has a wide range of datasets and tools available. And if you get hooked and want to learn more, the Census Academy[7] is available to give basic training on how to use these data.

While the census site is a fabulous starting point for research, those who are interested in learning a bit more should also visit **data.gov.** Produced by the U.S. General Services Administration, Technology Transformation Service, this platform serves as a clearinghouse for data collected and managed by the U.S. government. The site offers specific subsites on key topics, including:

- Agriculture
- Climate
- Ecosystems
- Energy
- Local government
- Maritime
- Ocean
- Older adults' health

These subsites offer access to specific datasets, toolkits, and contact information for the relevant agencies. While these certainly don't have the same broad applicability as the census data likely will for consumer insights researchers, it's easy to find relevant nuggets on here that can help inform your primary work.

Finally, your searches should always include visits to websites for governmental agencies. Working on something political? Check out the Federal Election Commission at www.fec.gov. Developing a campaign for a new medicine from a pharmaceutical company? Hello, Food and Drug Administration (www.fda.gov). Partnering to conceive a new public health campaign? Look for data from the Centers for Disease Control (www.cdc.gov). Looking for information on the GDP in Azerbaijan or the United Kingdom? The CIA's World Factbook has you covered (https://www.cia.gov/library/publications/the-world-factbook/). Want to get a list of local FM radio stations in a target market? You can do that on the Federal

Communication Commission's website (www.fcc.gov). And if you aren't sure which government agencies might be relevant for you, you can check out the master list on www.usa.gov.

While most of the time the U.S. sites can give you the necessary information to move forward with your projects, there are international sites that can be useful as well. The World Bank (www.data.worldbank.org) offers access to global development data—and even if you're not a data jockey, some of the reports here can be quite useful. The World Health Organization (www.who.int) tracks health statistics for its almost 200 member states, and UNICEF (data.unicef.org) offers a vast array of data, statistics, and reports for issues related to women and children that can be sorted by topic or by country.

Other Publicly Available Datasets and Reports

There are places you can turn outside of government sites for mass-data collections. One of the most valuable is work done by the Pew Research Center, a nonpartisan "fact tank that informs the public about the issues, attitudes and trends shaping the world" (www.pewresearch.org). The main site is organized into discrete areas, including:

- U.S. politics
- Media and news
- Social trends
- Religion
- Internet and tech
- Science
- Hispanics
- Global
- Methods

Each of those tabs then is separated into publications, topics, question search, datasets, methodology, and "our experts," allowing users to find relevant information no matter how much (or little) expertise one has in data analysis (see figure 3.2). Be forewarned: The information on this site is absolutely fascinating, and it is all too easy to go down a rabbit hole of interesting-but-not-relevant fact trails that can become quite a time suck!

Figure 3.2 The Pew Research Center is a leading public research organization, covering a range of topics and issues in the United States.

One last resource that might be of help to you: If you are looking for data and analysis related to politics, sports, or science, check out fivethirtyeight.com. Originally created by Nate Silver, the site has grown to be a go-to place for smart data analysis looking at global trends in these areas. And if you've decided that data deep dives make your heart go pitter-patter, their data are available for you to play around with. One particular shout-out has to go to the FiveThirtyEight team for the effort they put into explaining their methods and creating accurate and effective data visualizations. If you want inspiration for how to do this task well, this is a great place to start.

Media Coverage and Content

The last section of resources to review are those that will help you research and prepare through collecting media, including mainstream press, social media, and digital content. Again, there is an ever-growing list of companies who do social media monitoring and senti-ment analysis, which can be useful if you have an established contract with those companies. In case you don't have access to one of these resources, however, there are ways to get some basic information without having to spend money.

As often is the case when it comes to tech questions, Google (www.google.com) will be your best friend here. While any search engine is worth reviewing, Google offers a wide range of products and services that can help facilitate your secondary research. You can set up a Google Alert (www.google.com/alert) so you are notified when your brand is in the news— or their competitors are, for better or for worse. But maybe the coolest thing you can do on Google in terms of secondary research is use the Google Trends (trends.google.com) program to "explore what the world is searching."[8] Put in anything you want—a brand, a topic, an industry sector, your ex who you kind of hope is now viral for the worst reasons—and see what happens. The results will show you the peaks and valleys of interest over time, as well as how interest varies by subregion. Perhaps the most helpful element for our purposes: Related search terms are shared as well as both topics and queries. This will let you expand your search

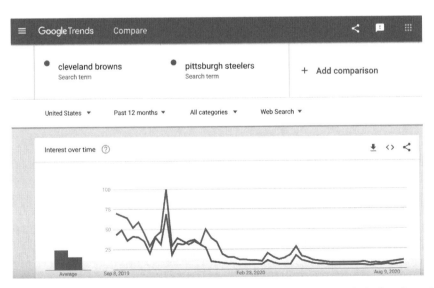

Figure 3.3   A Google Trends graph showing interest in the Cleveland Browns and Pittsburgh Steelers over a one-year period.

to see what else might be considered relevant. If genius is sparked and you want to compare, you can do so quite easily—just click on the "compare" box and type in your new additional query. Check out the comparison of the Cleveland Browns versus Pittsburgh Steelers search interest over time in figure 3.3.

Think about what you can glean from this, looking at the times when interest peaks and when it declines. There is a surprising amount of information you can ascertain this way, and this is both free and easy—the holy grail of secondary sources.

Finally, don't underestimate how important it is to get a sense of the public face of your brand through their various **paid**, **owned**, and **earned** media. In the "nonpublic" section of this chapter, I noted the importance of making sure you check out your client's social channels and digital platforms. This will include looking at what they have in terms of content strategy guides and other internal documentation, but you need to make an effort to see what the public sees as well. Make sure you go to Twitter, Facebook, Instagram, and any other social channel your client uses to see what they are putting out there—and how people are responding. You can do this just by looking at the public sites, but it is important that you get a good sense of how these channels are run and how they engage with audiences. You'll be surprised to see how often there is a disconnect between what the brand *thinks* is happening and what it looks like from the outside.

BEST PRACTICES AND KEY TAKEAWAYS

Secondary research often can be overlooked. Our excitement to jump into the project means we are anxious to get right into the mix—especially if there is a tight deadline that seems impossible to meet if data collection doesn't start right away. While it can be tempting to skip this step, it's not worth it. To do your job well, it is essential that you take a minute, pause, and develop a plan to do your secondary research. Spend time looking at both nonpublic and public sources to gather the information you need. Look at what they have and check out any proprietary resources to which you have access. Play around online, looking at public databases to learn about the audience, the market, the brand, and the sector. All of this will help you go into your primary research smarter and better prepared than you could ever be otherwise. By spending time doing your secondary research well, you'll be positioned to hit the ground running when you meet with your client and launch your primary research.

NOTES

1. Mintel Group Ltd. (2020). *About Mintel.* https://www.mintel.com/about-mintel
2. MRI-Simmons. (2020). *About.* https://www.mrisimmons.com/about/
3. WARC. (2020). *About Core WARC.* https://www.warc.com/about-core-warc
4. Wunderman Thompson. (2020). https://intelligence.wundermanthompson.com/
5. Claritas. (2020). *Prizim Premier.* https://claritas.com/prizm-premier/
6. United States Census Bureau. (2020). *Quarterly services survey overview.* https://www.census.gov/services/qss/about_the_surveys.html
7. United States Census Bureau. (2020). *Census academy.* https://www.census.gov/data/academy.html
8. Google. (2020). *Google trends.* https://trends.google.com/trends/?geo=US

KEY TERMS

Earned media: Media coverage that is sparked by a company's efforts to get coverage, usually through some form of public relations or publicity campaign

Nonpublic sources: Secondary material with limited access

Owned media: Media controlled by a company, such as its own website and digital presence

Paid media: Media coverage that is paid for by the company or brand, such as advertising messages

Primary research: Research that you are conducting to answer specific questions your client has, usually to inform a business decision

Proprietary resources: A type of nonpublic sources, proprietary secondary resources are data collected by a company with the purpose of sharing data only with subscribers or other paid audiences

Public sources: Secondary research sources that can be accessed by anyone who wants to find it, typically including governmental or nonprofit research databases that provide raw data as well as analysis

Secondary research: Research that exists outside and independent of your research project

4

Applied Research Ethics

It is impossible to overstate how important it is for researchers to have a clear understanding of the ethical issues and challenges in our field. Yet all too often, consumer insights professionals have not had any real grounding in what the ethical expectations for them are. Some might have been exposed to academic research ethics, which includes oversight from a university's Institutional Review Board (more on that in a bit). But when you're working in the professional world, there is no IRB to review your proposal to make sure what you are planning to do is ethical and responsible. No one is going to be looking over your shoulder, asking you to think through the ways your work might affect your participants. And you, as a researcher and human, might be asked to do things that you aren't quite sure you're super comfortable doing. It's unfortunate, but it happens—and you need to be prepared for how to respond.

That is why this chapter is so important. Researchers have an obligation to do what is *right*, not just following the letter of the law. Ethics are about your behavior, not your morals—it's not just about *knowing* right from wrong but also about *doing* the right thing in any given situation. This requires a sufficient level of preparation and forethought so you are equipped to make the best possible decision in a critical situation. You won't be an expert in research ethics after one chapter, and if you *do* decide to go into consumer insights for a living after graduation, you should spend more time reading, thinking, and preparing. But this will give you an overview of what to consider and why, along with specific information on scenarios where this can happen and what the outcomes might be. Ethics can be tricky. There isn't always one "right" answer for what to do. Sometimes you'll feel pressured to ask questions that don't quite feel appropriate for the audience (e.g., asking someone who recently was diagnosed with a terminal disease about life insurance) or to do work on a product you find troubling or distasteful (e.g., cigarettes or other tobacco products). Ultimately, you are the one who has to sleep at night, so you need to think about how you will respond in those situations—and know that there are good people who would choose either path.

This chapter is designed to orient you to the different concepts and conditions that are central to discussions of ethics in research. We will start with the most important piece—why this matters—and move onto the key principles of ethical research. Next, we will review privacy laws and legal implications of research and then discuss the particularities of conducting research online. Finally, we will review an ethical concern not related to human subject research but still really important: avoiding plagiarism and promoting intellectual honesty. The examples in this chapter are drawn from real experiences, although names and details have been changed to protect those involved (see—ethics!). But know that all researchers face ethical decision points on a regular basis. The information in this chapter will help you be equipped to make the best decision for you in those moments. And when in doubt, remember the Golden Rule: Do unto others as you'd have done to you. This most fundamental of ethical principles is a good guide for life generally and research specifically.

WHY THIS MATTERS

Imagine you are required to participate in a research study for extra credit in your "Introduction to Communication" class. You're told to report to the lab where this study is taking place at noon on a Tuesday. You show up and a perfectly nice grad student smiles as she introduces herself as the research assistant. The two of you chat as she gives you the paperwork to sign. She notes that you're a little bit late to arrive (you didn't think you were, but maybe the times were mixed up?) and that you need to get started as soon as possible if you want to have time to complete the study and get your extra credit. You don't have time to read the whole permission form, but this is for school, so it has to be legit, right? You sign, she takes it, and you follow her down the hall.

She leads you to a small room with large speakers. You sit in the chair and wait for the researcher to come in. When he does, you realize it's the professor from your class—good thing you hurried so that he isn't running too far behind! He tells you that you're going to be testing other students in the class to see what they have learned and hands you a series of note cards with questions written on them. At his instruction, you push the microphone button in front of you and read the first question. After a moment, you hear a click and then a voice comes through the speakers. The answer is incorrect. Your professor points to a buzzer on the table that you then press. Suddenly, a yelp comes through the speakers—"Ouch! That hurt! You didn't say this would hurt." Your professor assures the student that this is a regular procedure and asks if they want to continue, reminding them their extra credit is dependent on completion. They say yes. You still aren't sure this is a good idea, but your professor confirms you that you won't be held liable and your classmate won't even know you were the one pressing the button—so you ask the next question. Wrong again. Buzz. The yelps have become shrieks. Your professor turns up the knob to increase the electricity in the shock, so when the next wrong answer comes in, the screams are louder. You don't want to hurt your classmate, but your professor wouldn't let anything *really* bad happen, would he? As he keeps turning the knob higher and higher and the screams get more panicked, you realize—he isn't going to stop, and you are causing real pain. What do you do?

While this may read like the plot of a bad movie, it's actually an adaptation of the now-infamous Milgram Experiment. A psychology professor at Yale University, Stanley Milgram, wanted to understand why the rank-and-file Nazis followed the terrible commands that came from their leaders. Most of us, when asked, would say we were incapable of participating in that kind of horror. But Milgram's experiment showed otherwise. Most of the people who participated continued to press the buzzer as the screams increased, unaware that the cries they heard were from a confederate—someone in on the experiment who was acting to make it seem realistic.

This study had admirable aims: to understand the nature of obedience to those in authority. It had a useful outcome: the establishment of the agency theory, which is helpful in understanding why people follow orders from those in authority. But, as researchers, we need to ask: At what cost? What harm was caused? And does the study matter enough in terms of building knowledge about the world to accept the risks and potential harm? Ultimately, we have to ask: Was it worth it?

While this was an academic study conducted for academic purposes, it is still an excellent example of the ethical decisions faced by researchers. In an applied setting, you may have a client that wants you to see how to most effectively persuade a child to want and ask for a new toy. Or your client might be looking to develop a new fast-food treat that will have zero nutritional value but the taste will be unbelievable—with no more than 3,000 calories! A case can be made that it is ethical—or unethical—to do either of these projects. After all, maybe the toy will have educational benefits for children, and in the latter example we should trust adults to make their own nutritional decisions. But when the situation occurs, you need to think through how to do these projects as ethically as you can—assuming you decide to move forward. (For the record, I might pass on the first one but definitely would do the second.) The questions detailed at the end of the Milgram example above—the cost, the harm, the worth, and does it matter—are at the core of all ethical decision-making in consumer insights research.

The question of "why does this matter" and the implied correlate—is it worthwhile?—is the crux of what we are asking ourselves during this process. If the research doesn't matter—there are no stakes to the outcome—then really no research should be done. Research should be *purposeful*. The purpose can be business driven, such as how to increase awareness of a product or effectively communicate a new position to your target audience. It could be to test a new type of cereal or to gauge the best direction to go with a revised logo. Or it could be something for the public good, such as exploring strategies to maximize donations to an organization dedicated to preventing child abuse. The purpose can be broadly defined, but there should be a purpose. And as a researcher, you have an ethical obligation to do the best job you can for your client, your participants, your research team, and yourself. Each of these will be explored in turn.

Client. Your client has entered a contract with you, and you have made a commitment to them to do the best possible work you can. That means being upfront, transparent, and accurate. You can't cut corners or misrepresent data to fit your story, and you must spend time ensuring that what you *do* tell them addresses the business questions they had at the start of the project. If you realize you are going to run into trouble, you are ethically responsible for letting them know early and working with them to figure out a solution. Unethical research practice can permanently damage your relationship with your client and also mar your professional reputation. Eventually, word will get around, and you'll be looking for a new line of work.

Participants. The Milgram study demonstrated the impact of authority on obedience, and the connections here are worth noting. When conducting research, you are the authority figure—participants trust you to take care of them and guide them through your process. If you ask them to do something unethical, they might follow your lead—no matter how much they might regret it down the road. This means you need to be very careful about how you ask questions and how much room you give participants to opt out. If you are asking someone about their sexual history—even if they knew the topic when they agreed to participate in the study—it might get uncomfortable. It is unethical to keep pressuring someone to respond when they clearly don't want to continue. Let them say no and honor their decision. The relationship between researcher and participant should be one of mutual respect, and the responsibility for that lies with you.

Your research team. Almost always, you will be part of a team when doing your research. This means you have other people counting on you to do your part and do it well. It can be tempting to let someone else handle more than their fair share, especially if you are feeling overwhelmed by all of the other responsibilities on your plate. Resist that temptation. You have an ethical responsibility to your team to do your job to the best of your abilities, and failure to do so will cause tension in both the short and long term. Be a good team player, and make sure everyone looks good.

Yourself. You know that feeling where you lie in bed, unable to sleep, because you keep playing over something that happened that day that just feels wrong? You know in the pit of your stomach you made a mistake, and you just want to be able to go back and fix things—but you can't. When you're a researcher, it can be helpful to think about how you'll sleep that night based on the decision you make. If you think it will make you feel awful and keep you awake, you have a really good reason to fix the situation while you still can. But if you are comfortable that what you are doing will let you sleep—and your participants or clients or teammates or whomever else is involved in your debate—then carry on. While simple, this gut check can be an incredibly powerful way to chart your ethical course. Trust your judgment. Don't be afraid to ask questions and talk decisions out with your colleagues or your boss. And at the end of the day, do what you need to do so you can close your eyes at night and rest easy.

KEY ETHICAL PRINCIPLES

While this book focuses on applied research, it's useful to start with a brief discussion on the ways academic research approaches ethics—particularly since you likely will be doing research either in this class or in others. Universities in the United States typically have an Institutional Review Board that is charged with reviewing human subject research. Usually made up of faculty from a range of disciplines and representing a variety of methods and paradigms (see chapter 1 if you need a review), the IRB will review proposals created by affiliated scholars who are planning to conduct research with human subjects. The board typically is housed in a university-level department rather than individual schools. Make sure you familiarize yourself with how your university approaches the IRB in case you need to complete paperwork and gain approval before proceeding with your research.

Because ethical scholarship and research are paramount, the IRB likely will require you complete some sort of training program. Over 2,000 organizations—both universities and corporate entities—are members of the Collaborative Institutional Training Initiative (CITI Program). CITI provides online training modules and certifications for the conduct of ethical research. Certifications typically are valid for three years, and regular refresher courses help ensure researchers stay on top of the latest ethical recommendations and procedures. Grounded in the requirements and recommendations of major governmental and nonprofit organizations, the CITI program offers a robust introduction to the history of and issues around human subjects research. A complete list of organizations that subscribe to the CITI Program can be found on their website: https://about.citiprogram.org/en/subscribing-organizations/. Look for your university so you can make sure you know whether you need to complete this program. If yours isn't listed, check to make sure you are not subscribed elsewhere.

Academic research ethics requirements are based on the **Belmont Report** (see figure 4.1). Published in 1979, this report was the result of extensive work by the National Commission for the Protection of Human Subjects of Biomedical and Behavioral Research. The commission was charged with identifying "the basic ethical principles that should underlie the conduct of biomedical and behavioral research involving human subjects and to develop guidelines which should be followed to assure that such research is conducted in accordance with these principles."[1] This report identified three basic ethical principles that must be followed: respect for persons, beneficence, and justice.

Respect for persons. Also known as "autonomy," this ethical principle states that researchers must respect the rights, values, and decisions of participants. In other words, this means researchers allow participants to employ self-determination—that, knowing the risks, benefits, and procedures that will be employed during the research, they independently decide to do so. This ethical principle also means that vulnerable populations who might not have the cognitive ability to make that decision, such as children or the elderly, need to be given special consideration and protection.

To ensure this can happen, researchers need to ensure that your participants have **informed consent**. This means that persons, as much as they are capable, get to decide whether they want to participate in the research. Gaining informed consent involves three key elements:

- Do participants have enough *information* to make their decision?
- Can participants sufficiently *understand* the information in order to make their decision?
- Is participation *voluntary*?

Beneficence. This is a really fun/fancy word that basically means to do good. It often is considered in conjunction with *nonmaleficence*, another fun/fancy word that means to do no harm. When considering this ethical principle, we are reminded that it is not enough to simply

Figure 4.1   The Belmont Report established the ethical principles we follow as research practitioners.

Complementary expressions of beneficent actions:
1) do not harm
2) maximize possible benefits 3 minimize possible harms

44   *Chapter 4*

do no harm—we actually need to do good as well. The Belmont Report makes clear that this is an obligation, noting the "complementary expressions of beneficent actions in this sense: (1) do not harm and (2) maximize possible benefits and minimize possible harms."[2] Ultimately, this means we need to balance the possible good with the potential harm and work to ensure that the good outweighs the bad. In the context of the Milgram experiment, the good that came out—better understanding the ways people respond to authority—was a legitimate good. But did it outweigh the harm to participants? That's a continual debate.

Justice. The final ethical principle identified in the Belmont Report, *justice* in this context means "'fairness in distribution' or 'what is deserved.'"[3] In other words, people who are equals should be treated equally, which can be operationalized in several ways. From the report, this can mean:

in what situation are people not considered equals?

- To each person an equal share;
- To each person according to individual need;
- To each person according to individual effort;
- To each person according to societal contribution; and
- To each person according to merit.

The question of justice is one that cuts across all components of a research study, including ensuring no systematic bias is introduced in recruiting, the conduct of research, or analysis. Granted, these terms don't exactly roll off the tongue, but the principles are strong and continue to be relevant decades after the Belmont Report was issued.

APPLIED RESEARCH ETHICS

While these ethical principles are closely tied to academic research and are formally required only in that context, they are important for all researchers to consider across any setting. They are also closely tied to the code established for professional researchers. Our industry organization in the United States, the **Insights Association (IA),** has its own code of conduct adopted in April 2019. Created through a 2017 merger between the Market Research Association (MRA) and the Council of American Survey Research Organizations (CASRO), IA was "established to foster and promote the interest of the industry and profession, serves organizations and their research-related employees including researchers, analysts and data scientists, as well as individual research professionals not affiliated with member organizations."[4] Recognizing the international nature of research ethics, IA's 2019 Code is informed by those developed by other national and global research associations, including the International Chamber of Commerce/European Society for Opinion and Marketing Research (ICC/ESOMAR) Code.[5]

The IA's code is intended to self-regulate the industry and ensure ethical research across all members. It is rooted in four fundamental principles:

1. Respect the data subjects and their rights as specified by law and/or by this code.
2. Be transparent about the collection of Personally Identifiable Information (PII); only collect PII with consent and ensure the confidentiality and security of PII.
3. Act with high standards of integrity, professionalism, and transparency in all relationships and practices.

4. Comply with all applicable laws and regulations as well as applicable privacy policies and terms and conditions that cover the use of data subjects' data.

The code outlines thirteen sections that researchers must or should consider. The first set covers responsibilities to participants, including duty of care, primary data collection (transparency, notice, and choice and informed consent); passive data collection; use of secondary data; data protection and privacy; and children and vulnerable individuals. The next set focus on responsibilities to clients, including honesty and transparency and research quality. The code then covers the responsibilities to and of corporate researchers (those working in internal research and thus serving as both client and researcher), subcontracting, and responsibilities to the public, including research for public release. Finally, the code reviews legal requirements and professional responsibilities.

This code is a useful tool for researchers working in applied settings, and I encourage you to look at it both in this class and when you are working with or as a researcher in the future. This includes a comprehensive examination of an emerging (and somewhat tricky) area: ethics surrounding the use of social media posts—even public ones—in your research. If you are considering scraping or collecting social media content from identifiable users, make sure you really consider the ethics of that decision. Is there a reasonable expectation of privacy? Could this cause harm? Are you treating the subject with respect? Beyond our own ethical considerations, you'll also want to check the ToS (terms of service) for the platform to make sure you do not run afoul of their rules and regulations.

One final note: because the code also details sanctions the IA can impose on members found in violation of this set of protocols, ranging from a warning to expulsion. Decisions can be made public, which is a useful tool for ensuring others don't make the same mistakes.

Gaining Consent

Both applied and academic research codes of ethics require that you gain consent from your participants. But what does this look like in practice? In academic work, you likely will have a template to follow from your IRB. This template typically is fairly lengthy, including upfront information on the study title and the principal investigator (PI). The consent form likely will then include purpose, procedures, potential benefits and risks, alternative procedures, privacy and confidentiality, future research, compensation (if applicable), a reminder that participation is voluntary, and information about video or audio recording. The consent form will include contact information for both the primary investigator and the appropriate university department. If your study is with minors (generally between 13 and 18 years old in the United States), there might be an additional form that is written in appropriate language for that audience that will be signed in addition to the parental consent form.

In applied research, particularly when using qualitative methods, this can be a little less formal (see figure 4.2). If you are using a recruiter to find your participants (see chapter 1 for more information), they might have a template they use that the future research subject completes before the research begins. Or, other times, you as the researcher may bring a consent form for your participants to sign.

These forms typically will be straightforward and focus on ensuring a clear understanding of what is required, what the participant will received (typically a cash incentive or some form of gift card) and what the potential risks and benefits will be. Because gaining informed consent is essential to the conduct of ethical research, you do need to make sure you have written

---

CRC Inc. Consent Form
Last updated: 5/21/21

Please ask us any questions you may have before agreeing to take part in the interview.

Introduction: Thank you for participating in our research study. CRC Inc. is conducting research on behalf of a client that is interested in the educational experiences of college-aged students. The purpose of this research is to uncover ways universities and partners can better meet those educational needs to maximize student retention.

Our notes and recordings of your interview: To ensure that we capture the information you provide to us as completely and accurately as possible, we would like to take notes and make audio and video recordings of your interview. We will not share the notes or recordings with anyone except members of our research team for this research study. Our research team is limited to employees of CRC Inc. and our client ("Research Team").

Your information will be treated with the utmost care and confidentiality. We will remove all information from transcripts of your interview that someone outside of the Research Team could use to directly identify you. Only our Research Team will have access to the original audio or video data. We or our client may use information or quotations derived from your interview in future reports, publications or presentations about the research study but, if and when this information is used, it will *not* identify you as the source.

Risks and benefits of your participation: We will use our best efforts to protect your identity and limit any privacy or other risk of your participation. Your participation and the input that you provide may benefit current and future students and the broader higher education community more generally.

Participation is voluntary: Participating in this interview is completely voluntary. You may instruct us to stop your interview at any time for any or no reason. Once you stop the interview, we will exclude subsequent actions performed by you from our research study. You also may instruct us to destroy all record of your participation at any time for any or no reason without explanation. To terminate your participation at any time, please contact [NAME] at CRC by telephone at [555-555-5555] or via email at informedconsent@crcresearchinc.com.

Confidentiality: Your last name, address, and other personal information will not appear in any transcriptions, and they will not be released to anyone without your prior written permission. Research records will be kept in a secure location, and only our research team will have access to them.

Compensation for Participation: As compensation for your participation in this interview, we will mail you a check in the amount of $150 by standard U.S. mail to the address that you provide to us. We will mail your check upon conclusion of your participation in the interview. You will have no right to any additional compensation for our use of the information collected from or about you in connection with your participation.

Your Statement of Consent: I, the undersigned, have read this consent form. I confirm that all information provided by me is truthful and based on my own experiences, opinions, and observations. I acknowledge that I was offered the opportunity to ask questions about my participation and all of my questions were answered to my satisfaction. I am voluntarily participating in this interview and agree to have information collected by CRC Inc. during the interview process (including recordings) I the manner described above. I acknowledge that CRC Inc. will send the compensation check approximately two weeks after my interview.

Consent Signature_____ Date_____

Your Name (Please Print)_____

Figure 4.2   Example of an informed consent form used in applied research.

any documents in language that is understandable to your participants. That means thinking through age, education levels, and native language—if your audience is likely to have limited experience with or knowledge of English, you need to think about how to proceed. This can mean having translated documents or an interpreter present, depending on what your methods look like and what works best for your study. While the solution won't always be the same, you always need to think about how to ensure your respondents are informed about what expectations are for them and this study.

That said, in my experience, the purpose of the study tends to be masked in these permission forms to minimize the risk of priming the respondents or letting them know too much in advance about what will be happening. For example, if you were doing research for General Motors, you likely would not want the participants to know from the jump who the client is; if they do, every single answer—even those about cars or car buying in general—will be conditioned by how they feel about General Motors. Instead, you want to keep this fairly general—for example, "Automotive Study." This will give them a bit of direction about what will be covered without giving too much away.

The IA's Code of Ethics, reviewed above, includes specific information on how consent is to be approached. According to this code, researchers must (all quoted):[6]

1. Obtain the data subject's consent for research participation and the collection of PII or ensure that consent was properly obtained by the owner of the data or sample source.
2. If known at the time of data collection, inform data subjects if there are any activities that will involve recontact. In such situations, the researcher must obtain the data subject's consent to share PII for recontacting purposes. Recontacting data subjects for quality control purposes does not require prior notification.
3. Allow data subjects to withdraw their consent at any time.
4. Obtain consent from the data subject prior to using his/her data in a manner that is different from what the data subject has agreed.

As you can see, the emphasis here is on ensuring data are kept private and respecting the confidentiality of participants. Which leads to an important distinction: What do we mean by *confidentiality* versus *anonymity*? And does it matter? (Yup. It does.)

Anonymity versus Confidentiality

While we may think of confidentiality and anonymity as being practically synonymous in daily use, they have very different meanings in research and should never be used interchangeably. In research, **anonymity** means that the respondent *cannot* be associated with their data—absolutely zero identifying information has been collected, and it is impossible to connect the participant with their responses. This is incredibly difficult to guarantee at all, but it is practically impossible to guarantee when conducting qualitative research. In qualitative research, you usually are looking at the person whether in person or through an Internet stream. The person also has to be in contact with you in some way. So while maintaining anonymity would theoretically be possible in a very Jason Bourne kind of way, it is highly unlikely this would ever happen in real life. While it is more feasible to conduct anonymous research in quantitative work—for example, not using unique links, collecting IP addresses, or asking for any other identifying information—it often is easier (and safer) to just say you are guaranteeing confidentiality.

Unlike anonymous data gathering, **confidentiality** means that while you *could* connect someone to their responses, you promise that you won't do so. This means you would still guarantee to keep their names and any identifying information private; any quotes or specifics attributed to the participant would use a code word or some form of category identifiers (often age and gender along with any other pertinent variable). This lets participants feel more comfortable opening up and being vulnerable without you making promises you can't keep. And it should go without saying, but just in case: If you promise confidentiality, you have to abide by it. You can't say you'll keep things confidential and then show materials created in focus groups that have names on them. And if you *do* need to show their faces or use their names, this needs to be cleared with the participant upfront while gaining consent—and then you don't promise confidentiality, since you won't be able to do that. You just assure participants that they (and their data) will be treated with respect and care.

Privacy Laws and Legal Implications

Legislators in the United States have been scrambling to keep privacy laws updated as digital platforms increase in both availability and usage. Most of the laws that you might encounter in research are related to the passive use of publicly available data, including material that has been shared on social media platforms such as Twitter, Facebook, or Instagram. These laws often are created by individual states and it would be impossible to cover all of them in a textbook like this. That said, you are responsible for knowing the laws in the areas in which you are working. Make sure you are clear on the state's laws on recording subjects—even though you know that you will ask permission to record because you are an ethical, well-trained researcher, there are some states where it is illegal to record someone without their permission. Ethics tend to be stricter than the laws, so if you are conducting research ethically, you should be fine. But just to be on the safe side, do some basic research to ensure you are on the right side of the law as well. A great place to start is Georgetown Law's Privacy & Information Law Research Guide (see figure 4.3 for an overview of the site).

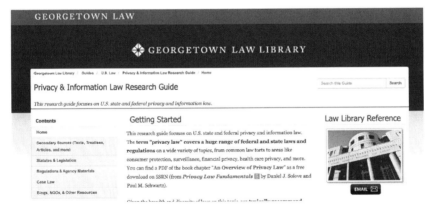

Figure 4.3   The Georgetown Law Library is an outstanding resource for researching laws related to privacy and information.

This site provides a comprehensive overview of where to find federal and state laws on privacy issues, and it can save you a ton of time and effort—and headache down the road if you inadvertently run afoul of the law.

When preparing for or conducting research, remember that some industries are more heavily regulated than others. If you're working in food research or pharmaceuticals, for example, you'll need to be familiar with a whole host of regulations that do not apply for sectors like fashion or home improvement. Be sure to investigate what you need to know and which laws or regulations you need to follow based on what you are researching and where.

Conducting Research Online

While quantitative research has been utilizing the Internet for years, it's only in the last decade or so that qualitative has started moving online. Increasingly, qualitative research is being conducted through computer screens rather than face-to-face. Virtual ethnographies and online depth interviews allow for a cost-effective way to understand your audience, with the added benefit of no travel and a greatly reduced rate of attrition or no-shows. Online research can be a fantastic tool for researchers, but it does come with a specific set of ethical concerns. Some of these may seem familiar to you if you've taken an online class. Think about your experience in that environment, where you are not quite sure what to expect and are trying to figure out how to do your part the best you can. Couple that with the usual tech problems and you can see where these can be stressful for participants. Therefore, as ethical researchers, we need to do what we can to make these online experiences work so that we can get the data we need and the participants still feel respected, comfortable, and engaged. We will get more into specifics on how to do that as a moderator in the next few chapters, but from an ethical perspective, make sure you are considering the impact of what you are asking the participant to do. If you are going to ask them to get up and find things in their house, they need to know in advance so they can be wearing clothes that are conducive to that exercise. (And by that, I mean pants. They need to be wearing pants. Or at least shorts. Standards, people.) You also need to let them know if you need to see the space around them or if they can use a "fake" background or blur it out.

Really think through the ways the ethical principles we discussed from the Belmont Report apply to an online environment. How do you ensure autonomy and that the person knows what they are getting into? How do you continue to show respect, even if their house is pure chaos and their kids are screaming in the background? (This happens. A lot.) How do you ensure you do no harm and instead do good? How do you ensure justice, treating people who are equal in relevant respects equally? In other words, how can you manage to mitigate the unexpected—which is going to happen a lot more often in the uncontrolled environment of someone's house than if they are in a sterile focus group suite or interview room—while still trusting them to be active participants in your research? This can be tricky and it requires preparation and fore-thought. Ethical researchers must go into each situation prepared to deal with the unexpected in ways that maintain respect and dignity for the participant. That doesn't change when you go virtual—it just looks different in terms of how to prepare.

Accurate Representation of Ideas, or How to Avoid Plagiarism

We touched on plagiarism in the last chapter, and it will come up again in section IV of the book, but I'd be remiss to write an entire chapter on ethics and not once talk about the importance of attribution and avoiding plagiarism. It is absolutely essential that you always cite information and ideas that come from other people. Attribution is a beautiful thing—it allows you to build on existing knowledge or present innovative new ideas, even if you didn't come up with them yourself.

When you are using other people's words or ideas, **make sure you have their permission**. Your participants usually have given you permission when they signed your consent form, but if a concept central to your presentation of findings came from someone outside of your research team, cite them. If you are using findings from previous research studies your client shared with you, cite them. If you are using an interesting phrase that you read in a magazine article about your topic, cite it. Make sure you include the author's name, year, and where you got it—and *cite everything that should be cited.* Sharing other people's ideas as your own is stealing. Copying someone else's words and pretending you wrote them is stealing. Always cite. And if you aren't sure? Cite. Give credit where it's due. Again, think of the Golden Rule—if you wrote something and it was used by someone else for their own gain without attributing you, how would that feel? Not great, right? Don't do it to others. It's not hard to cite. Do it.

BEST PRACTICES AND KEY TAKEAWAYS

There were so many times as a consumer insights researcher that I wish I had a chapter like this to review. I loved my job because I loved people, and I wanted to make sure I did right by them—but I was never quite sure what that meant exactly. I would be talking with someone about life insurance and they would break down in tears, because it turns out the barrier to purchase wasn't what we thought (the doctor's exam) but something else entirely (thinking about dying and leaving your loved ones behind to cope, which was unimaginably difficult to consider). Or I would be listening to teammates prep for focus groups to test a new children's educational television show, which I know was important research but still felt a little weird—and I knew I needed to leave those groups to the specially trained researchers who knew how to work with kids in a way that was supportive, safe, and productive. I never felt pressured to work with clients I felt uncomfortable with, and I respected the business decisions my bosses made, but the uncertainty about ethics was something that weighed on me over time.

If there is anything you take away from this chapter, I hope it is that ethical research requires preparation and forethought. You need to really think through your project and do what you can to ensure you will maximize benefit and minimize harm. One more example: In one of my early years as a professor, my graduate-level qualitative research methods class did a project on better understanding the experiences and needs of international students at our university. During our first in-class meeting after starting data collection, several students noted that their interviewees had cried during their sessions—some were truly bereft. What we had not realized was how very lonely being an international student could be, particularly since we were holding the class during fall semester and many were still finding their way in a new country and completely new environment. We immediately added information on our university's psychological services, global education counselors, and support groups for graduate students in hopes that we could help alleviate their pain. We also changed the consent form to better address the risks and potential harm and rethought how we asked for questions and examples. We had caused harm, and even though it was completely inadvertent, it was awful. Since then, I've worked even harder to see potential issues and triggers in the questions we ask and the way we ask them. After all, that's just following the golden rule.

NOTES

1. U.S. Department of Health and Human Services. (2020). *The Belmont Report.* https://www.hhs.gov /ohrp/regulations-and-policy/belmont-report/read-the-belmont-report/index.html

2. U.S. Department of Health and Human Services. (2020). *The Belmont Report.* https://www.hhs.gov /ohrp/regulations-and-policy/belmont-report/read-the-belmont-report/index.html

3. U.S. Department of Health and Human Services. (2020). *The Belmont Report.* https://www.hhs.gov /ohrp/regulations-and-policy/belmont-report/read-the-belmont-report/index.html

4. Insights Association. (2019). *IA code of standards and ethics for marketing research and data analytics.* https://www.insightsassociation.org/issues-policies/insights-association-code-standards-and -ethics-market-research-and-data-analytics-0

5. ICC & ESOMAR. (2016). *ICC and ESOMAR international code on market, opinion and social research and data analytics.* https://www.esomar.org/uploads/pdf/professional-standards/ICCESOMAR _Code_English_.pdf

6. Insights Association. (2019). *IA code of standards and ethics for marketing research and data analytics.* https://www.insightsassociation.org/issues-policies/insights-association-code-standards-and -ethics-market-research-and-data-analytics-0

KEY TERMS

Anonymity: A participant *cannot* be associated with their data; zero identifying information has been collected and it is impossible to connect the participant with their responses

Autonomy: An ethical principle stating that researchers must respect the rights, values, and decisions of participants and allow for self-determination; also known as "respect for persons"

Belmont Report: Published in 1979, this report identified three basic ethical principles that must be followed: respect for persons; beneficence; and justice

Beneficence: An ethical principle stating that research must "do good"; this principle often is considered in conjunction with *nonmaleficence*

Confidentiality: A promise to participants that while you *could* connect someone to their responses, you promise that you won't do so

Ethics: Researchers have an obligation to do what is *right*, not just following the letter of the law; ethics are about your behavior, not your morals—it's not just about *knowing* right from wrong but also about *doing* the right thing in any given situation

Informed consent: Persons, as much as they are capable, get to decide whether they want to participate in the research based on sufficient information and sufficient understanding; participation must be voluntary

Institutional Review Board: An administrative body established to review proposed research projects within an institution in order to ensure all human-subjects research is conducted ethically

Justice: An ethical principle stating people who are equals should be treated equally

Nonmaleficence: An ethical principle stating that research must "do no harm"; this principle often is considered in conjunction with *beneficence*

Respect for persons: An ethical principle stating that researchers must respect the rights, values, and decisions of participants and allow for self-determination; also known as "autonomy"

Qualitative Research Design and Considerations

You are excited to work with a brand new client: a fast-fashion brand that has grown to hundreds of stores in dozens of states based on a clear proposition—trendy clothes that are super cheap (and thus not expected to last too long). When you first meet, your client comes to you with a huge problem: They can't understand why consumers don't talk more positively about their products, and they don't know how to fix it. As you listen to them talk, you realize these people know nothing about their customers. They talk in stereotypes and caricatures, telling you their shoppers pick between paying their electric bill and buying a new skirt for a night out with the girls. They have difficulty articulating what they *like* about these customers but then wonder why people don't speak more positively about their company. At the end of the first client meeting, they sum up what they think is the root of their problem: They don't have a brand because they've never bothered to create one. Trying to be as polite as possible, you have to explain that they do, in fact, have a brand—it's just not one that any company would *want* to have. But, through consumer insights research, you will be able to help them understand their current brand and ideate around what their brand *should* be, all based on developing insights into the perceptions, opinions, and behaviors of their audience. The first step? Some serious qualitative research so we can develop a deeper, more meaningful understanding of their consumers and a better grasp on how they—the audience—perceive the brand both on its own terms and in relationship to other fast-fashion brands.

As we explained in chapter 1, qualitative research is the color in a coloring book, giving you depth and nuance around your RQs. It's often the first step in a multiphase research project, allowing a researcher to dig in and understand the consumer by giving them space to answer in the ways that work best for them. Using this information, you can then write a survey to quantify and measure the audience using their own language and meaning.

In this section, we will introduce and review qualitative research design (chapter 5), talk about best practices in qualitative data collection (chapter 6), introduce some creative exercises to help you dig deeper into your consumer's attitudes, values, and beliefs (chapter 7), and then review how to conduct qualitative data analysis and present your findings (chapter 8). In other words, we are going to tell you what this is, how to do it, and then how to make sense of what you learned. Hopefully, you'll be able to apply these techniques in your own research so you can see this in action. If you do, make sure you take time for **reflexivity**, the critical examination of your research and your role in it. This is the time for some serious navel-gazing. Doing good qualitative research requires you to be open to critique from yourself and others. This is a skill—a craft—that requires honing and polishing. High-quality qualitative research can be an exceptional way to help make decisions that are grounded in consumer insights, but you have to be sure that you are truly representing their perspective rather than your own. Learning to do this well comes with a built-in bonus, however. The skills you'll develop over the next few chapters apply to almost any interpersonal situation. By being good at qualitative research methods, you'll be better at listening, observing, and asking good questions. Your meetings will run smoother and your interactions with bosses, professors, and peers will be more effective. These tools *work*, but they require effort and reflection. Put in the time and it will pay off. I promise.

WHY DO QUALITATIVE RESEARCH?

As the example above illustrates, we often do qualitative research because we need to know more about the *why* and the *how*, better understanding what is underneath the preestablished categories that quantitative research uses. At its core, qualitative research is intended to let your audience members speak in their own voice, giving you a chance to dig around and probe deeper to truly understand the target audience's thoughts, perceptions, and beliefs.

Ultimately, qualitative research celebrates the individual and recognizes that we don't all see the world the same way. Rather than having a set script to follow, you instead have a set of guiding questions that help you dig in and learn from your participants in a way that centers their experiences while staying focused on your RQs and the client's business objective. Good qualitative research, whether it happens online or in person, will help build understanding and deepen knowledge, and you will be able to better represent your audience's perspectives when making business decisions.

Benefits and Limitations

In my experience, research works best when you use qualitative and quantitative techniques to derive the benefits (and accommodate the limitations) of each approach. So while we talk about the benefits and limitations of qual here, bear in mind that some of these will be offset if you do quantitative research as well. That doesn't always happen—some studies only do qual or quant—but when you can do both, you'll often get the best results.

Benefits

While you will undoubtedly discover your own benefits to doing qualitative research, there are a few that consistently arise when talking with consumer insights researchers and those who use the information gained through these methods:

- **Flexibility and adaptability.** Qualitative research allows for huge amounts of flexibility in how you approach your research. You can adapt to your participant's language and experiences to get the best possible responses to your questions. You can also follow emerging paths that could lead to fruitful insights that break new ground for your client.
- **Open investigation.** When you want to investigate something new (a new product feature, for example, or a new type of digital news platform) or something that exists but you don't know much about, qualitative research gives you the freedom to discover without

preconceptions or limitations. Unlike survey writing, you don't have to know a ton going in—you really can open the floor and hear from participants in their own words about their own perceptions, beliefs, and experiences to gain some initial insight and understanding. This is particularly useful when you need to learn about the language people use around a certain topic or how to define/use certain terms; by having this information at hand, you can then do better research across all methods.

- **Dig deeper.** Qualitative research allows you to dig below the surface, going beyond the logical answers that participants often start with. Rather than taking those rational answers at face value, qualitative work lets you probe to find out what is going on beneath, tapping into the emotions that underpin and inform decisions and perceptions.
- **Fun and engaging.** You may never find this on any other list of benefits of qualitative research, but I would be remiss if I didn't acknowledge how *fun* it is to do this work—to get paid to ask questions and engage with people from all walks of life. No two days are ever the same. You never know what you will see or hear during focus groups and interviews. You get to meet fascinating people and often work on interesting projects and incredibly cool brands. Honestly, there are times I still can't believe I got to do this job for a living, in large part because of how much I loved it. This work really, truly is fun—and I hope you find that to be true for yourself too!

Limitations

While the benefits for qualitative research are impressive, there are limitations as well. In this section, I am focusing on the overall limitations that you'll find no matter if you are working in person or online. Later in this chapter, I'll address some of the specifics around each of those modes.

- **Limited scope.** Because qualitative research is so centered on understanding unique experiences, it can be difficult to expand your knowledge to a broader population. There is no way to say how "true" what you have learned is for the entire audience; you really can only speak to general insights.
- **Questions about rigor.** For those who are untrained in qualitative research, this looks really easy to do—they think anyone can jump in and moderate a focus group without preparation and training. This means you have some really bad research out there that is not conducted professionally or with appropriate rigor. And when that happens, it makes all qual research look unreliable and uncertain. We'll talk more about rigor in a little bit, but know that these charlatans can make people question the entire field. To help counteract this, we need to work hard to make sure we are using best practices and holding ourselves to the highest ethical standards in our research.
- **Researcher influence.** The very nature of qualitative research—having a researcher asking questions and guiding conversations—means the researcher is intrinsically bound to the project. This can affect your findings in two ways. The first, **reactivity**, means the very act of observing changes the behavior itself. In other words, participants behave or respond differently because they know they are part of the research or they are reacting in some way to the person in the room. The second way a researcher can affect the findings is by asking questions or interpreting findings in a way that introduces **bias**—you find what you want or expect to find rather than truly understanding the audience's perspective. We will review some strategies for mitigating these issues, but it's important to remember that the researcher does affect the data.

• **Time consuming.** The old adage—it can be good, it can be fast, or it can be cheap, so pick two—holds true in qualitative research. Good qualitative research is time consuming. Even if you are conducting all of your research online so you don't have to worry about travel, you still have to build in time to craft your research guide, recruit participants, schedule and conduct your interviews or focus groups, analyze your findings, and then share your insights with your client. This takes a lot of time and you need to be prepared for that.

QUALITATIVE METHODS

Now that we've covered the benefits and limitations, we are ready to get to the really good stuff! One organizational note: This chapter gives you an overview of each method, while the next one focuses on how to do the actual data collection. Throughout this section, however, I encourage you to get creative and try things out. Getting your hands dirty, so to speak, will help all of this make more sense and give you an idea of how consumer insights work in practice. So, as you read through these next few chapters, think about how qualitative methods might fit into a research project you can conduct. If you're doing one for your class, fabulous—these will spark some ideas for how you can proceed. And if you're not, think about how these might be useful to help make sense of a situation in a group or organization—what perceptions do the university community hold about the online presence of your student media? How can your Ad Club grow membership? What opportunities are there to improve recruitment for your Greek community? Doing qualitative research to understand these or other questions will both help you develop some experience with these methods and, hopefully, help your organization find meaningful ways to improve.

As we go through each of these, I'll draw out specific differences and suggestions for conducting each method online versus face-to-face. Most of the time, the same general principles apply, so unless I note otherwise, feel free to assume that what I am referencing works for either mode.

Interviews

Interviews happen in a **neutral context**, meaning the physical space where you hold it doesn't really matter. You just want to find someplace relatively quiet and private—and the more personal the information you'll be asking, the quieter and more private you want it to be. If your research is face-to-face, you can find a coffee shop or other place where it's not unusual to sit and talk for quite some time. Or, if you are going to be discussing something that requires more confidentiality or privacy, you can rent an interview room from a focus group facility with the added bonus of being able to have the discussion videotaped without it being too disruptive. You don't need a huge amount of space for face-to-face interviews; just a comfortable place for you to sit and talk.

Increasingly, however, researchers are moving interviews online. This method is ideally suited to digital spaces, since these can be cost effective and more easily scheduled since the participant's travel time to and from the interview don't need to be baked in. For the client and research team, these save money by reducing the need for travel to a range of markets across the United States; because you can interview anyone, anywhere from the comfort of your home or office, you have the flexibility to schedule someone from California right before you interview someone from Delaware. You do want to make sure you give some direction for where the participant chooses to do the interview, however—make sure they are somewhere they won't be interrupted and can be open in their responses. Bonus: Your clients often can virtually "sit in" and send the moderator questions and notes as the interview flows.

Broadly speaking, there are three types of interviews you are likely to do:

- **In-depth interviews (IDIs)** are the bread and butter for most consumer-focused studies. Lasting anywhere from one to two hours, IDIs are intended to do a full deep dive into the perceptions, experiences, and behaviors of your participants. These guides typically would follow the same structure as a focus group guide and a project using both methods likely would have quite a bit of commonality between the two. Because you have the time to build intimacy and rapport with your participant, IDIs are ideal for making sense of deeper questions, developing strong insights, and centering individual responses without the risk of group think that comes with focus groups.
- **Expert interviews** are exactly what it says on the tin: Interviews with experts (including opinion leaders) in whatever your study is about. Often, experts are busy, so you won't be able to get a long period of time with them—the rule of thumb we used was 30–45 minutes. You want to use this time as effectively as possible. The good thing is experts already are in the head space of whatever your topic is—after all, they're experts—so you don't need to do all of the build-up required for a more general audience. You can dive right to the heart of what you need to know, letting you get maximum bang for your buck in the time you do have available. One note: When you are interviewing experts, you need to be incredibly buttoned up and hyper-prepared. They expect you to have done your homework, and you need to ensure you've brought everything you need to the table.
- **Clarifying interviews** are brief (around 5 minutes max) question and answer sessions that typically happen during an observational experience, which will be discussed more in the participant observation section below. The participants are not pre-recruited; you just meet them through the course of your observations and you ask a clarifying question or two. These sometimes will turn into full-scale interviews; if someone has a lot to say, you can collect their information and reach out to schedule a full interview down the road.

Interviews are an excellent place for novice researchers to get experience, and they are particularly useful when budgets, time, or client preferences lead to online-centered research. Sometimes, however, you need to get deeper into your topic than interviews will allow, and you need to move away from the neutral context to get the required data. In those instances, you'll want to use ethnographies.

Ethnographies

Also called "ethnos," **ethnographies** in consumer insights research refers to research that uses the context—the surrounding environment—to add richness and relevance to the discussion. Rather than meeting in a neutral environment, an ethno would take place in a store, in a home (as seen in figure 5.1), in a restaurant, or some combination of spaces like these, depending on what your RQs are and what locations matter most. Because your participant is actually *in* the physical space, their answers tend to be more detailed and deeper than what you would get in an interview.

While there are a number of reasons for this, the most obvious and important one is that you reduce the need for recall. Memories are imperfect, no matter how clear and exact we believe

Figure 5.1   During an in-home ethnography on moms and fitness, a participant talks to the researcher through her collection of finishing medals.

them to be. When you are doing an ethno, your participant doesn't need to spend mental energy recalling the exact layout of the grocery store or how they go about putting groceries away when they get home. You are in the moment, experiencing this with them. You're watching and listening as they talk you through their thoughts, reactions, and motivations, explaining their behaviors in real time. In this environment, you can ask specifically about store signage or layout or foot-traffic patterns or anything else that matters to your client's business question. It's a remarkably effective way to gather information and generate data.

When we talk about going out in the field with your participants, we sometimes refer to it as being in situ, which is just a fancy Latin way of saying "in the situation." (Or, for a more direct translation, "in its original place or position.")

The specific activity you are doing might also be used as shorthand; for example, you can do **shop-alongs** in clothing or grocery stores (as seen in figure 5.2). These terms can be really useful for making clear to your client what you are doing and why. When we plan shop-alongs, we often will go to multiple locations. For example, if you're doing research on shoe shopping, you might start at the store where your recruited participant usually shops and then go to one or two competitors for comparison. And, of course, at least one of those—usually the regularly shopped one, but not always, depending on your RQs and defined target audience for your research—will be your client.

While ethnographies work best when you can actually be face-to-face, it's possible to do these virtually and still get good results. Technology has opened up opportunities to live-stream shopping experiences, letting you ask questions and get answers using digital platforms designed for research (or, if you're doing this on the cheap for school, FaceTime or Zoom

Figure 5.2 During an in situ ethnography on moms and fitness, a participant talks through the appeal of a display window at the starting point for a number of rigorous hikes.

and headphones will work!). Just be sure you are making clear to your participant what they will need to do and how you will work together. If you're doing what would be an in-home ethnography, make sure they are prepared to get mobile and show you around. Ask for a tour of relevant spaces. Have them stop to show you and describe anything that sparks interest on your end. These data will lead to excellent probes when you get more into your discussion. Really use the space to your advantage, even online. You'll be amazed at how much you can learn by looking carefully and critically at an environment.

Participant Observation

While ethnographies use the context offered by an environment to spark better discussion, there will be times you just want to be in a space to watch and learn. That's when participant observation comes into play. In this method, you are in the space where the action happens, so to speak, but you're there as an observer—you're not just asking someone about their experience watching a football game; you are there experiencing it yourself. You can watch the population present and see what happens. This method is particularly useful when you need to identify certain patterns, such as how patrons make their way around stores (how long do they linger, what draws their attention, etc.) or how crowds behave (e.g., fans at a football game). At times, you'll want to ask some clarifying questions of those around you, so just read back up to the interview section to be reminded of what those are. But most of the time, participant observation is there for you to get the lay of the land and start making sense of how things work in practice.

One ethical note: In all of the other methods discussed in this chapter, the participants are pre-recruited. They know they are participating in research and have agreed to do so, and they have signed an informed consent document to make clear that they know what they are getting into. In participant observation, however, you aren't wearing a sign announcing your status as a researcher. You're just there, watching. If you do ask a clarifying question, make sure you explain you are a researcher and what you are doing. Remember the ethical principle of autonomy here: Participants have the right to make their own decisions. Duping someone into being a research subject is unethical. So, when in doubt, be clear that you are there for a purpose. Be honest, and you'll be surprised at how open people will be to helping you out.

Focus Groups

For a long time, focus groups served as the mainstay of consumer insights research, a catch-all solution that was wielded whenever qualitative data were needed.

Focus groups have become such a part of the American perception of market research the method even is lampooned on late-night television, like the classic *Saturday Night Live* skit shown in figure 5.3.

This overuse meant that some clients—and researchers—burned out on groups. The saturation meant that you had less skilled moderators out there plying the trade, leading to watered-down data and less relevant insights. Now, however, focus groups have been reinvigorated. Often used in tandem with other qualitative methods included above, focus groups provide an opportunity to use group dynamics and conversations to your advantage. Rather than having one person at a time respond to your creative testing, a group discussion can bring out a multiplicity of voices and perspectives. These discussion-based comments and critiques help build to really useful insights, often taking the moderator in unexpected directions and offering a bounty of quotes and visual data to use in your report (more on this subject in the next three chapters).

Figure 5.3   During her first appearance as host on *Saturday Night Live,* a bewigged Melissa McCarthy played an overeager focus group participant as part of a now-classic sketch.

When holding a focus group in person, you'll want to keep your total number of participants to no more than eight—ideally, somewhere between six and eight should be your target. This gives enough voices to have a good discussion but not so many people that the dynamic becomes difficult to manage. If you go above eight, it gets much harder to get everyone involved and ensure that all participants have sufficient "air time" to share their points of view. Plus, with nine or more people in the room, you're much more likely to lose at least a few to sidebar conversations. Another rule of thumb: Unless you have a specific reason to do so, you don't want your participants to know each other. Having friends or family members in a focus group environment makes it difficult to establish a true balance in the group; these existing relationships will affect the dynamic, no matter how talented or prepared the moderator is.

If you do have a reason for people to know each other in advance—for example, you might want to have women bring their "workout buddy" for a group on a new women's fitness venture—you'll want to make sure everyone in that room has their workout buddy with them. So instead of eight individual recruits, you'd have four **dyads** (pairs). For some particularly sensitive topics that still require some sort of group dynamic, you might want to consider having smaller "buddy groups" where everyone is a unit. Research on social narratives around menopause, for example, might recruit one woman and then have her bring three friends—or even hold the group in her house or a more comfortable location. You can be flexible with how you structure these. You just need to be really thoughtful about what will best create the dynamic you need to get the best possible data.

While focus groups increasingly are offered online, these can be trickier to moderate than one-on-one interviews and/or ethnographies. You'll want to consider "homework" participants can do in advance to ensure they are ready to go when the group gets started, such as pulling together pictures or relevant items from their home to share or answering a written set of questions in advance. As is the case with other online qualitative research, make sure they have a quiet place to go where they will be uninterrupted. Ensure in advance that they have a working camera and microphone and have downloaded and tested whatever platform you are using for your research. Tech issues can be a huge barrier in these groups, and it's hard enough to get a good dynamic without someone popping in and out to try for a better connection. And if participants will be using their phones, remind them to make sure their devices are charged and still have a charger on hand in case it's needed.

Online Communities

There are times where online research allows you to do things you could never do in "real life," and online communities are a great example of this. Some brands have set up entire online communities where they recruit brand or product users to join as members. These often have the look and feel of social media platforms, and participants can use this as a social outlet as well as an opportunity to provide feedback on potential product developments, advertising concepts, and possible partnerships. Because participants are recruited for an extended period of time, it's possible to observe shifts in their behaviors and attitudes over time—something much more difficult to do in other forms of qualitative research, particularly in terms of getting feedback on different iterations of messaging and products based on earlier feedback. Participants also build relationships with each other and the researcher, allowing for deeper discussions and the trust needed to be open to creative activities and techniques. Furthermore, participants are engaging from their own home, meaning you are reducing the barriers to participation. This allows for a broader audience that can be highly specific to your needs engaging with material that you wish to present. Researchers can either observe reactions and conversations or actively engage through direct questioning, depending on what their needs are for a particular project goal. While these communities can be expensive to set up and maintain, the constant stream of data—both organic and that created in response to a specific prompt—can be invaluable.

ENSURING RIGOR

It is essential that qualitative researchers work to ensure rigor during their research. When we talk about rigor in research, we mean holding ourselves to the highest of standards and doing things the *right* way rather than the easiest. I'll be honest: There will be times you will be sorely tempted to cut corners, maybe by classifying someone inaccurately to meet a certain criterion (age, race, etc.) that is proving hard to recruit, or maybe by letting participants bring friends to focus groups to make it easier to fill available slots. But when those temptations arise, stop. Take a breath. Remind yourself that this is worth doing right, and by holding yourself to a high standard, you will come out of this fully confident that you are giving the best possible insights and recommendations to your client. But what does "rigor" mean in practice, exactly? How do you ensure rigor? What are the best practices you need to employ to get your research done on time and on budget, while still making sure you are working the best way rather than the easiest? All great questions with surprisingly straightforward answers.

Ways to Ensure Rigor

When conducting qualitative research, there are some general recommendations for ways to ensure rigor. Some of these will come up again and again over the rest of this section, but all are worth remembering and following.

- **Record everything.** As discussed earlier, our memories are faulty. After you've done six or seven interviews or focus groups, they all start to blend together. If you record all of the sessions, you'll be able to go back and check quotes and discussion points to ensure you are accurately reflecting and representing what your participants had to say. Just make sure you have their permission to record.
- **Take good notes.** We are going to talk a lot about notes in upcoming chapters, but trust me—notes are your best friends when you are conducting qualitative research. Take notes on what you see, what you hear, and what you think is going on. Notes are a great way to keep a good record of your research in case of technical issues, but they are also your first phase of analysis.
- **Triangulate your methods.** Using more than one method helps make up for some of the limitations of others. This goes beyond using both qualitative and quantitative methods. Interviews are great, but maybe you want to supplement those with focus groups to get more voices and conversation. Or maybe your focus groups should be paired with ethnographies so you can do more probing and get deeper, richer data. Or you do a combination of online interviews and in-person ethnographies so you can get value from both methods. When designing your research, consider how you can use multiple methods to **triangulate** data and findings. Think about this as if you're on a cop show and you need to find a missing person—you'll use pings from cell phone towers to triangulate their location. That's what you're doing here in a less dramatic and slightly lower stakes fashion. By using multiple methods, you can circumscribe where the audience really is within the emotional landscape.

- **Have multiple moderators/interviewers.** A good research team will have multiple people who can moderate groups and interviews, ensuring that you minimize the reactivity that might come with one person's specific approach. For example, my moderating style tends to be superfast-paced and highly energetic. The rooms are filled with laughter and chatter, making it sometimes difficult to follow. I was often paired with an extremely effective moderator named Justin. As a researcher doing data collection, Justin was my polar opposite in just about every way. His style was incredibly laid-back. He'd stay fixed in his chair, nodding along as his participants talked. He'd occasionally throw in a drawn-out "Yeeeahhh, riiiight" to encourage responses, but he was a man of few words. As a research team, we knew that if Justin and I both got similar data, we could rest assured that we were on the right path and that we had minimized the impact of the researcher as much as possible.
- **Use bracketing to mitigate potential bias.** As researchers, you need to engage in constant **bracketing**. When the research starts, you need to write down all of your existing biases and beliefs—what you *think* will be learned and why. Keep checking in with this as your research moves forward so you are warding off potential bias, whether implicit or explicit. This bracketing is essential for staying as true to the participants' perspective as possible. Without this step, it can be incredibly easy to just find what you want to find—and that's something critics of qualitative research often fear.
- **Keep your RQs and business objective on top of mind.** It's easy to get so caught up in research that you forget why you are doing it. Being rigorous means staying true to your RQs and what you are trying to achieve for your client. This laser-sharp focus will save you time, money, and effort—all of which are invaluable.
- **Trust your research team.** Research works best when you have a research team you trust. Make sure you are listening to each other and that everyone's perspectives are valued and welcomed. Just because I hear something one way doesn't mean I have a lock on the "true" meaning; there's a chance someone else on my research team interpreted it differently and their interpretation is better. Build on each other's ideas and trust each other to do the right thing for your research.
- **No shortcuts.** This final way to ensure rigor seems like a no-brainer, but it's worth reiterating. Do this right. Do this well. Put the time into each phase of research, from this early design stage through to your analysis and presentation. Don't cut corners because you've procrastinated and are up against a deadline. Plan wisely and spend your time well. Ultimately, that will allow you to produce rigorous, useful research.

BEST PRACTICES AND KEY TAKEAWAYS

Not to beat a dead horse (weird expression), but doing qualitative research is really, really fun. This is a chance to learn about interesting people talking about interesting things. Sure, there will be some dud focus groups where the conversations never really take off, or you have participants who make your life really challenging (more on that in the next chapter). But most of the time, this work is rewarding and engaging—but you need to put in the time, energy, and effort to do it really well. Over the next three chapters, you'll learn about best practices in data collection (including writing guides and conducting research in the field), how to use creative exercises to improve your research, and then how to conduct analysis and present findings. I recommend reading through all of these before you get started so you are fully prepared to do the best job you can. And, as always, remember to keep the faith. Doing qualitative research may seem overwhelming at times, but you will be thrilled with the results. The rewards are worth it.

KEY TERMS

Bias: When you find what you want or expect to find rather than truly understanding the audience's perspective

Bracketing: As a strategy to reduce bias, researchers identify existing biases and beliefs—what you *think* will be learned and why—before research starts

Clarifying interviews: Brief (around 5 minutes max) question and answer sessions that typically happen during an observational experience

Dyads: Research with two participants paired up

Ethnographies: Research that uses the context—the surrounding environment—to add richness and relevance to the discussion; abbreviated as "ethnos"

Expert interviews: Interviews with authorities (including opinion leaders) in whatever your study is about

Focus groups: A research method that provides an opportunity to use group dynamics and conversations to your advantage; the group format allows for a multiplicity of voices and perspectives

In-depth interviews (IDIs): Long-form interviews that typically last anywhere from one to two hours; ideal for making sense of deeper questions, developing strong insights, and centering individual responses without the risk of group think that comes with focus groups

In situ: Research that happens "in the situation"; associated with ethnographies

Participant observation: In this method, you are in the space where the action happens (meeting room, sports stadium, concert venue, movie theater, etc.) as an observer

Reactivity: The very act of observing changes the behavior itself

Reflexivity: The critical examination of your research and your role in it

Rigor: Holding ourselves as researchers to the highest of standards and doing things the *right* way rather than the easiest

Shop-along: The specific activity researchers engage in with; for example, you can do in clothing or grocery stores

Triangulate: Using multiple methods to help address limitations of others

6

Qualitative Data Collection

You're sitting in an empty focus group room, waiting for a colleague to bring the participants in the room. Your client is in the back room behind the two-way mirror, and if you squint hard enough and lean the right way, you can almost make out the silhouette of someone moving around back there. You look at your guide, taking one last peek at the list of questions you have prepared. You're ready.

There's a knock at the door and your participants come filing in. You tell them they can sit anywhere, and they slowly make their way to an open seat. Once all are in, your colleague closes the door behind them. You're on.

Two hours later, you've wrapped up your group. The discussion flowed and the participants were wonderful. As you walk in the back room, the clients and your colleagues give you high-fives and a smattering of applause. The best part? You know without a doubt that you knocked it out of the park. This research absolutely helped address the business questions at the core of your research. You've done your job, and you've done it brilliantly—and your clients could not be happier.

Doing high-quality qualitative research can offer a rush like few other things people get to do in their professional lives. Knowing that you've nailed it—that you've asked the right questions in the right way to get the best possible data—is incredibly gratifying. You get to know that what you've done matters, and you are on your way to a successful final product for your clients. It's an amazing feeling, and one I hope all of you get to experience online and in person—whether as the **moderator** (the person leading the focus group), a member of the research team, or someone on the client side who gets to see what *real* consumers think and feel about their product, brand, or service.

But despite how effortless really good moderators make this look, doing qualitative research well is hard. Really, really hard. You need to be completely prepared and project confidence about what you are doing and how you are doing it. You need to be ready to encourage quiet people to talk while subtly discouraging those who are dominating the conversation. And you need to be constantly monitoring multiple fronts: The participants and their conversation, the clients and their reactions, and—most important—what kinds of data you are collecting. This chapter is designed to help you get the basic tools you need to eventually be really, really good at this—but it takes commitment and practice. As you are reading through this chapter, think about how these techniques would work. Imagine yourself in the room, both as the moderator and as a participant. And if you get a chance to moderate, take it—even if it's not something you think you'll want to do in the future, the experience is invaluable.

The techniques, strategies, and recommendations I write about in this chapter are the product of my years of conducting qualitative research both as a consumer insights researcher and as an academic as well as recommendations from some of the best researchers in the business. As is the case throughout this book, bear in mind that there will always be other ways of doing this. When you go into your first research experience, whether as a researcher or on the client side, pay attention to what those techniques are. This chapter will give you the foundations to conduct great research both in person and online, but you will always do well by watching, listening, and asking—the three fundamental principles of good qualitative data collection. And, as you might expect, good qualitative research starts with a well-crafted instrument.

WRITING AN EFFECTIVE INSTRUMENT

There are as many ways to write a **guide** (in academic research, used interchangeably with **instrument** or **protocol** to define the list of questions and instructions used to frame the discussion) as there are qualitative researchers. The way I am going to show you in here is grounded in my own experience and what I have used in teaching my classes for the past decade-plus, and it has proven to be effective time and time again. In fact, the example included in figure 6.1 was written by one of my former students who has been wildly successful in his research career—and he still uses the model he learned in our class.

While I am going to go through each section step-by-step, keep in mind that guides, like all elements of qualitative research, are **iterative**. This means it can change as you go—the guide you use in the first focus group likely will look different by the eighth one, even if you don't formally rewrite it. Think of a good instrument as a really strong draft—you get it as far as you can, get approval from your client, and then launch the research. Some things will work, some won't, and you'll need to adjust either on the fly or in a post-group/interview. And in qualitative research, that's totally okay—you just need to get good data to answer your RQs.

When writing a guide, the first thing you want to do is have all of the necessary information in the **header**, including the date when the guide is submitted and the project title. You then want to include your **RQs**, particularly when you are drafting the guide—this will help you stay focused on what you need to achieve during your available time. You will likely want to remove these before heading into your fieldwork, however—you don't want the participants to find out early what you are studying!

The next element is a table that identifies relevant sections and how long each is expected to take. This will allow you to see the total timeline for the group or interview at one glance, helping you stay on task as you move through data collection and reduce the risk of running out of time.

During the development stage, this **timetable** helps you ensure you're allocating time appropriately. If you know you need to spend a lot of time learning about the category in general, you'll want to spend the bulk of your time in the "up front" sections, whereas specifics to your client will go faster later in the group. This timetable will change as you write but setting it up as you start will help you start to break down how you will spend your time. This also forces you to think through each of the sections you'll cover in your guide. Writing out what the learning objective is for each of those sections to help bridge your overall RQs to your specific

BRAND X Unscripted Genre
Discussion Guide Flow

DISCUSSION FLOW:
Note: This is not meant to be a script. It will serve as a guide for the key areas of discussion and probing.

Area of Focus	Estimated Length
Introduction	10 minutes
Viewing Habits & Homework Review	20 minutes
General Unscripted Deep Dive	30 minutes
Subgenre Deep Dive	15 minutes
Mapping Back to Brand	20 minutes
Ideal Unscripted Platform	15 minutes
Wrap-Up	10 minutes
TOTAL	**120 MINUTES**

INTRODUCTION

- *Moderator will introduce self and review guidelines for the group – explain session is being video and audio recorded – there are colleagues in the back room – encourage open and honest answers – moderator is unbiased.*

- Thanks for joining us today. We are going to be talking about a variety of fun things today – so you can relax and be assured that there are no wrong answers – we just want your honest feedback.

- Before we dive into all the fun stuff, let's start with a quick round of introductions. Please tell me your first name, where you live, who you live with and your current favorite TV show.

VIEWING HABITS & HOMEWORK REVIEW

- Speaking of TV - How are you watching TV? [PROBE: Cable, Satellite, Streaming, etc.]
  - Please tell me what subscriptions, TV, streaming services, websites and apps you use to watch shows and videos? How does it differ by type of content/genre?
    - Which are your favorites? What do you tune to first?
      - Which do you pay for? What makes something worth subscribing?
    - Are there any you used to use but no longer use? Why did you stop?
    - Any you're considering subscribing to any but haven't yet? What is the appeal of these? What's holding you back?
      - How do you decide what's worth paying for and what's not?
  - Let's talk about traditional cable/satellite vs. streaming? What are your thoughts?
    - What do you like about cable? What do you like about streaming?
      - Does the content differ between linear and streaming providers (e.g. Netflix, Amazon, Hulu)? [PROBE: high quality, more variety, etc.?] Do

Figure 6.1   Example of a focus group timetable and cover sheet.

guide content. Once you have all of these orienting elements in place, you're ready to move into writing the actual content—and this is when things get really fun!

Guide Structure

As you can tell from the timetable example above, your guide should be set up as a **funnel:** You'll start with broad, general questions and then move toward your specifics. This structure offers a chance to get intel on the category and general behaviors without **priming** the participants by letting them know too much about who the client is. For example, if you are doing research for Target, you'll likely want to have a broader understanding of how your audience feels about big-box shopping in general before you talk about Target specifically. If they know from the start that they are doing this research for Target, all of those early responses will be through that specific lens, meaning you've lost your opportunity to get a "cold" read on their experiences and opinions without your client in mind.

In addition to starting with the widest part of the funnel, you'll want to throw out one or two **softball** questions that are easy to answer. The first few minutes of the research should be spent building rapport between you and the participant (or participants, in the case of focus groups). These questions should be relevant to your topic but not hard to answer—you don't want anything too detailed or personal, which would shut down your participant because they aren't ready to answer that kind of question yet. Keep it easy—you're laying the groundwork for future discussion by getting your participant into the right headspace, but you aren't making them work too hard before they are invested in you and what you are doing. If you're in a focus group, this also is when you want to establish a solid conversational dynamic, so include questions that will encourage responses from others in the room.

Once you've gotten through a few softball questions, you can start moving into more of the general category or sector information. Think about the "big picture" information you need to know. This is where you find out about overall preferences and perceptions, behaviors and beliefs. As a general rule of thumb, this will be about the first third of your guide, but, again, this can be longer or shorter depending on how much specific detail you need to answer your RQs. The further you get in your guide, the more detail you can ask for—someone who has been thinking and talking about their television use for twenty minutes is *much* more likely to be able to talk about a specific viewing experience than someone who just got off work and is still thinking about the traffic they fought on the way to your meeting. Let the conversation build as you move through the funnel and let the questions progress to the more specific brand and product information you need in a way that feels organic. Make sure you've written transitional questions in your protocol—that way, it feels like you are naturally moving from one subject to another rather than an abrupt change of subject that can feel weird and disruptive, reminding the participants that they are doing research rather than having a conversation.

Finally, at the end of your protocol, you need to include a **clearinghouse question** that gives your participants a chance to share their ideas that have been bouncing around during your research but they never had a chance to say. This usually is a variation of that exact idea: "Is there anything I *should* have asked you about, but didn't?" is fairly standard. Save a few minutes at the end for this. It's amazing what you'll learn when you open the floor and give participants a chance to share.

Tips for Writing

Writing a guide is like writing a book: No two people will always follow the same process. Over time, you'll figure out what works for you. As you start, however, here are some tips that my students have found useful over the years:

- Always write out the **ethical considerations** you will want to include in your introductory spiel. It's easy to forget to remind participants about what is expected of them (no right or wrong answers, I am an independent researcher, you are being recorded, people are watching—you know, the good stuff required for informed consent!). It's essential you cover these, so you want to have them listed so you don't forget.

- Start with an **outline** for each section, beginning with topics in bullet form, then moving to sentences and then questions. This lets you craft the questions with the purpose in mind, rather than writing a question that you aren't really sure serves the purpose.
- Think about how to **keep things moving along.** You'll want to go back and look at time allocations as you develop and iterate your guide to ensure you aren't belaboring something early on and thus boring your participants without gaining any new data.
- **Build in transitions** between sections. This should feel like a real conversation, so work on crafting organic-feeling transitions so each section flows into the next.
- The next chapter explores **creative techniques** for uncovering insights and deeper meaning, and you'll want to make sure you read that carefully to build in relevant exercises that will help advance your research. Certain creative exercises also give you time to go in the back room and check in with your client and research team, so you'll want to make sure you have at least one or two opportunities to keep your participants busy while you get direction on what you need to investigate further or how to manage the group.
- Once you have a basic question structure in place, write in **probes** that will help you dig around to elicit more information. Good probes will help you develop deeper understanding around your topics, but you need to plan for what you want to probe around. This is particularly useful if you have a participant who is reticent to talk or extremely succinct in their responses. Probes ensure you know how to keep digging to find out more and learn what's underneath superficial answers. These also have the added benefit of letting your client know where you are planning to take the question—the "rabbit holes" you plan to go down, according to noted researcher David Lawson. This makes sure you're all on the same page about what details to pursue before you go into actual data collection.

One final reminder that qualitative instruments are, by definition, iterative—but that doesn't mean half-baked. You need to really think through how your guide will work in practice. Play out the conversations in your head. Test out the ways you are approaching questions. Bounce ideas off your research team. But never, ever send something to your client or go into an actual research encounter with a guide that has not been fully developed. Your iterations are meant to improve and polish, not fix something that was poorly done in the first place. Once you have a solid instrument and the client has signed off, you are ready to start collecting data.

GENERAL BEST PRACTICES

By now, I am sure you are starting to suspect that I am really, really excited about qualitative research—and it's true. I love it. I love asking questions that people will answer, no matter how nosy it might seem. I love that I get to help people understand what they really feel about something that matters to them, often surprising them with their own insights. And I love getting to meet all kinds of people from all walks of life, spending time learning about who they are and what makes them tick. So it might be a surprise that my most important piece of advice for you is about making sure you manage that enthusiasm. In fact, I feel so strongly about this that I've created a two-part rule for it and, in the great tradition of brand professionals everywhere, named it after myself. With that build-up, I introduce you to the **Coombs Rule:** *Be cool; don't be weird.*

Yup—that's it. Five words (assuming you don't count a contraction as two words, but I am writing the book, so I get to pick and am going with five.) Two sentences. Three punctuation marks (including the highly controversial contractional apostrophe). But if you can follow this rule, you'll be off to a great start in your training.

While this rule may seem unnecessary, *so many* of the things I am about to tell you can make you seem really, really weird and off-putting if you don't keep the Coombs Rule in mind—and weird can quickly slide into creepy. It definitely is possible to tank an interview by aggressively maintaining eye contact, or to convince an entire focus group that you are nervous and unprepared because you keep twisting around and fidgeting in your chair. You'll also hear people say things that make no sense or are completely off track, and your instincts will be to laugh or say "huh?"—which will both embarrass the participant and pretty much guarantee no one else will want to make themselves vulnerable by talking. Very uncool, and really, really bad for your research.

This is why practice is so important. If you approach this as *training*—the same way teachers train in front of a classroom or doctors train for surgery—you will be amazed at how fast you can start collecting quality data. The people who wind up seeming weird and/or desperately awkward are the ones who try to wing it. No matter how socially uncomfortable you are, proper preparation and the deliberate application of the tools presented in this chapter *will* equip you to do good research and do research well.

Record, Record, Record

Now that we've established the Coombs Rule, there's a quick corollary: *Confidence is key.* A confident researcher is one whom participants will instinctively trust. They know they are in good hands and that you can guide the conversation to get where you need to go. Remember, consumers agree to take part in your research because they want to be part of the solution. Even if they are primarily motivated by an incentive, most want to actually earn it. If you are flailing and uncomfortable, they will recognize that and react accordingly. Preparation leads to confidence, but it's not enough. Even if you don't actually feel confident, your participants don't need to know it. As the saying goes, fake it 'til you make it.

One caveat, however: Confidence is appealing, but arrogance is not. If you come across as a cocky know-it-all, the participants rightfully will wonder why you're even bothering to ask them anything, since you already have the answers. Balancing humility and confidence can be tricky. But always remember that your job is to get the best data possible. That can only happen if your participants trust you to lead the conversation and believe that you genuinely are interested in and value what they have to say. This ties back to the ethics we discussed in chapter 4. Respect for persons is a huge part of doing research, and having confidence tempered by humility is central to achieving that.

By now, you know that conducting good qualitative research means being cool and not weird, confident but not cocky. Not only are you having to think about your demeanor and appearance, but you're also worried about getting good data and asking the right questions, hitting all of the established RQs and developing understanding of topics relevant to answering the business question driving the research. You're simultaneously trying to build rapport with the participant (or, in the case of focus groups, participants) and watching time so you don't go over. This is a *lot* for one person to do at once, and your focus on the short term—good conversation, managing dynamics, and so on—can make it difficult to take good notes. Beyond that, taking extensive notes is a great way to be weird and thus in violation of the Coombs

Figure 6.2 Moderators will use a whiteboard to record ideas and information from participants. (Getty: vgajic)

Rule—much like at the psychologist's office, seeing the person in charge desperately scribbling gives the participant cues about what you think is important or, worse, can make them start to overthink why you aren't writing other things down. So, then, how do you make sure you don't miss important points? How do you go review the data during analysis (covered in chapter 8)? And how do you recover that amazing quote that brilliantly summarized your ideas? The answer is simple: Record whenever possible.

There are different ways you can record what is happening in your qualitative work. If you're doing this work online, the software you are using typically will have both audio and video recording options. In person, you ideally get both video and audio, whether through fixed cameras in a focus group room or by doing a screen capture for digital work. If video isn't possible, you can make do with an audio recording. You miss the nonverbals, but at least you can get the quotes right. Whether you are online or in person, you always want to have a second person there to take notes. The notes offer a backup in case of tech failures and also let you have an avenue to write down impressions of what is happening that may exist outside of the words spoken. Finally, the extra person provides at least some semblance of security, especially for in-home ethnographies or IDIs that might be held in more remote places. And remember: All of these recordings—including the notes—become data for your analysis. Live notes are an amazing way to keep track of what was said *and* what it felt like in the room, which can be super useful in the analysis phase.

Now that we've established the baseline best practices for qualitative research, we're ready to go in the field.

DATA COLLECTION: IN THE FIELD

In research, we talk about the time spent actually engaging with participants as being **in the field**. This is when the proverbial rubber hits the road, and it is a time often characterized by late nights and early mornings, long flights and seemingly endless hotel hallways. It's also when you really start to see the payoff for your work and you are reminded that it is all worthwhile. In this section, I will review best practices for conducting interviews and ethnographies and moderating focus groups.

Across all of the methods discussed, moderators or interviewers need to think about their presentation and appearance—after all, in qualitative research, the moderator is part of the research process. Before you go into the field, think about the target audience recruited for your project. You want to dress in a way that will feel comfortable and familiar *to them*, selecting appropriate clothing that will allow you to fit in with the participants. While you always want to look professional, you don't want your clothes to become a distraction or point of interest; in a room full of people in jeans and T-shirts, wearing a designer dress and expensive shoes likely will make it harder for them to trust and relate to you. Likewise, if you show up to a focus group with a room full of HR executives in a concert T-shirt and ripped jeans, they might not take you seriously. That doesn't mean losing your identity—you shouldn't wear anything that makes you feel uncomfortable or unnatural. But when possible, you should dress to align with your audience. Ideally, your appearance helps you fit in and not stand out—you don't want to be a distraction. This includes jewelry. Don't wear jewelry that will clatter or clunk on the microphones. It's amazing how loud a couple of bangle bracelets can sound when piped into a back room! And finally, remember that you will often be in a confined space with your participants. Wearing an overpowering perfume or reeking of cigarette smoke is a surefire way to have your participant call things off early due to a splitting headache. Remember that our job is to be as neutral as possible, so look (and smell!) in a way that helps facilitate conversation and engagement rather than contributing to an unproductive situation.

Conducting Interviews

In the last chapter, you learned all about the three types of interviews commonly conducted in qualitative research: clarifying, expert, and in-depth interviews (IDIs). No matter what type of interview you are conducting, however, you want to keep a few ground rules in mind. While these hold true for all of the face-to-face (whether digital or in-person) qualitative methods we will be reviewing, they are central to the successful conduct of an interview.

Perhaps the most important thing to remember is that you are not the star. A lot of people who go into qualitative research do so because they really like talking to people, and we all know that the best conversations have active engagement from both sides. In research, however, our goal is to have the interview *feel* like a two-way conversation—but when you look at the transcript, you realize that the participant did the vast majority of the talking. Good research is done by centering the participant, meaning your job is to ensure that you are finding out what *they* think rather than leading them to the answers *you'd* like them to have. This can be hard—we sometimes hear what we want to hear, and if you aren't careful, you can miss the points they are trying to make. We'll talk about ways to prevent and preempt this later, but it's up to you to ensure that the participant is central rather than you.

A second rule of thumb—one that is essential to follow the Coombs Rule—is to internalize the guide. You don't want to memorize it, since you'll sound like a robot. And you definitely don't want to read it, since there is no way for that to feel organic and natural—instead, you'll have a constant reminder to your participants that this is a formal interview. Rather, you want to internalize it. Your interviewee brings up something relevant later in the guide? Awesome, you can just flow into that part of the discussion and then start backup when it feels natural.

Your interviewee is terrifyingly quiet and you aren't sure you'll be able to get the data you need? Not awesome, but internalizing the guide means you have lots of different ways prepared in your mind to get them to open up. Internalizing your research instruments gives you flexibility and allows for maximum responsiveness, all while allowing you to really focus on what the respondent is *saying* rather than what you need to ask next. This is well worth your time.

Finally, when conducting interviews, you want to really stay conscious of **body language** and use it to your advantage. Even if you are online, pay attention to what you are doing. Keep your feet planted toward your interviewee or your camera so you don't fidget, and make sure your body is facing them too. Don't cross your arms over your chest. This can be interpreted as blocking yourself off from the conversation, and you want to communicate openness. Maintain eye contact in a way that feels natural—but be careful that you don't wind up turning the corner to creepy. Generally, you want to let the interviewee set the tone—work to make them comfortable and read their body language to gauge how you should behave. If an interview is going really well, you'll often find that you are mirroring each other's body language—this a fabulous sign that you've built a strong enough rapport to take the interview where it needs to go.

Online interviewing isn't a huge departure from face-to-face. You're still working to build a relationship with your participant and keep them at the center of the conversation. The main difference is making sure they have any materials they need for your group; for example, if they'll need to draw a picture, you want to make sure those supplies are nearby. You also need to be careful about lags in audio and video. It can be easy to step on responses with an encouraging probe because the lag times make communication difficult. Spend some time in the beginning of your interview or focus group getting a sense of how much lag time is happening and adjust accordingly.

Conducting Ethnographies

While interviews can lead to fantastic insights, the opportunity to do an ethnography—to really be able to draw from environment and context—is invaluable. Since ethnos typically are one-on-one, conducting a good ethnography uses quite a few of the same skills as an interview. You'll still want to center the participant and ensure the interviewee (not you) is the star. Because you are conducting your research in a relevant environment, however, you want to think about ways that you can leverage the space, place, and items around you to ask better questions. Imagine you are doing research on healthy eating. You're in your participant's kitchen and you see a framed picture advertising a local farmer's market on the wall. That is a great cue to ask about shopping outside of grocery stores. Or take a moment to have them walk you through the organization in their cupboards. Look to see how foods are arranged. Ask where they keep healthy foods versus indulgences, meal ingredients versus snacks. If they have kids, ask to see where they put foods their kids *want* to eat versus the special treats that they want to dole out more infrequently. Sure, you could ask questions about this in an interview, but doing it in the context of their *actual* kitchen with their *actual* foods allows for deeper, much more personal questions. Look around for anything that could help you better understand this person and their life, and then use those observations to ask the best questions and probes you can.

When you are doing an ethnography, make sure you are really focused on the subtle physical cues your participant conveys—even if they don't know it. I remember doing research with a mom in a grocery store who had her toddler daughter in the cart. She was a fabulous respondent, and her kid was cute as could be, until we reached one of the middle aisles. Suddenly, the mom's eyes started darting around and her pace picked up. Her daughter started clapping her hands and pointing. I followed the mom's eyes to the signage—we had hit the cookie aisle, which her daughter clearly recognized. Her nonverbal cues—the pace, the eyes—helped me understand the tension between her daughter's desire for cookies (and her desire to keep the peace while shopping) and her own healthy eating goals. Again, this is something that has much more import and impact when in situ—but you have to be watching to know what to ask.

Because the situation is so important, doing online ethnographies requires considerable planning. If you want a tour of a kitchen, you need to make sure your participant is prepared to move. This means making sure they are using a portable camera or their telephone so they are mobile during the research. You can also prep them to have some materials at hand; perhaps you tell them to bring three things that they would save in a fire, for example, or have supplies to do some sort of creative exercise or writing. This isn't impossible; in fact, these can be incredibly useful. You just have to make sure you both are prepared in advance to make sure things run smoothly.

Interviews and ethnographies are a great place for new researchers to start to get experience. They give you a chance to get comfortable asking questions and probing appropriately to get the data you need, and you can build confidence in your skills before you need to perform with clients in the back room. Eventually, however, most qualitative researchers will take on focus groups. Everything included in this section applies, but there are more complex concerns that come with this larger-scale data collection.

Conducting Focus Groups

As discussed in the last chapter, focus groups are ideal for understanding group dynamics—but for that to work, you have to have a skilled, practiced **moderator**. A successful focus group goes beyond just having a good person leading the discussion for a couple of hours, however; it also means a ton of prep work before, doing, and after the session. Right now, we are focused on what this means when you are in the focus group suite, preparing to make sure that all goes smoothly. You likely have clients there with you, so it's important you come across as calm, cool, and collected—if you exude professionalism and competence, both the clients and your participants will be much more likely to trust you to successfully lead this experience. Make sure you have all of the materials you might need in the room. Have a digital clock ready—and if you need to use your phone, make sure you have it set so that no alerts pop up that could distract you or your participants. Once you are ready to start, a colleague likely will bring the participants in from the waiting room. When they walk in, you should be sitting in your seat with a straight back and your feet firmly planted on the floor—no slouching or twirling in your seat for you! Smile and welcome your participants, inviting them to sit where they want.

Once everyone is in, your colleague will shut the door—and then it's game on. Your job for the next two hours (or so) is to build a group dynamic that is engaging, respectful, collaborative, and open. You want participants to be able to agree and disagree with each other, and you do *not* want it to feel like you are a teacher calling on recalcitrant students. Establishing this in-group culture requires effort from the very start.

Starting the Group

When running a focus group, it is important to set the right tone early. Make sure you are addressing all of the ethical information and considerations that participants need to know, even after they've signed off on informed consent forms. There are a few key items that the moderator must address to ensure all participants are properly prepared for the group. Here is a loose script a moderator can follow:

Thank you for joining us today! I'm excited to have you all here, and I can tell this is going to be a great conversation. Before we get started, I have a few reminders I want to share, and then I'll cover a few ground rules. First, I want you to know you are being recorded—there are video cameras in the room. This is just for our research purposes, so we can be sure we are accurately reflecting what was said in today's group.

You might also have noticed the mirror on that wall. It's not just a way to make sure your hair looks good, although it is amazing the things you'll notice about your appearance over the next two hours! It's actually a two-way mirror, and members of my team are back there so they can hear what you are saying too. Occasionally one of them might come in here with a note for me, so wave hi! You might also hear them laughing or chatting, in which case you might also see me wildly gesturing at them to turn it down a notch.

So the last thing is that I want to reassure you that nothing you say in here will be right or wrong. I'm not going to get a raise if you love something and I'm not going to get fired if you hate it—my job is just to talk to you to hear what you think. And that part is really important—the focus is on you, not other people. So don't worry about what your neighbors or your family might think—we just want to know what you think. Sound good? Great!

Now, obviously, you'd adapt this for your own personal circumstances—if there are no video cameras, you can omit that part or replace it with information about how the group is being recorded. This language and these protocols aren't set in stone, but you need to be absolutely clear with your respondents about any recording that is happening.

Once the ethical information is made clear, you want to get the group underway. It's essential that you set the tone early by articulating ground rules that set up clear expectations for participants. Here is an example:

Now that we're ready to get started, I want to set a few ground rules. We really do want to hear from each of you, so please feel free to bounce ideas off each other. It's really boring for me to just ask questions one by one, and this will be way more productive and interesting for all of you if it's more of a conversation. So if Joe says something and Debbie wants to build off it, follow up! Or if Debbie says something and Sue disagrees or sees things a bit differently, that's great too—just make sure you're being respectful and not interrupting. Okay?

Once you've finished these introductory pieces, you're ready to officially launch the group! It's important to remember that these first minutes are essential to the overall success of your group. It bears repeating: As moderator, you want to project confidence—let your participants know they are in good, capable hands. You also want to project energy—if you are pitching a group that is going to last anywhere between one and two hours, you need to reassure participants that it won't be two hours of pure drudgery. Pay attention to your body language. Sit with your feet firmly planted on the ground. Make sure your arms aren't crossed in front of your body. Don't fidget and watch out for tics you may not even know you have (playing with your hair, jewelry, etc.).

As noted in the guide development section above, you want to come out of your ethics and ground rules with a softball question—one that every person in the room can answer without much thought. This often is something straightforward: Tell me your name, where you're from, and what your favorite movie is. That last part—favorite movie—should be adjusted to something in the general ballpark of what your groups are about.

Once you ask that opening question, your job suddenly gets much harder. You stop. You lean back in your chair, and you wait. It's imperative that you let the silence go on, even if it feels interminable. It's at this point that you need someone in the group to go first voluntarily. If you call on someone, you've just set the expectation that no one should talk until you tell them to. Keep smiling and keep your body language open, making eye contact with the participants around the table. Eventually (and usually within just a few seconds, even if it feels like you could run a solid 5K while waiting!), someone will go first. Then second. And then after that, it just goes around the room, falling into a natural pattern. Once everyone's taken their turn, you're ready to go!

Maintaining Good Discussion

Getting things started in a way that sets the right tone is a huge part of ensuring a successful focus group. If that goes well, the rest of this is so much easier. Every moderator approaches this "middle bit"—which really is about four-fifths of the overall group—differently, depending on the client, the participants, and their own personal style. That said, there are some general guidelines that I have found useful over the years:

- **Be flexible. Adapt.** There will be times that participants want to take the conversation in different ways that you had planned, sometimes unwittingly jumping ahead a section or going back to something said earlier. As long as it's relevant to the RQs, adapt. Go with it. Since you've internalized the guide, you can still make sure that you are ticking all the boxes in terms of data, insight, and discovery.
- **Watch your time**. It is entirely too easy to lose track of time and wind up spending an hour on category material and running out of time to get to specifics. Always make sure you have a sense of what time you need to wrap up and move on, particularly if you have important client-specific questions that must be addressed. It is so easy to get sucked into a really interesting, rich discussion and let it go too long—but then you run out of time to get to other pieces you need to cover. Again, internalizing helps—but you also really need to keep an eye on the clock and make sure you're managing time well.
- **Be respectful**. There are times when participants will say or do things that you can't quite believe or wrap your head around. Sometimes probing will help clarify or demonstrate relevance, but that doesn't always happen. In those cases, I usually just use a quick, neutral phrase—"interesting," for example—and then ask someone else a question to get us back on topic. Remember the Coombs Rule: This is where you really need to be cool and not embarrass or shame your participant, even if it's inadvertent.
- **Good relationships lead to good data**. It is remarkable how quickly and easily you can build rapport and relationships in a focus group room. In my experience, the best moderators are the ones who make the effort to build connections with their participants. The focus group attendees *feel* like they know the moderator, which means they are more likely to open up and share.
- **Pay attention to group dynamics**. It can be really easy to let a talkative person (or two) dominate the group, especially if they are saying all the things you want and need to hear. But you're there to hear from the group, which means you need to make sure you're calling on the quieter people and helping them get the airtime to say what they think as well.
- **Use private collection methods as necessary**. If it looks like group think—everyone agreeing out loud even if they might not inside—is taking over, or you are having difficulty drawing out some of your participants, you might want to use private collection methods to help

spark more conversation. Hand out paper or note cards and ask participants to write down their thoughts or responses. You can then call on the people you know you need to hear more from. Usually, having something written down boosts their confidence to finally speak up.

- **Don't forget the clients**! Clients usually are in the back room, watching, listening, and forming their own opinions. Moderators should work with their research teams to build quick check-ins into the guide so the clients can share their thoughts, perceptions, and suggestions for how to proceed. If the tech is available—for example, you have an Apple watch—your teammates can also text the moderators questions from the back in real time that can then be asked directly. This needs to be used judiciously, however, to not overwhelm the moderator or derail the research.

Again, these tips aren't going to fit for every moderator in every circumstance, but they offer a solid starting point for moderating.

Managing Difficult Participants

Most of the time, the people in your focus groups will be happy to be there and ready to go—after all, they signed up for this! Every once in a while, however, you'll have a participant who makes it difficult to get the data you want. Sometimes it comes from a good place. They are overenthusiastic and overly talkative, dominating the conversation and making it difficult for anyone else to get a word in edgewise. In a negative scenario, the participant is disruptive in a more malicious way. Maybe he's derisive about the topic or mocks other people's responses. Or perhaps she is just outright rude, making it uncomfortable for everyone in the room. When these situations happen, a moderator needs to be ready, willing, and able to help mitigate and manage the situation.

This isn't always easy to do. It can be hard to not just let something go, and we tend to worry—perhaps too much—about offending someone or hurting their feelings. What a good moderator needs to remember, however, is that the data always take priority. To make sure that happens, you need to have a good group. Perhaps even more important, we need to make sure we are following the Golden Rule of Research: Do No Harm. In trying to minimize offense to someone who is behaving poorly in our group, we can put the other participants in an uncomfortable, awkward, or even emotionally painful situation. Even in the best-case scenario where someone is just dominating the conversation with no ill intent, it can be incredibly frustrating to be someone else in the group who never gets to share their own point of view. We need to make sure we are working toward the good of the whole and working in our client's best interests at the same time.

In this section, we will review the five steps you can take to help deal with difficult participants. For our purposes, we'll be managing a situation with a participant named Paul. Paul is in his seventies, retired from a blue-collar job, and he doesn't have a lot of time for or patience with the "bells and whistles" on vehicles. Since the focus group you're moderating is on ideation for possible option packages that can be offered for a new model of cars, this means Paul is in his element. Every suggestion others make is immediately shot down, and he keeps pointing out how these options just lead to more expense down the road when they inevitably break. The other participants are visibly frustrated, and the group is quickly heading downhill. What can the moderator do?

Five steps for dealing with a difficult participant. As you know, focus groups generally are held either with a living-room set-up (couches and chairs arranged in a conversational style) or, more traditionally, with participants sitting around a table. The moderator will be at the head of the table, and the participants are sitting around the perimeter. In this first step, the moderator uses an extremely subtle technique in hopes that Paul naturally quiets down: **denying eye contact**. This is extremely easy to do, and it has the benefit of not putting the participant on the spot. No one but Paul will even notice it's happening. But eye contact often is interpreted as an invitation to speak, particularly when the person in charge is initiating it. By denying eye contact, a moderator will remove what Paul might perceive as an invitation to contribute. To do this effectively, the moderator will just slide past Paul when looking around the room. Look at the person to his right, then to his left. Look across the table and then back again. Make eye contact with anyone else in the room—just not Paul.

Often, this will be enough to get a participant to reduce their participation, particularly if it is employed early—when the moderator first notices this might be a problem. Sometimes, however, it's not quite enough, and that's when a moderator moves to step two: **verbal notice**. At this point, the moderator is still polite, calm, and friendly. The next time Paul interrupts or starts to answer the question before anyone else has a chance, you'll cut him off with a friendly—but clear—instruction to let other people have a chance to talk. Often, I'll say something along the lines of "I love your enthusiasm here, but I want to make sure we are hearing from everyone." I'll then call on someone else to talk, either asking the person that he interrupted to continue or asking another participant (usually across the table) to share their thoughts. This does two things: first, it is an overt action to let the participant know that their behavior needs to change; second, it allows the rest of the people in the group to know that the moderator is aware of group dynamics.

If after a verbal notice the participant continues to be disruptive and/or dominant, you can move to step 3: **"talk to the hand."** (It's more than a retro catchphrase, people!) In this step, you put your hand up between you and the participant. While still being polite, your voice is clearly more no-nonsense: "Paul, again, I appreciate you have a lot to say here, but we need to hear from other people as well." Turn to someone else, leaving your hand in the air between the participant and you, and once again call on someone else. Leave your hand up and don't make eye contact with the aggressor. While this is a more forceful response, remember that the other participants in the group likely are annoyed or offended by this repeat offender. You need to get the group back on track, and it won't be easy to do if the problem continues past this stage.

Rarely does a participant continue dominating or behaving derisively after step 3, but it can happen. When it does, it requires a bit more physical action. You've already denied eye contact, asked politely, and then asked directly; now, you need to try one more time to get them on board. To do this, you stand up and walk behind the person. This is step 4: **standing behind them**. You are careful to not touch him or her, but you will stand directly behind them. This makes it physically quite difficult for them to look at you; doing so requires turning around and twisting in a way that is incredibly awkward. You can stay behind them and moderate the group from there for as long as you feel comfortable, although usually a question or two will suffice.

Almost always, standing behind the participant is enough to get the message clearly and kindly that this behavior won't stand. Hopefully, this works. However, there will be times when it just isn't enough. Nothing will salvage this participant; there is no way to get them to be a positive, contributing part of the discussion. In those cases, it is essential that you get them out of the room as soon as possible. This is step 5: **removal from the group**. The best way to handle this is have someone on your team come in to remove them. Your teammate can enter from the back room and simply ask the participant to come out of the room to finish up via an interview: "Paul, we want to make sure we have time to hear all of your thoughts as well as the rest of the group, so why don't you grab your stuff and join me and we'll do an interview?" This approach allows Paul to save face, which is important in terms of both being respectful of Paul and ensuring the rest of the group does not wonder about what is happening or try to get him to stay.

I do want to emphasize that this is incredibly rare; in the years I've moderated focus groups, removal of the participant only happened once or twice. In the vast majority of circumstances, step 3 is the furthest you'll have to go. That said, it's essential that a moderator feel comfortable and confident, and they help ensure the rest of the participants have a positive experience as well. Having these steps in your back pocket is a huge asset for any moderator—and they can be pretty helpful in any sort of group situation as well!

Wrapping Up

I often like to build a wrap-up exercise into the final section of the focus group, giving participants a chance to summarize what they have learned and giving me a chance to do a final check-in with the clients and my research team before ending the group. We will cover more of these in the next chapter, but this is a great place for a creative exercise that will help end the group on a high note and provide an opportunity for your participants to reveal what their final thoughts are. This is particularly helpful when heading into the clearinghouse question discussed above: "What didn't I ask you about that I should have?"

Once participants are done, you can officially wrap up the focus group. This typically means giving them instructions on what to do when they leave (usually picking up their incentives and perhaps a parking voucher). If you will have participants for the next group waiting in the lobby, it's a good idea to ask your departing folks to keep quiet about what they discussed so that they don't spoil the opportunity for the next group.

Finally, the room is empty. You quickly gather materials you might need to hold onto—flip chart paper, artifacts from projective exercises, and so on—and go in the back room. Hopefully, your experience is akin to the scenario described at the beginning of this chapter.

CONDUCTING QUALITATIVE RESEARCH ONLINE

As discussed in chapter 5, more and more often, qualitative research is done online. Specialty platforms and programs exist to facilitate online interviews and focus groups while maintaining confidentiality, and researchers (and clients!) appreciate how much easier and cheaper it is to do this type of research without constant travel.

Generally, the same principles and practices that work for face-to-face qualitative research will work online as well; after all, people who are good at watching, listening, and asking questions typically aren't limited by the medium or mode of delivery. That said, there are some considerations:

- **Make sure participants know what is expected of them**. Will you use just audio or will they be on camera? What supplies should they have at hand? Will they need to play any clips on their browser? These are all things participants should know in advance so they can come prepared.
- **Be proactive to avoid tech issues**. Make sure you test run any software or platforms with participants who likely will be using their home computers or personal devices (telephones,

Figure 6.3   Online focus groups are increasingly common in today's research environment. (Getty: SDI Productions)

tablets, etc.). If they have to download and log in to something new, have a team member or your recruiter call them in advance to make sure everything is working and troubleshoot if needed. Remind participants to wear headphones and test their mics and cameras to make sure everything is working.

- **Be prepared for tech issues**. No matter how proactive you are, tech issues always will come up. Have a plan for what to do, including having tech support on call if needed (one of the benefits specialty platforms often provide). In advance, establish an alternate way of reaching the participant, and give them a number to reach you or the recruiter if they have problems. If you plan for trouble, you hopefully won't need it—but it will be a godsend if you do.
- **For focus groups, make sure you can mute microphones**. In the early days of the COVID-19 pandemic, countless memes made their way onto social media centered on the constant stream of unwanted audio from unmuted mics—including a legendary toilet flush from an unknown and unnamed Supreme Court justice. As a moderator, you want to be able to have some control over mics, and it needs to be fairly intuitive and easy so you can mute without wasting time during the group.
- **Have someone else from your team watching to take notes, and make sure you record**. It's really easy to move into the weird/creepy category online, and spending time writing down what your participant says is a great way to do that. Have someone else on your team there to write down key quotes and concepts, and absolutely record so you have a record of what was said.

BEST PRACTICES AND KEY TAKEAWAYS

Doing good qualitative research requires creativity and thoughtfulness, adaptability and commitment, preparation and planning. When this research is done well, it can lead to remarkable insights that can be transformative for businesses—or just give a strong indication of direction for a really pressing but not hugely significant question. As the person conducting the research, you need to be completely prepared, project confidence (even if you don't 100 percent believe it), and build trust between you, your participants, and your client. This type of research isn't easy, but when it works—it's magic.

As a final reminder, this chapter provides a foundation for how to approach writing a guide and collecting data, but my way isn't the *only* way. When you are out in the big, bad business world and working in applied consumer insights research, you'll be exposed to countless ways of approaching this work. Pay attention. See what works and what doesn't. Ask questions about *why* some things work and some don't. Integrate the techniques and strategies you find most helpful into your own work. And, perhaps most important, don't be afraid to *try*. Try new ideas and new techniques. Experiment. Refine. Polish. The best way for you to collect qualitative data is the way that works best for you—so trust yourself to figure that out.

KEY TERMS

Clearinghouse question: Asked at the end of each research incident, this question gives your participants a chance to share any ideas or information they want to share that didn't come up during questioning

Coombs Rule: Be cool; don't be weird

Funnel: Structuring a guide to start with broad, general questions and then move toward specifics

Guide: The set of questions and instructions used to frame the discussion in qualitative research (in academic research, used interchangeably with "instrument" or "protocol")

Header: The top of the qualitative guide/protocol with mandatory information (study title, date, etc.)

Internalize: Learning the guide thoroughly in order to maximize flexibility and flow

Iterative: Not set in stone; can change over time to respond to what is learned

Moderator: Research team member leading a focus group or other qualitative research

Priming: Revealing information that changes the way participants respond to later questions

Probes: Digging in deeper to participants' responses in specific directions to find out more and learn what's underneath

Softball questions: Questions that require little thought and are easy to answer; used to make participants more comfortable as they start their qualitative research experience

Timetable: How long each section of the guide is expected to take

7

Using Creative Exercises for Deeper Insights

A few years ago, I was conducting a research study for a small college. They had noticed a trend in enrollments where students would take classes for a semester, then leave, but then come back again a semester or two later. They wanted to figure out why this was happening and what, if anything, they could do to help.

Our first focus group started off well. The participants were responsive and chatty, and the conversation flowed. I had lots of good information and reasons that they would come and go—financial struggles, childcare concerns, changing work schedules that made it difficult to come to classes at regular times—all things that made sense and that the client had anticipated.

About 45 minutes into the conversation, I introduced one of the major creative exercises we had planned for the groups—a collage. I spread a pile of magazines in the middle of the table and dumped out markers and glue sticks around them. Each participant was given a large piece of paper taken from the in-room flip chart and told to draw a line down the middle. The collage instructions were clear: On the right side, show us the future: what it will feel like when you finally graduate; on the left, show us what it feels like right now as you try to get there. I left the room to consult with the clients. Even from the back room, we could hear the difference when people moved from the right—the fun, exciting, aspirational side—to the left. Things got quieter. A bit more somber.

After about 10 minutes I came back in. One by one, participants showed off their collages, walking us through the various elements and telling us stories about why they picked what they did. A young woman who had been fairly quiet throughout the group eventually stood up to take her turn. The right side was fairly consistent with what we had seen from other participants: A nice house, a person in business wear, and general trappings of a middle-class lifestyle. Prominently displayed on the left, however, was a still image from OK Go's "Here It Goes Again" video, in which the four band members do a choreographed dance routine moving between and among treadmills (see figure 7.1 for a visual).

When asked to explain, she was ready: "This is how it always feels. I think I'm finally making progress, then realize I'm just on another treadmill. I am never actually moving forward." That image—that explanation—resonated with her fellow participants, and the ensuing discussion was remarkable for its depth, clarity, and the level of vulnerability revealed. That moment with the collage took the group from good and useful to great and transformative.

83

Figure 7.1   An image from the OK Go video for "Here It Goes Again," used as part of a collage exercise.

At the end of the last chapter, I talked about the magic of qualitative research. Good creative exercises often are what make that magic happen. If you can find ways to get your participants to open up and move past the literal, logical answers, you often can uncover deeper, more meaningful insights than direct questioning ever could reveal. This chapter explores a number of these creative exercises. If you are doing qualitative research, whether for a client or just for your own practice and edification, try to bake some of these in. You'll be amazed at how valuable they can be.

GENERAL BEST PRACTICES

While you truly can get amazing results from creative exercises during interviews, ethnographies, and focus groups, it's important that you know when to deploy them and how to do it well. These exercises can be used to explore perceptions around brands, products, services—anything you need to understand in relation to consumers and their interior lives. In general, I recommend using creative exercises for two reasons: data and process. Since data are always the most important thing in research, let's talk about that one first.

Generating Good Data

The right creative exercise at the right time can elicit remarkable conversation and insights, generating the data that will help your findings transcend from serviceable to incredible. This often is used when you have a topic that people have strong, logical feelings about that they want to defend in strong, logical ways—even if they really are kind of neutral and/or more illogical in what they *really* believe. Let's be real: We all want to be able to say we knew all about the RPM and acceleration and brakes and safety features before we buy a car. But sometimes, all of those things are moderated by how much we really, really like the look. Or the brand. Or the color. We don't always make decisions logically, or at least not entirely logically, but we don't always want to admit that. Projective exercises help us get to what is *underneath*. They help us get deeper than the logical, rational answers so we can uncover the more compelling emotional wants and needs that often drive consumers in their decision-making.

Here's another example: I was moderating focus groups for a nonprofit that focused on Israeli-American relations. They had previous research indicating Americans felt a strong kinship and close ties to Israel, and they wanted to understand better what that meant. My boss, Boaz, was a physically imposing Israeli with a fabulous accent and total New York style. There was no way he could moderate the groups. So, he asked me to do it, since I was the "most American" person he knew. (Translation: I am from Ohio. Midwest FTW!) During the groups, we had participants yell out all of the countries they could think of as I scribbled them down on the flip chart. I kept soliciting more countries until we had a good list of about thirty countries, and, most important, Israel was on there. I then handed each participant a piece of note paper and had them divide theirs into three columns: care a lot, care a little, don't care at all. They then had to place all of the countries into one of those columns. As they wrote, I walked around the table, taking note of where "Israel" made it on each paper. We'd then talk about different countries were placed and why, again making sure Israel was part of the discussion. Invariably, it was in the "care a lot" or "care a little" columns. The reasons were clear and easily articulated, usually focused on the Judeo-Christian tradition and Israel's important role as allies in the Middle East. The next step was to bring in a projective creative exercise: an imaginary field trip. I told participants to imagine that each of the countries we had discussed and come to life. We were going on a field trip to the street where these countries now lived. We had Argentina's house, and Japan's house, and Australia's house, and so on. We'd stop in front of one house and they had to tell me what they saw.

Often, our first stop was Italy's house. The room would be loud and vibrating with energy as participants imagined what this would be. Do it yourself. Close your eyes and imagine what Italy's house would look like. If you're like our participants, this house is huge and probably made of brick or stone with a lush, green lawn. We go to the door, and it's opened by the mama wearing an apron, with a pot of red sauce at the ready. She invites us in to eat—*Mangia! Mangia!*—and we enter a house filled with lots of people, lots of food, lots of noise, and lots of love. After plates of pasta and goblets of chianti and more cannoli than we can consume, we have to leave. Participants usually were sad to go, although some were excited to see where we would go next.

I'd then tell them to imagine we have walked down the street and arrived in front of Israel's house. What did that one look like? The tenor in the room immediately changed. People would sit back in their chairs and cross their arms. The quiet was palpable, especially in the wake of Italian enthusiasm. Eventually, someone would speak up. "It's gray." "It's beige." Consistently, there was no color, no vibrancy. Participants would talk about how maybe there were armed security guards to check our passports before we went in. Some talked about bombed-out buildings around the house. When we got to the door, it was almost always answered by a male, often dressed in the traditional clothing of an Orthodox Jew. He would invite us in, and we would sit quietly while his wife brought in a small tray of food. The children would be off studying or, interestingly, often playing the violin. We would stay long enough to be polite, and then leave. Rarely were people sad to go.

It was fascinating to discuss these responses with the client, particularly because they were remarkably consistent across groups held all over the states. Their expectations had matched what was in the "care a lot" exercise—that Americans felt a strong connection to Israel. But what we realized was that Americans care about Israel as a country—an ally—much more than they feel a connection to the Israeli people. Our respondents knew very little about the natural beauty of Israel or its robust tech industry; instead, the images were of dated, fearful, deeply religious people living under the constant threat of violence—an Israel almost unrecognizable to our Israeli clients and colleagues. This insight was invaluable to them as they sought to build better relationships with Americans. And without these creative exercises, we would never have been able to get to this depth of feeling, belief, and perception. Our participants gave us very good, rational reasons for caring about Israel, and I am sure they meant those. But the field trip let us understand what that *meant* in a way we couldn't have gotten through direct questioning. Our data were better and our interpretation stronger because we used this approach.

Process

In addition to vastly improving the quality and depth of data, creative exercises improve your process—especially during focus groups. While your participants are making their collages or completing materials, you can pop into the back room to check in with the team for feedback and notes. They also are a fabulous way to reset your room and engage participants. If you notice you are losing your group, get up and walk around—they'll look to see what you are doing and start paying attention again. Doing a quick off-the-cuff exercise that lets you use the flip chart can remind your participants that their words and data matter, sparking new lines of discussion that can prove fruitful. For all qualitative work, these exercises help change the tone, break up the questioning and give participants a break, and let the moderator or interviewer have a few minutes to evaluate and assess what they've heard and where they need to go next.

Good creative exercises also serve as **stimulus** for your questioning. They provide remarkable opportunities to spark discussion and provide new avenues for investigation.

Creative exercises also often allow for the production of **artifacts** that can be extraordinarily useful during your analysis and presentation stages of research—just make sure you are maintaining the confidentiality of participants. The images gathered during collages or drawn during a "marketing exec" blast not only offer excellent data but also provide helpful visuals to add interest and depth to your work far outside of the data collection phase.

"Selling" Creative Exercises

While we tend to think about creative exercises as something for focus groups, they can (and usually should) be used with any qualitative research method. In the next section, we will review various types and examples of creative exercises that are commonly used, and you will quickly see some of the ways these can work with one-on-one research as well as groups. No matter how many participants you are trying to engage, however, you need to think carefully about how you "sell" these exercises to persuade your participants to actively engage. This can be a challenge. Some creative exercises—particularly those that require some flights of fancy—can make your participants feel quite vulnerable. They often force people out of their comfort zones and require different ways of thing and topic about the topic of interest. Thus, it is essential that moderators go in prepared to make them work. Here are a few tips:

- **Know what you are trying to get out of the exercise.** This will help you explain what the work will entail, thereby letting you answer questions that arise and redirect when participants go astray.

- **Practice, practice, practice.** Take the opportunity to pilot your creative exercises with those around you—your research team, roommates, friends, and family can all be useful faux-participants to let you practice your spiel and get comfortable with selling the exercise.
- **Have confidence.** No matter how wacky the creative exercise may sound, never let on to participants that you are anything less than completely confident that this will be a home run. If you aren't sold, they won't be either. Believe in what you are trying to do and let participants rely on your faith in the exercise while they still building their own.
- **Give things time to work.** It is perfectly normal for creative exercises to take some time to gain steam. If you're in a group setting, your participants may be conscious of not saying something silly or different from what others say. If you're in a one-on-one meeting, you may have a really literal participant who is uncomfortable with using their imagination to go outside the bounds of rationality. Keep the faith and keep probing to get them comfortable. You'll almost always get something. That said . . .
- **Know when to stop.** Even when they are going well, creative exercises will run their course. When you stop getting useful data or you have to finally accept you are talking to the world's most literal person, it's time to move on. Remember, time with participants is a precious commodity in qualitative research. You want to use it wisely. As we all learned from *Mean Girls*, don't spend time trying to make "fetch" happen.

TYPES OF CREATIVE EXERCISES

In this section, we will review some of the common creative exercises that my colleagues and I have used in our qualitative research. These are intended to give you some idea of what these exercises might look like and when to use them, but this list certainly is not exhaustive. Some of these are considered **projectives**: Exercises that require participants project brands or products (or, in the case of the field trip, themselves!) into an imaginary situation. This label often is used as a catch-all for non-direct questioning, but, for clarity's sake, I like to limit its use to those techniques that specifically require that type of projection.

Before we get started, two important notes: First, if you come up with a great idea for a creative exercise, try it. Test it with your research team. Experiment. See how it works and the kinds of data you get. We constantly were innovating and incorporating new approaches in our research and the vast majority of the time we found it worked. And second, the exercises I am including here all are ones that do not require technology. This is a conscious choice. Non-digital exercises can be done under almost any circumstances and some can be incorporated on the fly. They also are less likely to fail due to tech issues that might arise, particularly if people are using their own equipment (smartphones, cameras, etc.). This does not mean technology has no place here. You can do fabulous drawing exercises using high-end tablets, and if you make sure everyone has a smartphone, you can do polling through platforms like Kahoot. While my focus here is on tangible materials, this is not intended to limit your imaginations. Think of these as a starting point. I enthusiastically encourage you to think big and be bold in your own guide development.

Collage

This chapter opened with an anecdote about collages in focus groups, and I hope it gave you a good sense of what these projective exercises can do. Collages are ideally suited when you want people to visualize a situation—real or imagined—and show you what it looks like. We typically would have either preselected images or stacks of magazines covering a range of topics and genres so we had a good variety of pictures and headlines to use. We would never provide scissors—that kind of detail took too long. Instead, participants were instructed to tear out images and use the glue sticks to place them on their collages. We also included markers participants could use to write words, edit photos, or draw their own pictures. After about 10 minutes, each participant would then talk us through their collage and we would have short time for discussion. Once all were done, we could then talk about themes that emerged as well as new ideas that were sparked through this projective. These artifacts also provide a really useful tool for your analysis and presentation, looking at both what images are used and, equally important, what is missing.

While collages can be done in person, it's also possible to have them done at home, as seen in figure 7.2. This can be useful if you want the stimulus and discussion but don't have time for the actual creation in face-to-face research, but that also means these are suited to online research. Just make sure you give specific instructions to your participants about what materials to use, how much time they should spend creating it, and what expectations will be once they are in their research experience.

Drawings and Storytelling

Another visually oriented creative exercise you can employ is having participants create drawings around a specific question or topic. We've asked for individual pieces and comic strips or storyboards, depending on our RQs and what we needed to get out of the exercise. Drawings are fantastic if you need to get a visual representation of some component of your research, and the longer-form strips or storyboards allow for an emerging narrative as well. For example, you can have your participants draw your brand as a superhero and then tell you a quick story about that superhero's origin story or their latest feat.

One caution: If you are going to employ something like this, you need to make clear that you know not everyone is an artist and that stick figures are more than okay. As a nonartist myself,

Figure 7.2   Example of collage created based on the prompt "Imagine you've now succeeded in [goal]. What would your life look like?"

I like to foreground the importance of storytelling. If you have them focus on the story, it can take the pressure off the art. Stories can also be useful outside of the context of drawings. It can be helpful to have participants tell a story around your brand—perhaps they don't draw the superhero but just tell you about it instead. This can be faster and easier for some participants and often connects nicely with exercises designed to bring brands to life.

Drawing and storytelling don't have to edge into the fantastical. You also can do this by incorporating real-life situations that allow for more literal responses and scenarios. For example, imagine you are doing research on a vacuum cleaner that has a revolutionary new feature that is unparalleled at picking up pet hair. You could ask participants to tell you a story about the last time they tried to clean up pet hair. You can then follow up by having them tell you a story about how it would be different if they had this new feature on their vacuum. These stories become opportunities to probe and better understand the real benefits—both rational and emotional—that this product could provide.

Bring Brands to Life

As we saw in the Italy/Israel example above, it can be incredibly useful to incorporate projectives that **anthropomorphize brands**. Bringing brands to "life" in the minds of the consumer—whether in groups or during interviews or ethnographies—offers rich, meaningful insight into consumers' perceptions of brands on a wide range of criteria, including how relatable, personable, and appealing they really are.

In addition to the aforementioned field trips, bringing brands to life can include exercises like "brand parties": You're throwing a party, and all of the brands you've discussed are invited. The doorbell rings. You answer the door and [Brand X] is there. What are they wearing? What do they look like? Do they bring anything? If so, what? How did they get to the party? Do you want to talk to them? Who are they talking to? There are so many places to take this, and it can generate energy and excitement if done well. If possible, you want to be able to write down what people are saying so you can eventually compare across brand personifications. Typically, we would do three brands for whatever exercise we chose—our client and then two competitors. You'll want to have an advance discussion with your client to make sure you're covering the brands they want to know about, and you need to make sure all of the brands included are mentioned earlier in the conversation so their inclusion feels organic, especially if you have still not revealed who your client is.

Field trips and parties are two of the more common exercises to anthropomorphize brands, but I encourage you to get creative. Think about different scenarios where you might want to have a brand join you. Maybe they're the ones throwing the party rather than an invitee. If you're researching teen-centered brands or products, maybe you see where they would sit in the cafeteria and what "clique" they would join. The options are limitless, so have some fun brainstorming new ways to make this work. Trust me—it's worth your time.

Fill-in-the-Blank

One of my favorite "quick and dirty" creative exercises was to create a form letter of sorts with fill-in-the-blank options. For example, you could write the template for a love letter, and then have your participants fill it in based on their feelings toward your brand, as shown in figure 7.3.

Or, if you wanted to tap into feelings of deprivation, you could write an obituary and focus on what they will miss the most—and what they won't miss at all. Even the most reticent participant tends to enjoy these exercises. They are low stakes and yet still elicit really useful data, often crystallizing key ideas about the brand or media product and participant's emotions toward it. Think about how powerful it can be to have participants fill in an obituary that ends with this statement: "While my heart will always belong to [BRAND], I look forward to spending more time with _____ because they _____." This forces them to identify a likely replacement—and give you the reason why. That's invaluable data. Plus, clients love this—it's tangible, it's fast, and it leads to good discussions. These are great exercises to use toward the end of your research to summarize and transition to the final set of questions. If you're doing your research online, you can have your participants fill in digitally—just set it up in advance. If possible, you want to send this through your online platform rather than having participants click away. Hopefully, the chat feature will allow you to do that. And if they have to open something, you also want to be sure that you are not using programs your participants might not have. There's no point in sending something in Pages to a respondent who uses Microsoft. Make sure you are being as user-friendly as possible.

"Magic Wand"

Sometimes you need a tool that you can keep in your back pocket to use when you need to get your participants to get out of the literal and possible and into the ideal. In those situations, a

Soda Pop: A Love Letter

Dear _____ (favorite soda),

I am so grateful to have you in my life! Every time I am with you, I feel

_____. While I always want to be around you, my favorite

time to spend together is _____. I can't imagine doing

_____ without you. I always am _____ when

you are around, and it's even better when _____ is there

too!

While things are mostly amazing between us, we aren't perfect. If I

could change one thing about you, it would be _____.

Instead, you would _____. But please don't

take that to harshly, since you are still my favorite! In fact, the only thing

that comes close is _____, and that is just because

_____.

Thank you for always _____!

With _____,

Name

Figure 7.3 Example of a "fill-in-the-blank" love letter exercise.

magic wand can serve you well. It's a simple instruction: "You now have a magic wand and you can make the most perfect version of [X] that you can imagine. No limits. What would this look like?" You then just probe to understand why the things your participant mentions really matters to them. Even if they get completely fantastical, you can take the kernels of what they are saying to uncover insights and create a more practical set of recommendations. Bonus: Magic wand exercises require no preparation, no materials. You can use this as needed, even if it's multiple times in the same data collection experience.

Creating Lists and Organizing Data

While the magic wand is fantastic for ideation and creativity, there are times that you just need to get all possible criteria on the table and then see how they connect to each other. In those circumstances, I love to look for exercises that allow me to create lists and then have participants organize those data into meaningful categories. In the Israel example I shared earlier, I talked about how we had participants list all of the countries they could think of as a group and then organize those into three lists. There are countless variations of this type of exercise that are incredibly useful when you need to generate a robust pool of brands or products and then see how participants categorize them. Imagine you are having students list all of the criteria they look for when picking a class for their next semester. You can write down all of the items on a series of sticky notes that are randomly posted on the wall. Participants can then organize them into categories that they determine—class time, professor, required, and so on—and organize those categories in relation to each other.

These exercises are particularly useful when you are trying to prepare for a survey and understand both what matters to your audience and the "buckets" they use to organize their thinking. These work particularly well in individual research either face-to-face or online, but I would not recommend them for online focus groups, at least for novice researchers. It can be difficult to have a group activity like this when they are remote and don't have the physical tools to manipulate and organize, so other strategies might work better.

Other times, you'll want to think about list/organizing activities to help elicit a broader range of information. Rather than having participants generate lists and then create categories inductively, you provide the headers and they fill in the columns. One of my favorite exercises to use is called "plus/minus lists" (see figure 7.4). They are exactly what it says on the tin: You create a chart with two columns, one with a "+" and one with a "−" at the top.

You then ask participants to focus on one and then the other—fill up the "plus" column and then move onto the "minus." Every brand, every product, every experience has both good and bad points, but at times in research it can be difficult to get both. If your group is hating on everything, you can draw the figure and then immediately start recording their complaints and issues in the "minus" column. Once that gets exhausted, you then can say, "Okay, we clearly know what you don't like. Now let's talk about some of the things that should go on the positive side. What's something positive you can say about [brand/product]?" This also works in reverse. In some situations, participants will be loath to criticize the brand, either because they are true brand enthusiasts or, sometimes, because they don't want to offend or be "mean" to the moderator. These lists can pull you out of the one-sided spiral and elicit better data. And again, these don't require huge prep—you can do this live and on the fly, whether online or in person. You also can use whatever criteria you want as the headers for each column or on each page—this can be adapted to just about anything.

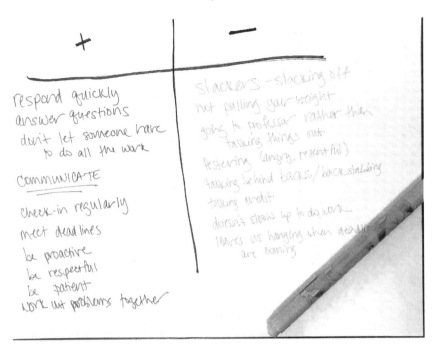

Figure 7.4   Example of a "plus/minus list" created to generate ideas around how to create a successful group culture.

Card Sorts

Card sorts work really well in person when you are trying to understand what criteria matter and how they are organized but want to allow for a more individualized response than the summary list might allow. To do this, you'll give each participant a stack of index cards and instruct them to write down all of the reasons they would want to do or buy something, what their criteria for evaluating a certain product is, and so on. You can then do two things: First, you can have them organize into whatever piles/categories they feel are appropriate and then name those categories, akin to what the "list" exercise explained above. Or, if you already know what categories you want these sorted into, you can bring in buckets or bins labeled accordingly. Participants can then each drop their index cards into the bucket they feel is best suited for that particular card. For example, if you are looking at criteria for shopping at a pharmacy, you can bring in buckets labeled CVS, Walgreens, and Discount DrugMart. They then sort their cards into the one they feel best meets that criteria. As you go through what was placed in each bucket by individual respondents, you can dig into brand perceptions as well as consumer needs.

Marketing Exec

One of my favorite ways to wrap up the group is to do a "marketing exec" exercise. By this point, participants likely know who your specific client is—the unmasking has happened, so to speak. In this approach, you ask participants to imagine they are a marketing exec for your client, and their job is to make a demonstrable improvement in whatever area you're researching and they'll get a huge bonus. (I like to use $10,000—it's enough imaginary money to show the stakes are high and worth working for, but not so high that it seems like it would never happen.) They have five minutes to create a marketing message that would get them to that bonus. That time keeps it short and focused on key concepts. Once the time is up, participants present their work and, in a group setting, the group can vote on whose idea(s) are the best and talk about why. This exercise works really well across all settings and has the benefit of creating fantastic artifacts for your analysis and presentation.

BEST PRACTICES AND KEY TAKEAWAYS

Creative exercises can be an incredible way to develop deeper insights and help participants get beyond the literal and rational answers that tend to come up first. These are essential tools for your work as a qualitative researcher, and I encourage you to try these out. I'm amazed at how often I wind up using these exercises in my everyday work and life, and I suspect that you'll find these come in handy when you're working with a group or organization and trying to make sense of a situation. As my favorite childhood church song says, "Be Not Afraid." The benefits far outweigh the risks.

Good creative exercises will help you get a deeper and better understanding of your audience, and these work best when they are tailored to your experience. Use your imaginations and your training to develop new iterations of exercises that will help you get the best data possible. And good data are essential for good analysis, which is what we will cover next.

Figure 7.5   Focus group members work together to develop ideas and shared understandings. (Getty: Milan Markovic)

KEY TERMS

Anthropomorphize brands: Bringing brands to "life" in the minds of the consumer to generate insight into perceptions of brands on a wide range of criteria, including how relatable, personable, and appealing they really are

Artifacts: Materials produced as a result of creative exercises, such as collages, drawings, and fill-in-the-blank results; these are useful during your analysis and presentation stages of research by offering visuals to add interest and depth

Projectives: Exercises that require participants project brands or products into an imaginary situation

Stimulus: Materials or ideas brought into a research experience with the intention of generating responses from participants

8

Qualitative Data Analysis and Reporting

As you may remember (lo so many chapters ago), one of the very first things you read about in this book is **that consumer insights research is focused on translating data into insight and insight into meaningful recommendations**. That happens through good data analysis and reporting—which means you need to think about, plan for, and engage with this phase of the process the entire time you're doing this research. From the minute you start putting together your research instruments, you should be thinking about and planning for your analysis and reporting—what will you need to know? What kinds of visuals will be useful? How will you be able to address your RQs? A worst-case scenario is finishing up in the field and realizing you've missed a big chunk of what you needed to learn, so all of these considerations go into your research planning. And along those same lines, you want to make sure you are continually doing analysis while you are in the field. While we talk about these as separate processes, they really need to go hand in hand to ensure you are conducting thorough, rigorous research that you can confidently put forward to address your client's business objectives.

That said, once you are fully out of the field, you need to be ready to do a deep dive into what you heard and what it means. You'll block out a period of time with your team to do a **debrief**, a lengthy period of time where you just sit and talk, debate, argue (kindly and respectfully), and push and pull at the data until you hit those a-ha moments that mark the beginnings of finding a really good, really relevant, really useful story in the data. This process requires flexible thinking and imagination and, like all creative processes, can be spectacularly frustrating. There will be times when you are convinced that no story exists in the data, no insights will be gleaned, and you've just wasted both your time and the client's money to come up with nothing new or exciting. But push through. Keep engaging with the data and your research team. Invariably, kernels of ideas start to spark. One person makes a comment—even an aside—that someone else picks up on and expands. The energy in the room builds as you realize that this may be it—you may have finally (finally!) cracked this story. And as you keep building, you may realize that some of it doesn't quite work—you don't have the data to support it, perhaps, or the specific point you are trying to make isn't connecting with the rest of the ideas presented. In those cases, you likely have to go back to the data, and that's okay. You've done a fabulous job collecting data, you've parallel-tracked and integrated analysis while you did so, and you know with certainty that your work is going to have a positive impact on your client's business. But to do that, you need to know how to properly analyze qualitative data.

To help you prepare, this chapter will cover two different phases in your qualitative research. The first part will cover what you should do *while* you are still in the field—the practices and procedures you need to employ to ensure you are getting the strongest possible data and ensuring rigor. The second, which will be the main focus of the chapter, reviews best practices for the "pure" data analysis phase and gives specific recommendations and tips for getting the best possible story out of your data. The last section of this chapter then tells you what to do with your work, including brief overviews of ways you can submit your findings and how to use that material to transition to the quantitative phase of research. Before we begin, an important reminder: Your job as a researcher is to provide the results of your best thinking and analysis, *not* to report data. If you don't deliver on the analysis, you haven't done your job well. So don't think of this chapter as one you can skim—this really, really matters.

GENERAL BEST PRACTICES: DURING FIELDING

As noted in chapter 5, it is essential that you integrate data collection and analysis during your qualitative work. This involves two main components: Talking initial thinking through with your team and clients (as appropriate) and writing really good notes during the research experience itself. "But wait!" you may say. "Doesn't that violate the Coombs Rule?" (I appreciate you remembering. Thank you for your diligence. #extracredit #influencer) The answer to that excellent question is nope, not really. There are two different kinds of notes that you'll use. If you are the moderator or interviewer, you'll want to only take **jot notes**, the quick ones you can scribble really fast so you don't forget an idea or a key takeaway, or maybe to write down the time so you can find a great quote in the recording later on. Sticking with these jot notes help you make sure you don't come across as a faux psychiatrist, and hopefully you have a teammate taking good notes unobtrusively during the fieldwork.

Once you are done with each instance of data collection, however, everyone on the research team who was there will want to take about 20 minutes and spend time writing **field notes**. These field notes let you create a record of everything you remember about the interview or focus group itself—what was said, anything that stood out, things you want to remember—but also serve as a first level of analysis. You should put in here any ideas that were sparked, either about how to iterate your guide for the next field experience or potential insights that you want to think more about. When I am doing my field notes, I tend to write my record of what I saw and heard in regular font and then *italicize my ideas*. That lets me keep the writing flow steady and the documentation in one place while also making clear what came from the participant versus my own thinking. It's important to note here that field notes are intended to be stream of consciousness—a true brain dump in the best sense of the phrase. Don't worry about it making sense or being well crafted. The idea is to get as much out as possible, letting your thoughts flow. This opens you up to ideas and seeing connections—something that you might have missed in the group suddenly stands out, or you see how two seemingly disparate points of discussion actually have a lot in common. These field notes also are invaluable in remembering fragments of potential ideas that spark while talking with participants. In the moment, you're often thinking about what went before and what is coming next, so you don't have a chance to follow and explore those little inklings. Field notes let you do that.

During your entire time collecting data, your team should constantly be spending time talking through what you've heard and seen, what has worked, to be changed. Eventually, you will start to reach **redundancy** on certain topics data are emerging. (Academic side note: In academic research you continue collecting until you reach redundancy; in applied research like this, you have a set number of interviews you plan to do from the beginning. Due to budget and timeline restrictions, rarely would that number change over the course of research. Unless something completely new comes up that is important enough to add additional research to your design, you stick with your original plan.) Once you have reached redundancy on a key point or line of inquiry, you should then start developing some initial themes or explanations. You can then test those during the groups or interviews, doing what we call **member checks**: checking your thinking with participants. This allows you to get feedback on your initial analysis and gives you an opportunity to dig more into what participants have to say from a more informed perspective. If you are doing research where the client is present, this also can be helpful in making sure they are buying in to the process.

Eventually, you will be done with data collection, ready to go back and start the full phase of analysis. What does that mean? What does that look like? All excellent questions. Let's dig in.

GENERAL BEST PRACTICES: POST-COLLECTION DATA ANALYSIS

When I worked for a consumer insights and brand consulting company in New York, our offices were in a loft in Tribeca. The researchers (like me!) were in the front bullpen space, where we could brainstorm ideas, bounce question wording around, test out projectives, and dance (obviously) as needed to get our wiggles out. The space had a glass-walled conference room that looked out over us, and that was where the debrief magic happened. We would block out three hours on our calendars, drag up flip charts and all of the artifacts from creative exercises we had shipped back from groups, and grab Diet Coke and snacks to fuel our thinking. The glass walls would be covered in collages and plus/minus lists and all kinds of notes, and we would have our laptops handy to check our notes and look up things we needed to learn. The flip chart in the corner of the room stood ready with multicolored markers ready for drawing, writing, and lots and lots of crossing out and arrows.

Some of my best memories from my years as a researcher took place in this small conference room. This was where I learned that I actually am creative, despite the fact I can't carry a tune in a bucket nor can I draw anything more complex than a standard stick figure. Being able to see connections between and among ideas, developing meaningful insights and recommendations, and working out compelling stories from our data to help answer our clients successfully answer their business questions was truly creative, and I wish I could bottle the energy and enthusiasm in that room. I have never felt as clear-sighted and purposeful as I did in those days, and I hope this chapter helps all of you have those experiences as well, whether your debriefs are happening online or in person.

As we move into the "how" of qualitative data analysis, a few thoughts/warnings. First, if you have done your job well, your findings often will have a *high "duh" factor*. They will feel intuitive and *right*, which can make you feel like you actually didn't find anything new at all. That's what can be so tricky about this. If your findings truly are grounded in the data, you will be crystallizing something that feels organic and natural—it fits with your client and their needs—even if it is something they would never have thought of without you and your

.ta. If it feels too revolutionary, however, you need to make very sure you take it back to your data—this often means you've pulled away from what the data actually tell you so you want to confirm, confirm, confirm by finding the data to support your thesis *and* looking for **negative cases** (experiences reported by your participants that fall outside your story). If you can account for those with what you've developed through analysis, your case is strong. But if you can't, you need to make sure that you're really dismissing an outlier and not ignoring an important theme that might disrupt your current thinking.

This leads us to our second point: **Data analysis is messy and nonlinear**. You need to be prepared to feel very strongly that you have made a terrible mistake in your data collection and you are now going to be fired and that everything is on fire. This is especially likely in cases where you haven't had the chance to do sufficient initial analysis in the field—you are now starting from a deficit, and it can be incredibly frustrating. But persevere. Keep your head in the data. Work with your team. Get more Diet Coke or Mountain Dew or whatever your beverage of choice is. If you keep engaging and playing with the data and potential ideas, eventually you will break through. You just have to stick with it. Eventually, themes will emerge. And while they might not be immediately correct, they will at least give you a starting point to pursue.

Finally (and most important), always keep in mind that your job is to **transform data into insight and insight into meaningful recommendations**. The first part of this is where most of our focus will be. This happens through **abstraction**: taking the concrete data and pulling them out of their immediate context to help find connections and derive meaning. This doesn't mean decontextualizing them entirely, however—the data don't exist in a vacuum, and you want to stay true to what the participants said. But as I said earlier, our job is to find the meaning in the data, and that means looking for patterns and meaning that transcends the literal. Your field notes, your data, and your thinking all come into play to make this happen.

In the Debrief

You and your team in the room are on a Zoom call, ready to jump into your debrief. As you start, I recommend rewriting your business objective and RQs on a piece of flip-chart paper and put it on the wall; if you're doing this online, make sure everyone has them handy. This helps make sure you keep focused on what you're trying to achieve here. It can be all too easy to go down a path that is interesting but not relevant. Keep your eyes on the prize. You also want to remind everyone about what is coming next. If you're just doing this phase of research, you'll be preparing for a final presentation. If you're moving into surveys or another qualitative phase, you'll be prepping for a **topline**—a "checkpoint" presentation that shows what you've learned and where you will go next in your research. Remember, by this point you'll have spent countless hours engaged with this data, so you know what's here. Go back to the beginning. Look at the early data that may have faded in your memory. Start to look for patterns. How do the disparate data points connect? How do they help explain each other? How do they hang together? During this debrief, you'll be using **inductive reasoning**, moving from the bottom—the vast amount of data you have—to reach the level of abstraction needed to identify key themes and insights that will help advance your understanding of the RQs. You get to this through talking, brainstorming, and debating. Use whatever tools and techniques you need to make sense of this. Running into a brick wall? Use a projective to see if you can find a breakthrough. Follow a spark that doesn't seem to quite work to see where you can take it. While that idea may not work, it could lead to something really good. This is where being part of a team is invaluable. It's always easier to play with concepts and ideas when you have other people to challenge and inspire you.

Debrief Roles

Over time, I've identified five roles that are incredibly helpful for a successful and productive debrief. These aren't roles that are assigned at the start; in fact, over the course of a debrief people often will take on different roles, depending on what is going on. But if you have each of these roles represented, you are positioned for a successful debrief.

- **Idea Ingrid.** You always need someone comfortable getting the group started and launching initial paths to follow. It sometimes can be difficult to get teammates to open up and share, especially when they are uncertain about the strength of their ideas. Idea Ingrid takes the reins on this task, offering up new ideas and suggestions to keep the room popping and help advance analysis.
- **Negative Nancy.** When you have someone chock full of ideas, you also need someone to point out when they just won't work. Someone needs to point out the flaws, and that's where Negative Nancy shines. This role prevents group think from taking over and stops a team from going with the first, easy answer. At times, however, the tension between Negative Nancy and Idea Ingrid can get a little heated. That's when you need . . .
- **Relief Ryan.** Always ready to break the tension and help manage the group dynamic, Relief Ryan is paying attention to the group dynamics as much as the data analysis. It's important that someone do this—you need to have someone who makes sure the team keeps moving forward productively. Relief Ryan is the one who will notice when someone (me) is getting hangry, or when everyone is just running out of steam and you need to take a break and regroup.
- **Collaborative Carl.** Often the unsung hero of debriefs, Collaborative Carl takes responsibility for finding the connections among the disparate strains that emerge during analysis. He is able to link some of Ingrid's ideas in ways that mitigate Nancy's concerns and makes sure that everyone on the team is being heard. If Relief Ryan is focused on group dynamics, Collaborative Carl's energies go toward the data advancing in a meaningful way as the team works toward uncovering insights and developing the story.
- **Leader Linda.** While all of these roles are important, every debrief room needs a Leader Linda to succeed. This person is the one who keeps the RQs top of mind and refocuses the rest of the team when they start going astray. She knows when to let lines of thinking unfurl and when they need to be reined in or refined. Without a leader, there is a risk that the group will not come to any sort of satisfactory outcome. Linda makes sure the team stays focused and makes progress during the analysis period and that they parallel track pulling out materials that will be useful down the road. We love Leader Linda. We *need* Leader Linda.

Again, these roles aren't fixed, and they might not always be present in every debrief. But I find it useful to have these in the back of your mind during your debrief. If no one is taking on a leadership role, you might need to do it. Or you might need to throw out ideas or (kindly and respectfully) point out the flaws in the ones that are being discussed. There are times you might see the connections that help explain the data, or you might crack a joke to break the tension. If things really aren't working in your debrief, do a quick mental review of these roles. If one isn't being represented, take it on. You'll be surprised at how quickly that can help change the trajectory of your debrief.

Physical Space

Depending on your team's arrangements, they can be done either online or in person. I always prefer the latter if at all possible; it is much easier to do this when you're in the same physical space. If you have to be online, however, insist that everyone turn their cameras on. Debriefs take trust and engagement. Seeing each other's faces helps build and reinforce that. To that end, if you *are* in person, arrange seating so you are in a circle. Look at each other. Make sure everyone is at the table, even if it's metaphorical. You should be surrounded by your data and have room to move and look at everything. Literally immerse yourself in your data so that you are re grounded in what you heard and saw in the field. If you're online, make sure everyone has access to any materials from your group through a shared drive and folders.

Debriefing

I wish I could give you a list of exact steps that you need to follow for a successful debrief, but unfortunately the messy nature of qualitative data analysis makes that impossible. Instead, I'm sharing some general guidelines—strategies and techniques that have worked for me and my teams in the past. As was the case with developing creative exercises, I highly recommend experimenting to see what works for you and your team. As long as you have faith in each other and the work you've done and you are willing to put the time and effort into doing this well, you'll be happy with the end results.

- **Brainstorming.** I recommend starting with a general brainstorming session. What stood out? What did you think really mattered? What ideas were sparked for you? During this process, refer back to your field notes. You'll likely have some good material in there to share. Don't be afraid to build off each other as well—this is where you have the chance to start finding connections.
- **Push and pull ideas.** Don't assume the first iteration of an idea is as far as it should go. Push at them. Pull. Think of ideas as Play-Doh that you can shape and reshape. Eventually, you might just get to the exact shape you need, but it's unlikely that will be the first version.
- **Be constructive.** There is no point in doing a debrief if no one is willing to challenge each other, but you need to make sure you're being constructive in your criticisms. Challenge each other to think deeper or differently, but always be respectful when doing so. It can be helpful to use neutral language in these situations—rather than "Uh, no" with an implied "you dummy," say, "Huh. I don't see it that way. Can you explain more?" Remember that you are a team working toward a common goal. Uncritical agreement is not ethical since you're letting your client down, but you also need to ensure your team comes through stronger than when you started.
- **Don't let outliers dominate your findings.** There will be times that you had a highly compelling and charismatic participant who had brilliant responses—but they didn't necessarily connect to what other people said. While you want to look for negative cases to test your insights and "big ideas," you don't want to let an outlier's perspective outweigh everything else. If you have an outlier, put that person to the side. Foreground other participants to make sure you're really representing the audience and not just one person. You can then come back to this outlier as a negative case—how does your analysis account for their experience? This lets you accommodate what you saw and heard without following the lure of what ultimately will be an unproductive path.

- **Don't beat up your client.** There will be times you have a metric ton of "minuses" on your plus/minus lists. We had one fast-fashion client for whom poop in the dressing rooms came up in multiple focus groups in different markets and shoppers didn't have a whole lot of positive to say. Coming up with positives was challenging. But think about your own experiences. If a professor only tells you all the things you do wrong and never tells you what you're doing well, how likely are you to listen to their suggestions for improvement? In my experience, not very. Clients are the same. They are invested in their business, which is why they brought you on board. So when you're doing your analysis, make sure you have good things to say as well as bad.
- **Look for the through line.** As you start to develop insights, look for the **through line**: the connection that links these concepts. Ultimately, that will lead to your overall story—the "elevator pitch" that incisively summarizes your analysis and gives you the hook on which to hang your findings and recommendations. This through line is what allows the client to make sense of your work, an essential step in conducting quality consumer insights research.
- **Always come back to the data.** Once you think you've found the through line and cracked the story, come back to the data. Look for illustrative quotes and exemplars. Do one more check-in for negative cases. Build this out so that you are confident you are representing the audience's perspective while still answering your client's RQs. Remember that you're looking for explanatory power, and you need the data to back you up.
- **Remember your ethical responsibilities.** As discussed in chapter 4, you have an ethical responsibility to your participants, your clients, and your team. If you cut corners in the debrief, you are behaving unethically. If you make up data to fit your story (rather than inductively developing your insights and thus story from the data), you are behaving unethically. Stay committed through the end. Spend the time you need to do this well. It's worth it.

If you follow these guidelines, you'll be well on your way to a successful debrief that will result in quality insights and a compelling through line/story. So, what's next? How do you share this with the client? The final section of this chapter will center on what you do if you are at a checkpoint in your research, where you will present topline findings to tee up the next phase of research. Final research products and presentations will be covered in detail in section IV (chapters 12–14), so you might want to skip ahead if needed.

TOPLINE RESEARCH REPORTS

As noted earlier, a topline research presentation is intended as a checkpoint as you move from one phase of research to the next. This gives you an invaluable opportunity to present your initial findings to your client and get their thoughts (and hopefully buy-in) before you move onto the next stage of research. While this can involve a client presentation (either virtual or in person), we are focused here on the types of written documents that might be created. No matter what type of document you create, however, you always want to make sure your work is put together in a way that someone up the corporate food chain can make sense of what you've done. Your reports shouldn't only make sense to someone who is in the trenches with you and deals with methods on a regular basis; this work needs to be accessible and meaningful to anyone who encounters it within the client's organization. This is particularly true for qualitative research, which lends itself to compelling visuals and storytelling.

To that end, when you are pulling your topline report together, remember that your role here is to be a **storyteller** and **interpreter**. Your through line that connects your insights is your story, and you need it to be compelling. Furthermore, you are there to interpret data, not just report it. Always keep in mind that your clients—whether internal or external—have hired you to represent the consumer and develop insights that will help them make good business decisions.

The ways you submit your deliverables to your clients usually will be determined in the initial RFP and written in the contract. While there are a range of ways your work can be submitted, the topline often takes one of two forms: a visual deck or a brief report.

- **Visual deck.** When we refer to a "deck" in research, we are referring to a PowerPoint-type slide presentation that is visually oriented and generally fairly light on text. This deck is focused on the key insights and ideas and is focused on communicating as concisely, efficiently, and compellingly as possible. Decks are incredibly useful for clients that tend to have shorter attention spans; as a research executive from IHeartRadio noted, if you are presenting to the people who were thinking about music during class instead of paying attention, you don't want to bury them in data. You want to craft this deck to communicate the essentials with qualitative data (quotes, pictures, etc.) included to illustrate your points.
- **Written executive summary.** For clients more invested in depth and detail, a written report generally is better suited either as a stand-alone or in supplement to the deck. At the topline stage, this likely is in the form of an executive summary, still focused on the core ideas but with more explanation and explication. While you could have a client ask for a longer report, those tend to be rare at the topline stage. This will be different when you get to the final report.

Both decks and written reports need to include basic information on the business objective and RQs as well as details about the research conducted. (For examples, take a quick peek at chapters 12 and 13 of this book—there is a ton in there!) This includes the methods used, the total N (number of participants) for each method, and breakdowns of any relevant demographics (gender, age, etc.). The next section will introduce your insights and/or the **themes** that emerged in your research. Finally, the last section will include any interim recommendations you'd make based on your data as well as plans for the next phase of research, including details about your anticipated methods and any key ideas you plan to investigate further. If you are giving recommendations, remember the three main criteria for worthwhile recommendations: (1) they must be *relevant*; (2) they must be *actionable*; and (3) they must clearly be *grounded in your data and insights*. Again, the more you can give here, the more likely you are to get buy-in from your client and ensure you have a successful final experience. If you aren't sure what you plan to do next, spend time thinking about it before submitting your topline. You want this to be as fully baked as possible to ensure the project moves forward smoothly.

In the analysis section above, I noted that you don't want to beat up your client, and it's worth another reminder here. You may be familiar with the "compliment sandwich," where you start and end with positives and then put the criticisms (or, in our world, "opportunities") in the middle. While this may read as disingenuous, it is really important that you put yourself in the client's shoes. If you tell them only about things that are bad, you can't expect them to keep listening. After all, if they really are that terrible, their business would have shut down by now. While you never should make things up, you *should* make an effort to find and foreground the good as well as the opportunities to improve. After all, if we are dedicated to doing no harm, that includes not putting the clients down. Be truthful, but be fair. That will get both you and your client into a space where you can make real, consumer-focused change rather than reach an impasse.

One final reminder: When writing, you need to really think about who your client is and what their expectations are. If you're presenting research to pharmaceutical scientists, they will have a different expectation for clarity around methods than music label execs. Likewise, music label execs will expect a visually compelling and professionally designed presentation, whereas the pharma team might appreciate something more straightforward that still looks polished and professional. Some research companies have a basic template and branded style they use for their presentations, but it's always worth making sure what you put together will be appropriate for your audience in order to most effectively communicate your insights and recommendations. If needed, you can always add an appendix with more data and detail, but it's better to have what they want and expect baked in. When in doubt, ask your contact for recommendations.

BEST PRACTICES AND KEY TAKEAWAYS

If you've put the time and effort in to collect top-notch data, you don't want to cut corners when you get to data analysis. This is where you get to really see your work come together. Again, it can be messy and laborious. There will be times you are convinced you'll never come out with good material. But if you persist, you will get there.

This textbook is structured to reflect the two main methodologies in consumer insights: qualitative and quantitative research. This wraps up the qualitative section and we will move next into quantitative research design, collection, and analysis. Before we do, however, I want to take a minute to reflect on *why* qualitative research matters so much. For large swaths of the population, this type of research may be the only time someone asks their opinions about, well, almost anything. This is an opportunity for them to affect change for something they probably care about, brands and products that play an important role in their lives. This is a joyful responsibility for us as researchers, and it is imperative that we take it seriously. We are the way consumers get a seat at the table, and that truly is an awesome responsibility. When coupled with our responsibilities to our client, it is incredible to think about how important this research really is. And once we have successfully completed our qualitative research, we will be able to take what we learned to craft surveys that help us quantify and measure the concepts that emerged as being relevant, important, and salient to our consumers. Pretty cool, right?

KEY TERMS

Abstraction: Taking concrete data and pulling them out of their immediate context to help find connections and derive meaning

Debrief: A lengthy meeting where a research team works through the data to generate insight and develop the story

Field notes: A record of everything you remember a qualitative research experience, including what was said, anything that stood out, things you want to remember; these also serve as a first level of analysis by including ideas sparked and thoughts on guide iteration

Inductive reasoning: An analytic process that starts with data and, through abstraction, leads to the identification of key themes and insights that will help advance understanding of RQs

Jot notes: Quick notes taken in the midst of the qualitative research experience

Member checks: Checking the team's initial analysis with participants, allowing for feedback and providing an opportunity to dig more into what participants have to say from an informed perspective

Negative cases: Experiences reported by your participants that fall outside your story

Redundancy: No new information or data are being generated on certain topics; in academic research, this is also called "saturation"

Through line: The connection that links insights generated in research

Topline: An interim presentation that comes midway through a research project or after each phase of research

9

Quantitative Research Design and Considerations

While the depth and richness that come with qualitative research are invaluable to researchers, there will be times that you Just. Need. Numbers. Maybe you need to figure out with a measurable degree of accuracy the size of your target audience in the population. Or maybe you need to figure out what concepts your customers associate with your brand, or what white space there is in the competitive landscape for you to move. In consumer insights, quantitative research—usually based on surveys—is an essential tool to have in your research toolbox.

With that said, I know that many of you likely went into your major because it probably doesn't require a huge amount of math. I totally get that the thought of statistics might make your head hurt and your stomach ache. And truth be told, I was with you. I am not a "math" person. But here is the amazing news: When it comes to consumer insights research, you really don't need to be. The math—the statistics—are done by someone else. Even if you're in a small research shop, you'll likely be able to contract with a "data jockey" to clean and weight the data and then run the statistical tests you need completed to do your analysis and make your recommendations. And for those of you who are exhilarated by numbers and statistics and mathematical equations? This chapter will help you see how that statistical analyses done by data jockeys (perhaps your future dream job?!) support the RQs and business objectives in consumer insights research. By understanding this, you will be much better prepared to be an effective partner with the rest of your team rather than someone who just processes data files and generates reports.

And now the news gets even better for people on both sides of that equation. (Get it? Math jokes!) By the end of this section, you'll be so comfortable with the stages of quantitative work that consumer insights professionals *do* execute that you'll be excited to dig into this kind of research. (I know, right now it sounds unbelievable, but hopefully by now you trust me.) In this chapter, we'll review why you do this kind of research and the benefits and limitations before moving into the basic principles of quant (sampling theory, error, and all kinds of good stuff!). In chapter 10, you'll learn how to write a survey, including specifics on structure and writing questions. Chapter 11 takes us to data analysis and presentation, where we review the statistical analyses that are commonly used in this type of research. As was the case with the qualitative section, all of these pieces work together—you need to know the types of tests you need to run while you are developing your survey instrument so you ask the right kinds of questions to collect the necessary data. So, while this is presented as a series of chapters, remember that these all intersect and connect to help design the best possible quantitative research you can in order to answer your RQs and address your client's business objectives.

As we go through this chapter, you may find yourself having to reread different parts for them to make sense, or you may find yourself struggling to stay focused and awake. (My feelings will not be hurt. I get it.) But stick with it. Spend some time thinking about the applications of what you are reading. Take a few minutes to write down what you *think*, I mean in your own words, and then come back to the chapter to check in on it. And don't forget to ask your professor when you need clarification. For most people, quantitative research isn't as intuitive as qualitative research—although some of you may find yourselves absolutely loving this. And once it clicks—once it all does start to make sense—you'll start to see how valuable this is for researchers and our clients.

My natural instincts are those of a qualitative researcher, but I can tell you honestly that there is something incredibly gratifying about doing quant work. I loved digging into the spreadsheets (for real) to find patterns and stories. The challenge is different but can be equally satisfying. So, as we get started, take a deep breath. Gird your loins. Let's go.

WHY DO QUANTITATIVE RESEARCH?

As made clear in the name, quantitative research is employed when we need to quantify something—find the numbers that help us get precise measures. And the two ideas baked into that last phrase—"precise" and "measures"—really summarize neatly the benefits of quantitative research. While qualitative absolutely is rigorous and useful, it does not help you figure out how many people are exactly aware of your brand or prefer your product versus your competitors. Quantitative research, however, gives you that precision in your measurements. You can quantify within a fairly narrow range both brand awareness and product preference. You can gauge how your target audience perceives your brand values in relation to your competition. You can understand the phrases or concepts most associated with your magazine or newspaper. You can track appeal of your commercial, television pilot, or full-length movie down to the second, determining what works and what doesn't. These precise, accurate measurements help inform decision-making in a way qualitative often can't. By having these types of crystal-clear data, your research team can make compelling recommendations that have real numbers associated with them. This is particularly effective when coupled with the depth and meaning of qualitative research in order to show the potential percentage-based opportunities for growth or improvement along with verbatim quotes and imagery. Ultimately, the potent combination can be particularly persuasive for clients seeking answers to their business questions.

Most of the time in consumer insights research, you will be doing **survey research**. This is by far the most common quantitative method used in terms of data collection. This approach allows you to then use a range of statistical tests and models to answer your specific questions (you'll learn all about these approaches in chapter 11). Because survey research is so predominant, it is our focus for this part of the book. You may occasionally find yourself doing some other form of quantitative research, such as a field experiment to test traffic flows or shelf arrangements in different stores or doing basic **A/B testing** to compare audience responses to two iterations or options of the same ad or product (Option A versus Option B). These research projects generally are so specific and narrow that they couldn't be covered well here anyway. If you understand these basic principles of quantitative research as outlined here, you'll be prepared enough to learn about and adapt to these methods in order to continue doing your job well.

Benefits

There are a number of benefits associated with quantitative research. As was the case in chapter 5 for qualitative, I am drawing out the biggest and most compelling for this chapter. When you get into the actual conduct of this research, however, you'll soon discover other ways quantitative research benefits your research project. With that disclaimer in place, let's review:

- **Standardization.** While this is also a fundamental characteristic of quantitative research and will be discussed more in that context in the next section, standardization also is one of this methodological approach's key benefits. Standardization means you can "set it and forget it," as the old informercials used to say. You create your instruments, determine your path, and then move forward. This reduces the possibility of reactivity, since the researcher's influence would be part and parcel of every participant's experience. This also means you don't have to worry as much about potential surprises that could emerge; you know what data will be there once data collection is completed.
- **Extrapolating results to the population.** This one is more complex than that statement indicates, and much of this chapter will be spent detailing the circumstances under which extrapolation (or, as it can also be called, generalization) can occur. But when you've met those conditions, you have the power to say that the results you got from talking to a representative sample of your population hold true for the population (as you've defined it) as a whole. So, for example, you can talk to 1,000 toothpaste users in the United States and get their opinions and then use those data to talk about the opinions of *all* toothpaste users in the United States. This is much more efficient (and far less costly) than actually trying to survey the entire population and allows researchers to make broader claims with reasonable expenditures of time and money.
- **Sizing audiences and summarizing results.** Because your research is standardized and you can extrapolate results under certain conditions, this is incredibly useful for actually sizing your audiences: How many, where they are, and what they want can all be understood in terms of percentages. This is invaluable intel when making business decisions, and it is something qualitative research just can't do. There are times hard numbers are needed—you need to know what percentage of your target audience is aware of your brand, for example, or what shifts are happening in music listening habits—and this ability to size audiences in terms of actual numbers can be incredibly useful when answering business questions.
- **Finding measurable relationships among variables.** When we talk about quant research, we focus on **variables**: an element or factor that can change or can vary in value/options. So, that might mean looking at the relationship between age and television viewing—each of those is a variable that is different for different people. If we do a survey where we find out each respondent's age and their television viewing habits, we can then use statistics to determine how age (variable one) is related to TV viewing (variable two). These relationships are incredibly useful to measure and understand when trying to understand what consumers do and why, and the beauty of quant research is you can define your variables in almost any way that is helpful to you. You'll just want to make sure you check with your data expert to ensure you have the right kind of measurements (and thus data) for your variables for the tests you want to run (more about that in chapter 11), but once you get the hang of this, it's easily done.

- **Drawing specific comparisons.** Quantitative research lets you draw specific, measurable comparisons between brands, products, audiences, and so on. Rather than having a "squishy" understanding of how your brand stands in comparison to your primary competitors, quant research lets you map and measure it. You can also test the effectiveness of different ads to see which is more compelling, drawing comparisons between perceptions and persuasive markers. Or you can establish how closely certain characteristics are associated with your brand versus the rest of your competitive landscape. No media brand, product, or service exists in a vacuum, so this kind of intel is remarkably useful for determining opportunity and white space.
- **Can be faster and more efficient than qualitative research.** This last benefit is the most practical of all the ones listed here. While fielding qual research often takes quite a bit of time, if you are doing a straightforward study with a broad enough population from which to recruit, you likely can get a survey written, fielded, and analyzed in a shorter period of time. The actual timeline depends on how easy or hard it is to find your defined population (**incidence**), the people who meet the criteria for your research and how many resources you can put toward recruiting and fielding, but you usually can get in and out in just a few weeks.

Limitations

Most of the limitations discussed in this section will feel intuitive after reading the benefits; these are the flip sides to the coin. But it is essential that you are aware of these general limitations to quantitative research so you can think about how to best mitigate and manage them, usually through triangulating with other methods (qualitative or quantitative, depending on your circumstances and needs).

- **No flexibility.** While standardization is one of the fundamental underpinnings of quant research, the lack of flexibility that comes with that is a huge limitation. This means you cannot adapt if something isn't working, and you can't investigate anything new that emerges without starting another phase of research. This also means it is essential to carefully **pilot test** whatever instruments you are using, thoroughly testing them with members of your target audience in advance to ensure your questions make sense, your language is clear, and you are not accidentally **priming** your respondents (inadvertently preparing them for what is coming up next and thereby changing the way they answer your questions).
- **No space for personalization.** Another consequence of standardization is that you have to use the exact same language for every single participant. While there are some tricks of the trade you can use to ask questions only of participants who fit certain criteria using adaptive structuring and skip patterns (those will be covered in chapter 10), this is limited—and you still need to have those questions developed in advance, and you need to have enough people answering them to be able to draw conclusions. You can't adjust question wording based on a respondent's unique experience—you need to reflect general categories that most people can fit into.
- **Large sample sizes are required.** To be clear, when we say "large" here, it's a relative term. Thanks to sampling theory (coming up soon!), you aren't going to have to talk to tens of thousands of people to draw your conclusions, but you *are* going to have to talk to way more people than you do for qualitative. As noted in the benefits, this often is faster than qual would be. But it can be expensive, especially when you are dealing with a low-incidence population that is harder to find.

- **Extensive knowledge and preparation are required.** While qualitative research is ideal for investigating new topics and ideas, you can't figure things out as you go in quantitative research (as noted in the bullet above). This means you have to be incredibly clear in what you are asking and how you are asking it. All terms need to be carefully **operationalized,** meaning you have clearly established and articulated definitions for key concepts and variables so everyone is on the same page. For example, if you are interested in learning about shoes, you need to make clear what *kinds* of shoes qualify. Does all footwear count? What about work shoes? Athletic shoes? Or general athletic shoes (tennis shoes) versus fashion sneakers? How about orthopedics or support shoes? Boots? Snow boots? Ski boots? Moon boots? Ankle boots? This could go on and on. As you can see, even something as seemingly straightforward as "shoes" in everyday conversation becomes broader and more complex when you are trying to quantify and measure. This means you need to carefully think about how you are going to operationalize each concept and variable to ensure shared meaning among clients, the research team, and your respondents.
- **Results can be easily overstated.** It is ridiculously easy to overstate the claims that can be derived from your quantitative research—after all, you have numbers! Hard numbers! And the story they tell can be so compelling that you can get a wee bit carried away in talking about how your data "prove" something. When you find yourself saying "prove," check yourself. Have you *really* proved this, or have you just found indicators and relationships? Are there no other possible explanations? It is extremely rare (if not impossible) for consumer insights research to prove anything. So, don't overstate. Don't talk in absolutes. And as Dwayne "The Rock" Johnson would say if he were a researcher, don't write a check your data can't cash.

BASIC PRINCIPLES AND CHARACTERISTICS

When doing quant research, there are some basic principles and characteristics you need to know and understand. By familiarizing yourself with each of these principles, you'll be better prepared to get into the nitty-gritty of the "inner workings" of quant that will be discussed in the rest of this chapter and the next two.

Correlation Is Not Causation

This really is a fundamental concern in quant research, but it also can be really difficult to keep in mind when you are talking about your findings, as noted in the last limitation bullet. At its simplest, this rule means that just because there is a relationship between two variables, it does not mean one *causes* the other. **Correlation** has real statistical meaning, and there are tests your data jockey will run to measure the relationships between and among variables. But for our purposes, the main thing to remember is that the surveys and research we will be doing at best show how different variables are related; they will not tell you the direction of that relationship (which one causes the other).

A commonly shared example of this is looking at the correlation between ice-cream consumption and drowning. These two variables are highly correlated; when ice-cream consumption goes up, drownings do too. Why would that be? Does ice cream cause drownings? Or, more logically, it could be that both ice-cream consumption and swimming go up during hot summer months—ergo, both go up at the same time and are related, but one is not *causing* the other. While this example is more clearly understood than what you might find in your data, the principle stands: You can talk about how your variables are related, but don't make causal claims unless you have run the appropriate statistical tests. (And the vast majority of the time, you won't.) At times, you'll hear researchers talking about **Occam's Razor** (also spelled "Ockham's"): the simplest explanation is usually the right one. At times, our instincts will instruct us to come up something really complex and convoluted to explain our data. The vast majority of the time, that will be wrong. Keep it simple. Keep it clean. You'll likely come up with the best explanation that way.

Standardization

Since we already talked a bit about standardization as one of the benefits of quantitative research, I am not going to repeat too much of it here. It is important to note, however, that standardization really is a basic principle and characteristic of this kind of work. This isn't just a "nice to have" benefit—it's essential to what you are trying to do with this kind of research. The beauty of quant research is that it gives you hard numbers and data that you can use to draw a clear picture of the ways your audience behaves and thinks, including their percep- tions of your brand and your competitive landscape. This is invaluable information, but it only works if you ask the same questions of everyone in your study. You need to make sure you are adhering to the highest standards of rigor. There are no shortcuts here. Once you have your language and your protocols set, you follow that path to the end. This can, at times, be frustrating; you realize a question is worded awkwardly or that you have inadvertently primed your participants with the way you've structured your survey, for example. And there may be instances where the problems are big enough that you do need to make a change midstream, such as you have a fairly narrowly defined audience and, after struggling to field your survey, you realize you have to expand some of your parameters to have enough people take the survey to be able to do your analysis. In the rare cases this does happen, you need to work closely with your client and your data experts to ensure you are not undermining the quality of your results. It's worth a reminder: The more you can pretest and pilot your survey to make sure it will work in practice, the better off you'll be in the long run. Shortcuts can wind up causing an awful lot of trouble.

Hypotheses versus Research Questions

Thus far, we have talked about the guiding purpose in our research as the RQs. And in applied research, RQs tend to be the focus throughout—they stay consistent whether you are doing qualitative or quantitative research. In academic research, however, you may find that hypoth- eses are more common in quant research. While RQs leave open the possible outcomes and results, a **hypothesis** proposes what the relationships between and among variables will be. When a hypothesis is proposed in academic research, it usually is grounded in either theoretical rationale and/or previous research. You may occasionally come across hypotheses in applied research, but they certainly are much less common than RQs—in fact, most clients would be quite surprised to see a hypothesis show up in a final report. Even if you have a tentative (or fairly concrete!) hypothesis about the relationships among variables in your study, you usually would not formalize it and test specifically to those results. Instead, you would use that sup- position or inkling to inform the questions you ask, the tests you run, and the ways you analyze and interpret your results.

SAMPLING AND SAMPLES

The main benefit of quantitative research is that you can take data collected from a small sample of people and apply what you learned to the entire population as you've defined it. Think about how cool this is, for real. It is rare that you are able to actually talk to everyone in your population, particularly once you expand beyond a few hundred people in a clearly delimited community—and even then, it's tough. The only way we can really understand and draw inferences about our populations is by using samples that we can then extrapolate to the population as a whole. In this section, we will talk about the two big categories of samples—probability samples that can be used to extrapolate to the population and nonprobability samples that can't be truly extrapolated but can still offer direction and insight, particularly when coupled with qualitative research.

As a reminder from earlier chapters, you'll start your research by defining your target population: Who do you need to talk to in order to get the answers you need to address your RQs and business objectives? Your target population—your audience—is the population we are referring to throughout this section. This can be really narrow: for example, women 18–25 who watch the Hallmark Movie Channel for at least three hours a week. Or you can make it much broader: adults who watch television at least one hour a week. This population is defined according to your research needs and generally remains consistent throughout your entire research project.

One preliminary note: If you *can* talk to everyone in your population, this is a **census**. The United States famously does a census every ten years, which I am sure you can recall from the "Secondary Research" chapter in the first section of this book. Most of us do not have the resources of the U.S. federal government, however, and thus we can't do research of that kind of scope. Think about even doing a census at your university. Let's say your university has 20,000 students enrolled on the main campus, all of whom are physically on campus at least two times a week for classes. Even under those circumstances, it would be extraordinarily difficult to conduct a census of all university students. Finding those 20,000 students and then getting them to take your survey would be so expensive and time consuming that it likely wouldn't be worthwhile. Ultimately, it would just be too resource intensive for what you'd get at the end—and that's with a relatively small and physically constrained audience. Think about the challenges if you are trying to understand Coca-Cola drinkers or fan perceptions of Harry Styles or heavy users of Instagram. It would be impossible to identify and find all of those people in those populations, let alone talk to them—and this is why sampling matters.

There are two main approaches to sampling: probability and nonprobability. Within those categories, there are a range of sampling strategies you can use, depending on what you need to learn and how you are going to use your data. Because our purpose is to help you develop a baseline understanding of the "whats" and "whys" of quant research in this chapter, each of these will be by necessity fairly short. You don't need to be an expert, but I do want you to know enough that you will be comfortable at least understanding what these terms mean and why you would use them. As a reminder, when you are designing your quantitative research plan, you want to think through *how* you are going to use the data you collect—what are the kinds of tests you will need to run to answer your RQs and address your business objective? What do you need to know at the end of this phase of research? More practically, how much time do you have? How much money can you spend? These questions will help guide you in deciding what kind of sample you need.

Probability Sampling

The gold standard of sampling is **probability sampling**. A probability sample meets four primary criteria:

1. The sample is **representative of the population** as you've defined it.
2. It is **selected according to specific defined procedures**.
3. **Every member of your population has an *equal* chance of being selected** to be included in the sample.
4. **The chance of being selected for the sample can be calculated**. (Not that you have to do it yourself—there are calculators for this!)

If you can meet each of these criteria in your probability sample, you can then confidently extrapolate your findings to your population as a whole. This is all thanks to years of statistical theory development. Scholars, scientists, and statisticians have been working on developing modern statistical theory since the late nineteenth century, and their work gives us the confidence to make credible claims based on what our data reveal. Before you start getting antsy, I am not going to dig into statistical theory or its history here (although it is FASCINATING, and I highly recommend digging in if and when you have the inclination). This is really just to reassure you that this is not something we throw around without real, credible science behind it. This stuff is legit, and we can trust what we learn through our research—particularly if we are using probability sampling.

    Simple random sampling. Simple random sampling is the most basic form of probability sampling. To do this, you select a random sample from your population. To do this perfectly, you need to have a **sampling frame**, or a list of every member of the population. While that might be possible (albeit cumbersome) if you are talking about students at your university, it would be nigh impossible to collect a complete sampling frame if you are looking at media usage (people who watch television) or consumption behaviors (people who drink soda pop). So, in those cases, we would assume the population is broad enough that a sampling frame is not needed; we can draw a random sample from the general population. To do this, you pick every Nth person, where "N" means "number"—so you'd pick every fifth person, or thirty-third, or ninety-second, and so on. Here is the tricky thing with the human mind, however: We are hardwired to look for patterns, so true randomness is quite difficult to achieve. If you want to do this, you'll want to use a random number generator. This is as simple as asking Google to pick a number within a range.

    If by chance you do have a sampling frame to use, you want to make sure that you do not accidentally introduce **periodicity**. Periodicity means there is something about the way your sampling frame list is organized that makes it more likely one "unit" on that list will be selected than another. For example, if you are using a student directory that is arranged in alphabetical order, you may get your total number of completed surveys done by the time you get to the Rs—which means anyone whose name comes *after* that did not have an equal chance at being selected. Boom! Not random. Or, if you are looking at a sampling frame organized by majors, students in agriculture or anthropology or astronomy will be much more likely to be selected than those poor, lonely, end-of-alphabet zoology majors. To prevent this problem, make sure you mix up the order of your list in advance. In the old days of paper phone books, this would mean literally sitting and cutting up names into tiny strips that could then be piled together, mixed up, and pulled. The idea of that makes my head hurt, but for those researchers, it was the best way to randomize a sampling frame. We can now use computers for these purposes, so just remember that you need to watch for periodicity if you are drawing a simple random sample from a sampling frame.

Stratified random sample. There are times where you will need to do a "deep dive" into one or more particular segments of your population; for example, you want to break your population out to really understand the differences among age groups or household income (HHI). In those cases, you'll want to do a stratified random sample, which allows you to set specific totals for how many people you want to make up each **stratum** (or segment) in your total sample. So, for example, you may want your sample to break out like this:

Table 9.1   Stratified Random Sample (One Variable)

Age Category	N
18–24	200
25–34	200
35–44	200
45–54	200
55 and older	200
TOTAL N	**1,000**

Or, if you want to get even fancier (I KNOW!), you can break these out by two variables, such as gender and age:

Table 9.2   Stratified Random Sample (Two Variables)

Gender	Age Category	N
Male	18–24	100
	25–34	100
	35–44	100
	45–54	100
	55 and older	100
	n (males)	**500**
Female	18–24	100
	25–34	100
	35–44	100
	45–54	100
	55 and older	100
	n (females)	**500**
	Total N	**1,000**

(Note that the capital "N" is used for the total number in your sample, and subsamples or strata would be denoted by a lowercase "n.")

When you are using a stratified sample, you can approach this situation either as a disproportionate or as a proportionate stratified sample. The example above is a **disproportionate stratified sample**; we used the exact same size for each stratum, no matter what the actual representation in the population for that group is. There are times, however, when you will want your strata to reflect your population in a more realistic way. That's when a **proportionate stratified sample** will come into play. So, for example, if your population is 63 percent female and 37 percent male, your proportionate stratified sample will look like the example in table 9.3:

Table 9.3   Proportionate Stratified Sample

Gender	N
Female	630
Male	370
TOTAL N	**1,000**

When you are making your decisions about your strata, you need to make sure you can fill each "bucket" enough to have a sufficiently robust sample to do the deep dives you need to maintain rigor and have confidence in your findings. This can get really expensive really fast, however, so exercise caution when designing research plans—unless you have a massive budget, you should only develop subsamples that absolutely are needed (rather than "nice to have").

Cluster Sampling

If you have ever watched exit poll information roll in on election night, you will have seen the results coming in from what is probably the most famous example of **cluster sampling**. In this sampling strategy, you start with a large group and then randomly select groups from within that group, then further select down using more randomization, until you get to a useful unit of analysis. So, for example, in exit polling you would start by breaking the state into counties, then counties into geographic blocks based on some characteristic (such as population density), and then blocks into precincts. Once the final precincts are randomly selected, you can then use a simple random sampling procedure to select voters as they leave the precinct. The "nth" voter you select is determined by previous voting information for that precinct (or multiple precincts, depending on the voting location) and time of day.

While exit polls are the ones we most often hear about in the media thanks to the election association, cluster samples also play a huge role in how we collect media usage data. The Nielsen Company uses this approach to build its foundational ratings information for both television and radio, moving from states to counties, counties to cities, cities to blocks, and blocks to individual households. This method is complemented by other methods of data collection, but this old-school approach helps ensure non-digital households are represented as well to best reflect the population in its data.

Nonprobability Sampling

While probability samples certainly are the most rigorous and scientifically valid approach to collecting data, there are times where that just is not feasible. You don't have the time or, more often, the money to collect data from a true random sample. Or your research doesn't really require that level of expense; your RQs only need directional information giving you some reassurance about the direction you should go, rather than specific hard numbers. In those cases, you would consider using a **nonprobability sample**. These samples do not follow the same scientific sampling procedures used in probability sampling, so you can't be sure every person in the population has an equal chance of being selected, nor can you calculate their likelihood of being selected. This means you can't calculate your sampling error, which means you shouldn't extrapolate to the population. Let me be clear: There will be times to use a nonprobability sample as part of your triangulated research, meaning you've paired your quant phase with a highly rigorous qual phase of research. In those cases, you likely will feel comfortable sharing hard numbers with your client, and that is totally acceptable—as long as your client knows what you're sharing and what the limitations are.

Convenience sample. Perhaps the most common form of nonprobability sampling is the **convenience sample**. In this approach, you find people from your population who are convenient to use in your data collection. Going back to our example of doing research at your university, this would be the equivalent of setting up a table in your student center or in the main quad and stopping people who walked by, asking them to take your survey. Sure, this *sounds* good—you'll get a great cross-section of students if you are in a central area, right? Unfortunately, not really. Imagine you set up every day for one week, from 10:00 AM to 3:00 PM. While that sounds great, it leaves out an awful lot of students. What about students who only take evening classes? Or online? Or those whose classes are on the other side of campus so they never make their way to the central areas? All of those students would be left out because you chose a convenient place to find participants. In professional consumer insights research, this is what you find when you have **mall intercepts**—companies that collect data for specific client projects in malls or other public spaces. The problems you saw with the on-campus example would apply here too, but writ large. You're talking about a very specific type of people who would be at malls at certain times and days, and mall populations vary greatly depending on which stores are open and available. While you can get some interesting directional research, particularly if you are doing research on topics that would have some natural connection to malls (movie theaters, retail, etc.), the data should not be considered as more than directional.

Volunteer samples. You may remember at various times seeing what looks like a survey question on a website: "Who do you like better? Elvis or the Beatles!" You pick one, and you immediately see how everyone else voted as well. Hijacking these polls is a favored pastime of both troll and fan armies—both will find an online poll and swarm it to get their favorite outcome. True story: This is how the United Kingdom wound up with an autonomous underwater vehicle called Boaty McBoatface. They opened a poll and the people spoke (and by "people," I mean people who found it hilarious to name an official British vessel something completely ridiculous). These polls are wildly unscientific because they rely on a **volunteer sample**: interested people voluntarily go to your poll and take it. They come to you, which means they clearly have some motivation for participating.

That said, if you are conducting research with a low-incidence population that otherwise will be really hard to find in the population, you may want to put links to your online survey places they will have at least a reasonable chance of being selected. Or, if they wouldn't be on your site, perhaps you could place links in other places they might go; for example, if you are an outdoor adventure recreation brand, you could put links on the websites of retailers where your target population might go to shop. But as we saw with convenience samples, you need to make sure that you are clear with your client about how that limits the ways you can extrapolate your findings to the general population.

Snowball sampling. The final type of nonprobability sampling that you likely will encounter in consumer insights research is **snowball sampling**. This approach is particularly useful with low-incidence populations. Think of this as an actual snowball—you start with a little bit of packed snow, and as you roll it around, it attracts more snow to grow bigger and bigger. If you have a starting point with members of your population, you can ask them to share the survey with others who might take it. Through this, they build your snowball—you get more and more participants because they are referring others to your study. This is often used when you are researching certain narrow occupational or recreational groups; you find a handful of professors who will share with other professors and then ask that second group to share with more professors, who share with more professors, and so on. Or you find an initial group of collegiate quidditch players, and then have them pass the link to other quidditch players they know or post in discussion groups or on Slack channels to help spread the word. If you are using a snowball sample in a professional context, you would likely not ever be able to do your study using probability unless you had a sampling frame; the incidence is just too low.

ERROR, MARGIN OF ERROR, AND CONFIDENCE LEVEL

When thinking about the differences between probability and nonprobability samples, the biggest advantage of a probability sample is that you can extrapolate your findings from your representative sample to the population. Why does this work? Because you can calculate error, which tells you how far off the results from sample are from what you would get if you actually conducted a census with the entire population. This acknowledges that sampling isn't perfect—it's not an exact replica of what you would find in the total population—but it allows us to make these broad claims without having to do the impossible (i.e., speaking to every Coke drinker in the country).

There are three types of error with which researchers typically are concerned:

- **Random error**. Random error is error that cannot be planned for or controlled in your research. For example, the survey taker is interrupted by their child while in the middle of the survey. Or they get online to get started when a neighbor starts blowing leaves. There are countless ways error can be introduced to a study, so if it is not related to measurement or sampling error (described below), it is categorized as random.
- **Measurement error**. Measurement error is derived from inconsistencies from the instrumentation or testing procedures; for example, you ask a leading or unclear question, or something about the order questions are in introduces a bias that then affects later answers. Because this type of error is related to instrumentation and procedure, it likely would be present even if you did a census—your data would be flawed because the ways you approached it introduced those flaws.
- **Sampling error**. Sampling error is what we typically talk about when discussing the error in quantitative research. Sampling error is the estimation of difference in results between what you find from your sample versus what you would find if you did a census and spoke to the entire population. Note that this does *not* mean you drew a bad sample; it just is what happens when you use sampling to understand your population. Most of the time in consumer research, we don't really know how far off we are from the population; again, the odds of you ever speaking to all consumers of Coca-Cola are infinitesimal. But when it comes to political polling, you actually have a result that you can compare to what your samples told you. How do we make sense of this? The margin of error.

Margin of Error and Confidence Level

When we calculate the sampling error, we talk about it in terms of the **margin of error** (or, in academic research, the **confidence interval**). The margin of error gives us the range where we would expect the "real" answer to be if we did a census with the population. This typically is represented as a plus/minus number that gives us the range (the interval) where you would expect the true answer to lie. So, for example, imagine you are a producer working on an aging television show. Your lead actor is caught on camera during a drunken brawl, and you need to decide if you are going to keep him on the show or cut your losses and move on. To help make this decision, your team does a survey to gauge his appeal and the audience's reaction to his altercation and ensuing apologies. When you survey a representative sample of your target population, you discover that 52 percent of regular viewers (your target pop) support keeping him on the show while 48 percent prefer you give him the proverbial boot. The survey is with 1,000 viewers and has a margin of error of +/−4 percent. So while this may *look* like clear direction to keep him on screen, the margin of error gives us a more nuanced picture. If you talked to every regular viewer of your show, you would expect the "true" response to fall in a range:

• Keep him: 52 percent (could be anywhere between 48 percent and 56 percent)
• Dump him: 48 percent (could be anywhere between 44 percent and 52 percent)

Knowing this, you now see that the *actual* support from regular viewers could actually be higher than the percentage that wants to see him go. To make this decision, you'd likely want to pair your survey with some qualitative research to better understand where the audience is as well as a data analysis of media coverage and social media sentiment. With all of these data in hand, you can get a sense of where the audience actually lies.

One more complicating factor: When you are presenting these data, you need to think about them in terms of how sure you really are that your data are accurate and that the true answer would lie within the margin of error. This means you need to talk about the **confidence level**: how certain you are that your range of answers are accurate in terms of what you would find in the population. This is expressed as a percentage, and researchers typically would expect to be at least 95 percent or 99 percent confident about the accuracy of their findings. When taken in sum with the example above, you could say, "I am 95 percent confident that between 48 and 56 percent of the population support this actor remaining on our program." Does it sound like you're hedging your bets? Sure. But it's accurate. Think of it this way: In survey research, we are in the business of forecasting, not prophesizing. So we can tell you what is *likely* to happen, but not what absolutely *will* happen. (Remember this during election seasons—this is when you really will hear bad reporting on survey data.)

While this is a best practice, it can also be overwhelming for your client. Thus, in consumer insights practice, we often are more direct than this. If you are using a probability sample, the confidence level should be included in the report. This will allow you to speak to your confidence in results and is important for accuracy. But the confidence level and the confidence intervals typically are not a central part of the findings. You want to make your research reports as straightforward as possible, and the inclusion of this information in your main narrative can be overwhelming and confusing. In academic research, however, this plays a much bigger role; scholars will clearly identify the confidence level so other scholars can evaluate the credibility of the findings.

Generally speaking, a larger sample size will lead to a smaller margin of error and a higher confidence level (in other words, you'll have a more limited range for "true" answers and you can be more certain that the "true" answer falls in that limited range). When you are determining your sample size, you need to think about both the acceptable range and how sure you need to be. You can then use an online sample size calculator to figure out what is the right size for you. My favorite is www.surveysystem.com/sscalc.htm, but there are a ton of options out there, and this is the tool I used to create figures 9.1 and 9.2.

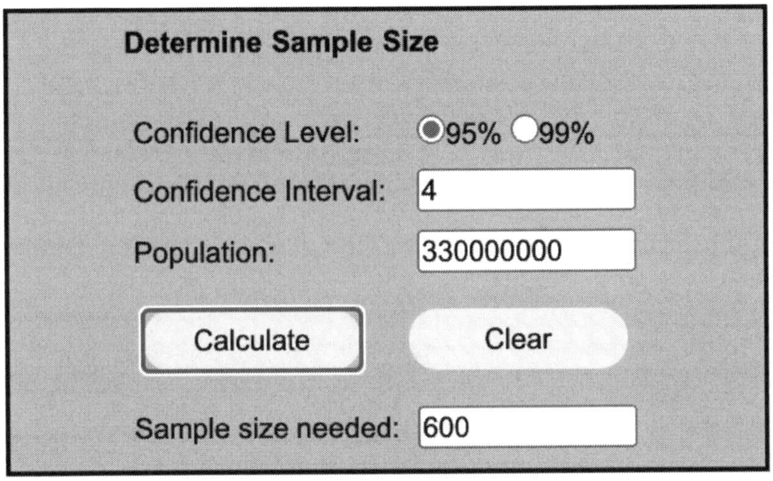

Figure 9.1   Example of a sample size calculator used to determine the sample size needed for the approximate population of the United States with 95 percent confidence and a +/−4 percent margin of error.

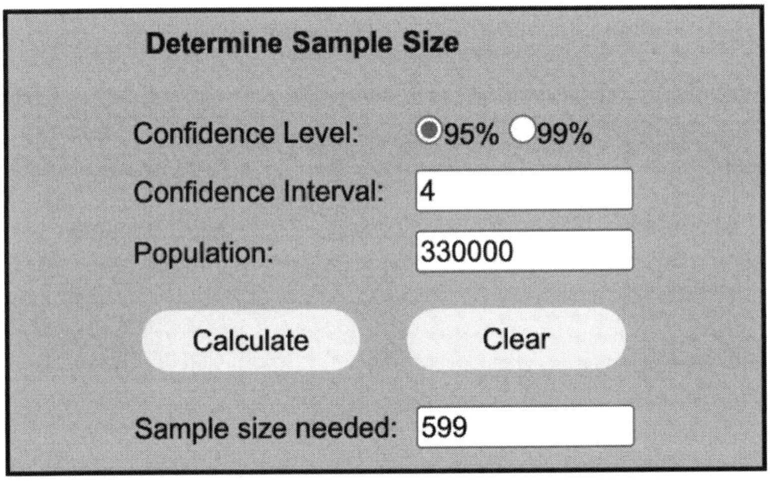

Figure 9.2   Example of a sample size calculator used to determine the sample size needed for a much smaller population (330,000) with 95 percent confidence and a +/−4 percent margin of error.

Spend some time playing around with these calculators. Plug in different numbers to see how things change. What you will soon notice is that, once you get to a certain population size, adding more on to your sample will have a limited impact on your population. There are about 330 million Americans (as of 2019). If you wanted to do a survey with a margin of error (MOE) of +/−4 percent with a 95 percent confidence level, you'd only need 600 respondents. If you want to take it to +/−3 percent with the same confidence level, it goes up to 1,040. But if you take the population size down to 330,000, you barely see movement in the sample size to hit those same MOE and confidence levels (95 percent confidence level goes down by 1 to 599, as seen below, while 99 percent confidence level only goes down by four participants to 1,036).

These sample size calculators can be used two ways: as seen above, they can be used to determine the sample size needed to hit your target MOE and confidence level, but you can also use them to figure out the MOE retroactively. Just pop in your sample size and confidence level, and voila!

One final note: While you will see margins of error and confidence levels reported in consumer insights research, these generally are not as much of a focus as they are in academic research. Applied research in general is more open to nuance and interpretation of results than academic research, which makes sense when you think about the objective: In applied work, you are trying to make the best business decision possible, but you have to do it in a timely fashion and with a modicum of certainty. To do this well, clarity is required. In academic research, however, scholars are more focused on building general knowledge and being completely transparent about their methods and findings. Having these metrics foregrounded is essential to that end goal.

In this next section, we review a few additional concepts that are central to quantitative research in academic studies that are less commonly considered in consumer insights research. While you might not find yourself referencing them regularly, it's still important to know and have a basic understanding of these concepts in order to have a better sense of what is going on "inside" your research. And an added bonus: If you find yourself at an agency or organization that likes to use academic research as a starting point for their own work (secondary research—woohoo!), you'll have a basic sense of how to read and interpret this work.

Three specific areas will be covered in this final section: validity, reliability, and the use of scales. Fair warning: The brevity and lack of detail in this section may hurt your professor's head and heart, particularly for those coming from more traditional academic backgrounds and who did not do consumer insights research. Treat them gently. Listen to them. This material really is important to know, and you are lucky (#blessed) to have a professor who can explain—and do!—this type of work for a living.

QUANTITATIVE RESEARCH FOR ACADEMICS

The three concepts covered in this section are all ones that help researchers understand that what we are researching is rigorous and precise. They help other researchers know that the data you are presenting are sufficiently tested to ensure accuracy and that you, as a researcher, have followed exacting protocols to confirm your data are as close to reality as possible. Academic research often repurposes instruments that have already been confirmed through earlier research, building on those previous studies either through replication or by means of application to a new (but related) area. While consumer insights research is almost entirely custom and bespoke, that is not the case in the academic world. This accumulation of methods and knowledge—central to the scientific method—allows for a calculation of and emphasis on validity, reliability, and replication and confirmation of scales.

- **Validity.** Validity is the extent to which a test *actually* measures what is *supposed* to measure. Ultimately, this speaks to the accuracy of your research and its components. Validity is an indicator to those reviewing your research that you have spent time and effort to ensure you are as truthful as possible. The validity of measures often is something you will look for in studies that have used similar (or identical) instruments that have already been confirmed to have high validity. When these measures are used, you can rest easy that you are measuring what you intend to measure.

- **Reliability.** While validity focuses on accuracy, **reliability** emphasizes how consistent or stable a measure is. In other words, if another researcher used your same measures in their own study with the same population, a reliable measure would find similar results. If your findings are completely different, that means your measure is unreliable and should not be used (or, if it is used, you need to be able to explain why it came out so differently).
- **Replication and confirmation of scales.** In quantitative research, **scales**—a series of related questions that use the same set of answer options—often are used to better understand complex phenomena. We will be spending a lot of time in the next chapter talking about how we build out scales (or batteries, or matrices) in consumer insights research, but in academic research scholars rely on similar scales that have been tested for validity and reliability. The common use of these scales allows for comparisons across studies, subjects, and audiences, which means different scholars can examine similar questions and draw meaningful comparisons with assurance that the differences are not due to measurement error.

Again, these concepts are not super likely to come up in your consumer insights work, and most of the time you will be constructing client- and project-specific measures that are designed for your specific RQs. And if you are using existing scales, they likely are proprietary to either the research company or the client and are not available in the public domain.

BEST PRACTICES AND KEY TAKEAWAYS

Hopefully, this chapter has persuaded you that quant research is not the terrifying beast that so many of us see it as when we think about research in the abstract. Now that you are hooked, the next two chapters will show you how to do it, first through writing effective surveys and then through understanding data analysis and the types of tests that are used to make sense of audiences, answer RQs, and address business objectives. Remember that these three chapters are intended to be considered as a set; to write a really good instrument, you need to know what you will be *doing* with the data to ensure you ask the right types of questions to use in your analysis.

KEY TERMS

A/B testing: A type of testing used to compare audience responses to two iterations or options of the same ad or product (Option A versus Option B)

Census: Research that includes every member of the population as a participant

Convenience sample: A nonprobability sampling approach wherein respondents are recruited because they are easy to access/find

Correlation: A statistical measure of the relationships between and among variables

Extrapolation: Generalizing the results from research with a representative sample to the population as a whole

Hypothesis: A proposed model for the relationships between and among variables

Incidence: How easy or hard it is to find your defined population

Mall intercepts: A recruitment technique used in nonprobability samples wherein participants are recruited in malls or other public spaces

Nonprobability samples: Samples that do not follow rigorous scientific sampling procedures and thus the results cannot be generalized to the population

Occam's Razor (also spelled "Ockham's"): The simplest explanation is usually the right one

Operationalization: Establishing clearly articulated definitions for key concepts and variables

Periodicity: Something about the way your sampling frame list is organized makes it more likely one unit on that list will be selected than another

Pilot test: Thoroughly testing research instruments with members of your target audience in advance to ensure your questions make sense, your language is clear, and you are not priming your respondents

Priming: Inadvertently preparing your respondents for what is coming up next and thereby changing the way they answer your questions

Probability samples: Samples that meet rigorous scientific statistical procedures so findings can be extrapolated to the population

Sampling frame: A list of every member of a population

Scales: A series of related questions that use the same set of answer options

Snowball sampling: A nonprobability sampling approach used with hard-to-find populations; once you find a respondent who fits your criteria, you ask for recommendations and assistance with recruiting

Standardization: All questions are asked the same way and in the same order

Stratum: Also known as a segment or subsample in your total sample, a stratum (plural: strata) is a way of looking at one part of a population as defined by the researcher

Survey research: Research that uses standardized questions to collect information from participants; the most common form of quantitative research in consumer insights research

Variables: An element or factor that can change or can vary in value/options

Volunteer sample: A nonprobability sampling approach wherein interested people voluntarily go to your poll and take it

10

Quantitative Data Collection

Writing surveys is equal parts art and science. You need to really center everything you do on your audience—how they think, the words and phrases they use, and the ways they engage with whatever it is you are researching. You also need to make sure you are writing a technically sound, scientifically rigorous instrument that will generate accurate data that can be used to answer your RQs and address your business objective. Make no mistake; this is a craft—and like all crafts, writing good surveys requires considerable skill, attention to detail, and thoughtful effort. Because you can't make changes once your survey is live and in the field (that pesky standardization bit strikes again!), you need to make absolutely sure that you have written good questions, placed them in the right order, and are collecting all of the information you need to do your job well.

Often (but not always), your survey will be written based on what you have learned in qualitative research. You will have had a chance to talk to your audience and find out what matters to them and the phrases they use. When this isn't the case, however, you need to make absolutely sure that you have done the necessary prep work to write the best possible survey for your client and their audience. This can be tricky—our instincts often are to write what makes sense to *us*, which isn't always what will make sense to the audience. Good researchers always keep the target population in the forefront of their minds when writing instruments, however. Remember that our clients absolutely are experts in their industries and thus will use terminology that would not be familiar to the everyday consumer; while someone who works in restaurants could automatically tell you what a two-top is, that phrase might not be as familiar to someone who regularly has dinner in a casual dining restaurant—and even THAT term is jargon! (For the record: A two-top is a table for two in a restaurant, and casual dining restaurants are moderately priced dine-in eateries that often have televisions in the bar like Applebee's, Outback Steakhouse, or the Cheesecake Factory).

As you start this process, remember to reground yourself in what your client's goals are for this project. Spend time revisiting the RQs and business objective. Review your topline presentation and any other materials you have available. If it has been a while, look at the secondary research again to see how you understand and interpret it differently based on what you now know. It's amazing what kernels you can discover when you come back to that information with additional context and information. Read through what you wrote in your initial bracketing experience and see if that needs updated or altered. Throughout all of these steps, keep a list of ideas and insights that you want to make sure are considered during the actual survey-writing process. All of these things will help you prepare to write an engaging, comprehensive survey that will lead to quality data analysis and compelling findings.

GENERAL BEST PRACTICES

Once you have regrounded yourself in all extant materials, you need to start thinking about what you need to cover in your survey. It's useful to approach this as systematically as possible. Remember that you are going to be writing something that will be used to make informed business decisions, which means you need to be as rigorous as possible when putting it together.

- **Start with a (long, long) list.** We will discuss the step-by-step process of survey creation below, but at the outset, you need to make sure you have as complete a list as possible of the topics and questions you want covered—and *why*. Remember that surveys are finite; participants won't stick with you forever, so you have a limited amount of real estate available for what you want to achieve. You eventually will need to prioritize, but for now, you want to focus on getting all possibilities on the table. This will let you start without as much worry about inadvertently missing a key question or variable.
- **Carefully define your population.** You need to know exactly who needs to be represented in this study, which means determining and defining any relevant variables that will be needed in your analysis. If you anticipate that you are going to want to do "deep dives" into a particular segment, you'll need to make sure you have the questions in your survey to identify members of that group. Missing out on something that winds up being potentially useful—education levels, for example, or household income—can undermine the quality of your results. Plan accordingly. This includes geography as well. If you are conducting research for a gas-station chain that is only in six states, you need to think about whether you want to talk only to people in those six states or if you want to expand more broadly. This decision will be made based on your RQs and business objective, but you need to know early where you will be looking for participants.
- **Know how you are finding your respondents and collecting data.** Historically, survey data were collected using random digit dialing to find people in your defined population to participate in your research via telephone. In the age of cell phones and spam blockers, this is much (much) harder to do. Most research nowadays takes place online, often using some sort of **panel**: pre-recruited respondents who have already been screened and are in an available pool from which you can select. Whether you are using an Internet panel, a phone survey, or some combination of the two, you likely will be partnered with an external company who specializes in survey data collection. This can be a company that can also host your survey (Qualtrics, for example) or they can be focused more exclusively on recruiting. Either way, you'll likely need support getting your sample filled.
- **Plan for your data analysis.** The statistical tests we will cover in the next chapter require certain questions be asked in certain ways. While we aren't going to get into too much detail here, work with your data experts and statisticians to ensure you are asking the right questions in the right ways to run the tests you need during analysis.
- **Communicate with your client.** A good way to wind up with a bad product is to leave your client out of discussions around what the survey should look like. If possible, have a quick meeting with them to make sure you're on the same page about what needs to be included.

While you don't want to inundate your client with information, you do want to make sure they are on board with what you are planning for both the survey instrument and your data analysis. Once the survey is in the field, options are limited. You need their buy-in in advance to ensure a successful outcome.

- **Operationalize key concepts and variables early.** Getting buy-in from your client includes ensuring a shared understanding of how you are defining key variables. You want to make sure you have agreement on such items as audience characteristics or the list of competitors that they want included in your instrument. Before you start drafting in earnest, be sure you have clearly operationalized all of these variables and that your client agrees. This (hopefully!) will forestall any future crises.

- **Focus on your flow.** A good survey flows naturally from one section to the next, and it feels like you are building as you go. If you have a good flow, participants are engaged and ready to keep going with you through to the end. When you are writing and testing your instrument, really spend time on the flow—make sure the question order makes sense, put in some written transitions between sections, and so on. Trust me—it makes a huge difference.

- **Think about human behaviors during survey taking.** Remember that real, live, actual people will be taking your survey, and you need to make sure you are crafting an instrument that is designed to maximize their likelihood of finishing the entire study. So, write questions that can be answered. Keep emotional responses in mind. Consider how they are going to actually physically take the survey; if it's likely via mobile devices, for example, you'll maybe want to limit question formats built for horizontal screens (ratings sliders, for example). Don't let your "survey creep" happen and eventually wind up with an instrument that just takes too long to complete. A good litmus test: Based on the incentive you're offering, how likely is a member of your target population to complete this? The best way to check to make sure all of this works? Piloting.

- **Pilot, pilot, pilot.** Our final bullet in this list: You *must* pilot your instrument at multiple points in the process to make sure it flows properly, your meaning and intentions are clear to your participants, the survey can be completed in a manageable amount of time, and you have written appropriate response options for each question. You also want to make sure your instrument works on a range of screen types and sizes, including mobile devices. This piloting can be super informal—leaning over to a colleague to ask if a question makes sense or having them run through a battery of questions really quickly—or watching a qualified participant actually take the survey to gauge their interpretations and responses and generate feedback that can be used to iterate and improve the instrument. All points on this continuum are useful exercises, but you definitely want to make sure that you have people outside of your research team pilot testing your survey to ensure you catch mistakes before you go live in the field.

PREPARING TO WRITE YOUR SURVEY

As noted earlier, when you are preparing to write your survey, you'll want to start with a comprehensive list of what you need to learn or ask about. Starting early in the project, I like to keep a page handy for this list that I can just keep adding to over time—you never know when inspiration will strike, so I'll jot down a word or phrase to remind me about what we might want to ask about when we get to the survey phase. This is a fantastic starting point, so even if you don't have one you've been using the whole time, I highly recommend just spending thirty minutes or so brainstorming. Get everything out. Remember that you will be writing closed-ended questions (more on that to come!), so you need to think about potential response options as well as questions. You can prioritize and edit later, but this initial "brain dump" will spark ideas and get you started on the right path. Think about how the human brain works. Once we start writing something, we naturally get committed to what we have on paper—no one wants to kill their darlings, as fiction writers say. It's also all too easy to get so into the weeds on a survey that you miss out on asking something really important. This list will help you guard against that happening.

Once you have your list, you'll need to start organizing. As was the case when developing qualitative instruments (interview and focus group guides in particular), I recommend starting with categories or subject headers—what are the broad areas you need to ensure that you cover everything and that the survey flows. From this point forward, you need to make sure you are working to avoid **priming** your participants. With its roots in psychology, priming means introducing something that then changes the ways your participants answer later questions. For example, if you let them know early on your survey is for Target, they will then answer all questions about big-box retailers—even those that you want to have more generally answered—with Target in mind. To help prevent this result, you'll want to make sure that you keep your survey as neutral as possible for as long as you can, which means clearly planning around section order.

Finally, you will want to think about how you will cover the requisite ethics in your survey while still avoiding priming. In academic research (which might apply if you are doing an in-class project, depending on how your university's IRB handles that situation), you typically would have an extensive explanation that covers the study's title, the potential risks and benefits, what the participant should expect during the survey procedure, and who to contact if you have any questions or concerns. In the applied world, the ethical disclosures vary greatly. Some are as simple as a heads up about who the survey is for and how long it will be, whereas others will need to give more detail based on the sensitivity of the topic. Be sure you check with your client and your team, so you know what ethical disclosures need to be included.

STRUCTURING YOUR SURVEY

Surveys often follow a fairly consistent structure. While you may come across examples that do not use this model, this general approach will give you enough background and context to apply the same thinking to other approaches. Remember that you want to tailor your survey to your specific project, client, and audience; there really is no one-size-fits-all template that will let you plug and play all the time. That said, these sections will be included—roughly in this order—most of the time in your research, so it's worth knowing what they are and thinking them through.

Before you get into your questions, I highly recommend putting your RQs and business objective at the top of your instrument as you develop it. This is a fantastic way to reground yourself in what you need to achieve and stay focused on what must be included. You will want to triple check that you've taken them out before you go live with your survey, but it's helpful to keep them front and center during your drafting process.

Screener

Survey instruments always start with a **screener**: the questions that determine who is qualified to take your study because they meet your essential criteria. Anyone who tries to take the survey but *doesn't* meet your criteria will be given the boot (in the gentlest, kindest, most grateful way possible—no need for bad research karma!). Imagine you are doing a study in which you have defined your target population as men 18–54 who drink iced tea at least once a month. Your screener would need to have questions included to learn their age, beverage preferences, and the frequency of beverage consumption. It might look something like figure 10.1:

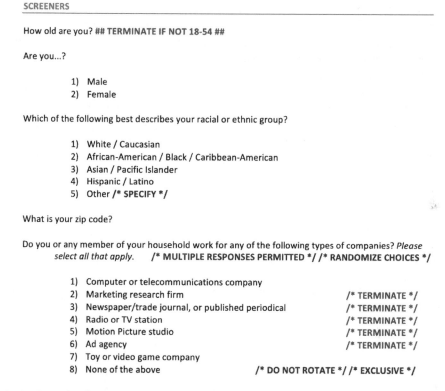

Figure 10.1   Example of a survey screener.

Anyone whose answers did *not* meet your criteria would be taken to the end of the survey, where they will be bid a gracious adieu. You might also put a question in to eliminate those who would have too close an association with whatever it is you are studying; for example, you'd want to eliminate anyone who worked in the beverage industry or in market research, since their expertise on the product (iced tea) or process (consumer insights research) would mean they likely had a meaningfully different experience that disqualifies them as representative members of the population. Some instruments will screen out potential respondents who recently completed a survey as well.

I cannot stress enough how important it is that you carefully think through the questions you will include in your screener. If your RQs require that you include a certain percentage of Lipton iced tea drinkers, you will need to include a question about brand usage or preference as well. "But wait!" you likely are thinking. "Wouldn't asking about Lipton tea lead to priming?"—which truly is an excellent point, and you all deserve more extra credit for your application of knowledge. And priming really is a real risk here. To mitigate that, you would **mask** your client by including a range of competitor brands in the same list, as is the case in figure 10.2—because a wide range of television channels/services are included, respondents won't be able to tell which is the focus of the study.

/* QNETWORKS */ Here we will present you with cards showing a number of television channels and/or services you may or may not have heard of. **Please tell us how often you watch the following channels and/or services** by clicking on the option below that best describes how often you watch the channel/service.

BOXES AT THE TOP
1) Daily
2) Weekly
3) Monthly
4) Have watched, but less than once a month
5) Heard of this, but do not watch
6) Never heard of this

CARDSTACK - SHOW LOGOS ON CARD AND RANDOMIZE ORDER

a) A&E
b) Animal Planet
c) ImagiNation
d) History Channel
e) National Geographic
f) Netflix
g) Paramount Network
h) Science Channel
i) Travel Channel
j) TruTV

MUST SELECT C1-C5 for (c) ImagiNation – OTHERWISE TERMINATE
MUST SELECT C1-C4 FOR AT LEAST 3 NETWORKS – OTHERWISE TERMINATE

RESPONDENTS WILL NOT SEE THE CODING QUESTIONS
/* QVIEWERCODE */ Viewer Code

1) ImagiNation Core Viewer **IF QNETWORKS IMAGINATION = ANY C1-C2**
2) ImagiNation Casual Viewer **IF QNETWORKS IMAGINATION = C3**
3) ImagiNation Potential Viewers **IF QNETWORKS IMAGINATION = ANY C4-C5**

Figure 10.2 In this example of a screener, the question is written to measure frequency of viewership for the client without letting the participant know which channel is the client.

Potential participants should select all of the options that apply to their iced tea consumption. You can have a code on the backend of the survey (something the participants don't see but gives you and the programmer a way to ensure appropriate progress through the survey) that kicks out people who do not drink Lipton to ensure you only have that brand. And if you are doing stratified samples based on brands, you could ask for a certain number of Lipton drinkers, Arizona drinkers, and so on. It's really cool stuff.

The Body

Your screener has weeded out those who are not qualified to take your survey, so you know for sure that anyone who made it through is part of your target audience. Phew. So now, you have to think about how to use your time as wisely as possible. The body of the survey is where you actually ask the questions you need to have answers to, but you really have to think through how you keep your participants engaged while getting them through the different sections. Most surveys are only around 15 minutes long; you can go a bit longer if you have a sufficiently compelling incentive to continue, but any longer than 20 minutes or so, and you start to see increased **attrition**, or people dropping out/quitting your survey. You want everyone who starts your survey to finish, so you need to make sure you keep them moving and that you are using your time as wisely as possible.

When you are constructing your survey, keep the funnel model in mind (as was the case in qualitative instrument development as well). You want to start as broadly as needed and then eventually narrow in over the course of the instrument. Not only does this flow make intuitive sense to participants, it also helps prevent **order bias**, or introducing bias through the order of the questions and responses. Priming is not just to be avoided in the screener; you also want to make sure that you are not accidentally priming by asking about your specific brand or product too early in the survey. As the saying goes, you can't put the toothpaste back in the tube. Once you have revealed who will be using the results of the survey, respondents inevitably will have your client in mind when answering all further questions. Make sure you want that to be the case once you have revealed who you are working with for this research. Be intentional in what you reveal.

When you are putting your instrument together, you also want to think about how you can use programming to tailor your survey based on what respondents have already answered. Consider the ways you can use **skip patterns** to ensure your participants only are shown relevant questions; if you answer "yes" to a question, you move onto the next set of questions, but if you answer "no" and thus the next set of questions is irrelevant, you skip down to the next applicable section. You also can—and should—consider times when **randomizing** and **rotating** questions or options in matrices and/or responses makes sense. This is a great strategy for reducing order bias; by making sure that everyone does not get the same order within every question, you reduce the likelihood that people will all just pick something early without reading through the whole list. Note that this does *not* mean changing the order of questions; those remain the same for every participant. This is about randomizing and rotating *within* a question to mitigate potential bias.

Softball questions. To help make sure participants move from the screener to the body of the survey, you want to start with softball questions. As was the case with qualitative research, **softball questions** are easy to answer and don't require a huge amount of thought. If you ask too much, too early, your participants will be tempted to drop out—especially if you don't have a compelling enough incentive. Even if they stick with you, there's an increased chance they'll start answering poorly or just not paying attention. These easy, no-brainer questions still need to be relevant, but it lets you get your respondents into the right headspace and encourages them to continue with the survey. This is a fairly quick section, only talking two or three minutes at most, but it is important for building engagement and investment with your participants.

Values, perceptions, and behaviors. Once you've hooked your respondent through your softball questions, you will then move into the first "meaty" section with questions that require a bit more thought and engagement. This often centers around queries about personal or cultural values (what matters most, how and what they prioritize, etc.) and information about behaviors (media usage, frequency, usage, etc.). Anything that you want to find out that is not tied specifically to your category or brand should be asked in here.

Category information. Once you have general behaviors and perceptions, you likely want to move into perceptions of the category (like we see in figure 10.3). For our iced tea example, you might want to ask about beverages in general, including what their motivations are for choosing different types of drinks. So, for example, you could ask your participants to rank different motivations for choosing iced tea versus caffeinated soft drinks versus coffee-based beverages. These perceptions tend to be quite broad—you really are focused on the *category* rather than specific brands.

Another example: If a movie production company is thinking about expanding into a new genre, they might spend quite a bit of time in this section of a survey to understand perceptions of genres and likelihood for audience members to go to the theater, rent at home, and/or buy for home viewing. For both of these examples, you would rely on the statistical tests we will be covering in chapter 11 to identify overall priorities and relationships. Participants will simply

/* **QATTRIBUTES**/ Which of the following statements/attributes describes the types of networks you enjoy watching? /* **MULTIPLE RESPONSES PERMITTED** */ /* **RANDOM ROTATE CHOICES** */ ## SHOW IN 2 COLUMNS ##

1) A good escape
2) A guilty pleasure
3) Action-packed
4) Aspirational
5) Authentic
6) Credible
7) Diverse
8) Edgy
9) Educational
10) Features meaningful stories and relationships
11) Features people like me
12) Fun
13) Gritty
14) Has compelling characters
15) High quality
16) Intense

17) Lighthearted
18) Motivational
19) Over-the-top
20) Relatable
21) Relevant
22) Reliable
23) Superficial
24) Suspenseful
25) Unique
26) Visually captivating
27) Trail-blazing
28) Smart
29) Optimistic
30) Takes me to new places
31) None of the above /* EXCLUSIVE * / /*DO NOT ROTATE*/ /* TERMINATE *

/* **END SERIES** */

Figure 10.3   An example of survey questions written to measure the association of characteristics with certain networks (as shown in figure 10.2).

be answering the questions; they don't need to do these rankings themselves. Remember that we want to ward off attrition by minimizing how mentally taxing it is to complete these surveys, especially in the first half of the experience.

Competitor information. At this point, you often are about halfway done with your survey. The competitor information section often is intended to uncover comparisons between your brand or product and your main competitors as well as aspirational brands—the ones who are in "white space" you potentially want to move into. The beauty of computerized surveys is that you can program to be responsive to earlier responses. As long as you have asked a question earlier to generate the needed data, you can limit the options they are presented with to brands they know or are familiar with and/or brands you need to know about. Competitor information usually is focused only on a handful of brands—at most—per respondent. Often, you will ask about your brand as well as one or two others. Because these often have fairly extensive question batteries, you want to make sure this doesn't feel too redundant or too tiring.

Brand information. The last real "content" section, this is where you focus on understanding specific information about your brand and the respondents' perceptions and behaviors around it. By now, they know who the client is so you no longer need to worry about masking; you ask direct and specific questions about your brand or product. These are really useful opportunities to ask **benchmarking** or **tracking** questions—ones a client includes in every survey with their target audience to show change over time. If it's a question that you are intending to ask in the future or one that you will use to measure effectiveness (such as awareness of your brand or usage behavior), it would be considered a **baseline** question since it gives you the starting point to evaluate change against.

Demographics

Once you have asked everything you need to know, you will then wrap up your survey with questions about demographics. I highly recommend putting these questions in a separate section on a new page along with an explanation that the information collected will only be used for statistical and analytical purposes and will not be shared. You likely will be asking for personal information in here, so you want to reassure your respondents about how you will use these data, as shown in figure 10.4.

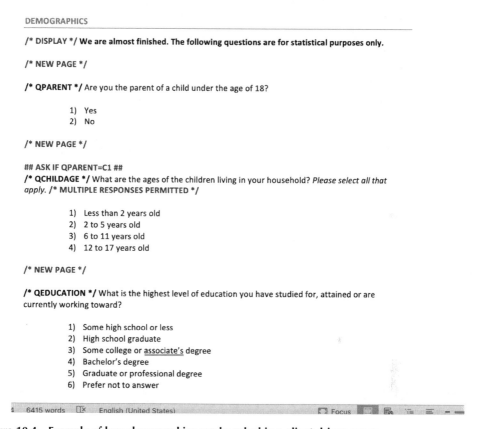

Figure 10.4 **Example of how demographics can be asked in a client-driven survey.**

As a rule, demographic questions should only be asked if the information is directly relevant and will be used in your analysis. Ethically speaking, you want to minimize how much personal information you ask for in this section. If you won't need it, don't ask it. You also should not duplicate any questions that were asked in the screener; this should all be new information. Typically, the demographic section would include questions on some or all of the following:

- Sex/gender
- Age
- Race/ethnicity
- Education
- Employment status
- Parental or guardian status (usually focused on children under 18 living in the household)
- Marital status
- Household income

Depending on your topic, of course, these items could change. Most of the time, your client or your company will have standard ways of asking these demographic questions.

Be careful that you follow best practices in how you operationalize and articulate your demographic variables. With items like age and household income, you'll want to provide a range of options rather than asking for a specific number (although some like to ask for the birth year and then code into categories on the backend). Some items require more sensitivity than others. For example, it is important that you think about the differences between sex (related to biological characteristics, so offering male, female, and intersex options) and gender (referencing the sense of self, so usually offering options like woman, man, or trans)—these terms should not be used interchangeably, so you need to be thoughtful in what you include in your instrument.

Race and ethnicity can be particularly tricky to ask about, so it is worth spending some time on advance planning for how to approach this question. If you want to map your research onto the U.S. Census, you often will use its ways of asking about race and ethnicity. As of the 2020 Census, "ethnicity" and "race" are asked separately. The first question—"Is Person 1 of Hispanic, Latino, or Spanish origin?"—is followed by this explanation:

> NOTE: For this census, Hispanic origins were not considered races. Hispanic origin can be viewed as the heritage, nationality, lineage, or country of birth of the person or the person's parents or ancestors before arriving in the United States. People who identify as Hispanic, Latino, or Spanish may be any race.[1]

As we see in figure 10.5, the next question asks, "What is Person 1's race?" In this response, participants checked one or more boxes as appropriate and were asked to identify their origins.

While the census's approach in separating ethnicity and race is fairly common, other researchers integrate the two and just ask participants to select all that apply. Here is an example of that:

- Which of the following best describes you? *Please select all that apply.*
  - Asian or Pacific Islander
  - Black or African American
  - Hispanic or Latino
  - Native American or Alaskan Native
  - White or Caucasian
  - Biracial or Multiracial
  - Other race/ethnicity not listed here
  - Prefer not to answer

Be sure you check with your team and your client before you go forward with any of your demographic questions. You may want to make sure you are using an approach that allows to compare findings versus earlier studies, for example, or your client may have specific breakdowns they would like to be able to use. This all needs to be identified and agreed upon in advance. You should also consider not requiring answers to these questions (as indicated in the last example above); some participants may be uncomfortable answering, so there can be an ethical concern about requiring information that creates psychological distress.

If you are looking for good ways to ask these questions or more analysis of why this matters, I encourage you to look at good examples that are available online from such prestigious (and noncommercial) organizations as the Pew Research Center. There is a robust discussion within the online research community about how to do this well (and why it matters), and I encourage you to check it out!

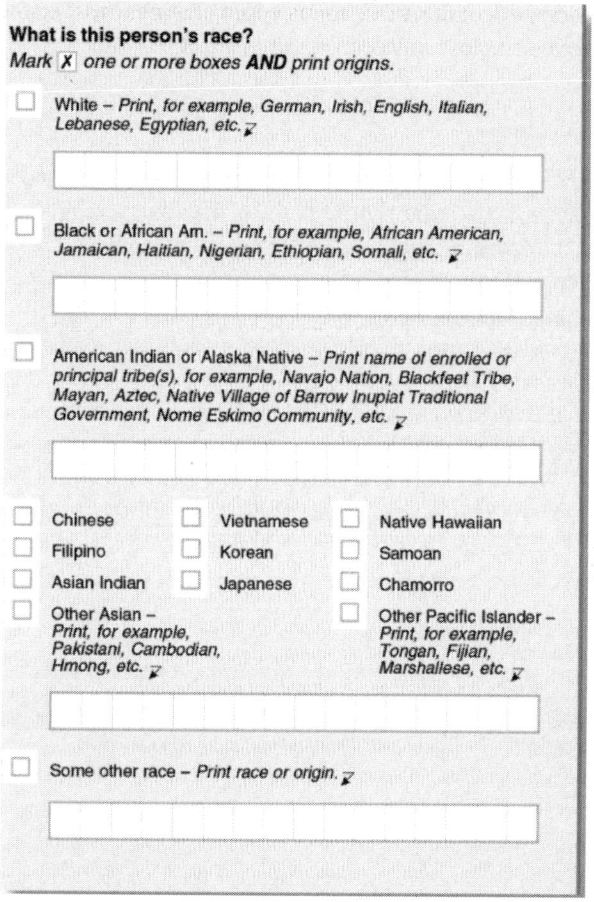

What is this person's race?
Mark ☒ one or more boxes **AND** print origins.

☐ White – *Print, for example, German, Irish, English, Italian, Lebanese, Egyptian, etc.* ⤤

☐ Black or African Am. – *Print, for example, African American, Jamaican, Haitian, Nigerian, Ethiopian, Somali, etc.* ⤤

☐ American Indian or Alaska Native – *Print name of enrolled or principal tribe(s), for example, Navajo Nation, Blackfeet Tribe, Mayan, Aztec, Native Village of Barrow Inupiat Traditional Government, Nome Eskimo Community, etc.* ⤤

☐ Chinese ☐ Vietnamese ☐ Native Hawaiian
☐ Filipino ☐ Korean ☐ Samoan
☐ Asian Indian ☐ Japanese ☐ Chamorro
☐ Other Asian – *Print, for example, Pakistani, Cambodian, Hmong, etc.* ⤤ ☐ Other Pacific Islander – *Print, for example, Tongan, Fijian, Marshallese, etc.* ⤤

☐ Some other race – *Print race or origin.* ⤤

Figure 10.5   The U.S. Census's race question used in the 2020 Census. (https://www2.census.gov/about/training-workshops/2020/2020-02-19-pop-presentation.pdf)

Editing Your Survey

Once you are finally done putting all of these sections, you may find yourself with the World's Longest Survey. You'll have dozens of fabulous questions that are guaranteed to generate essential data, and they absolutely, positively CANNOT be cut. It seems impossible. But again, friends, these are times you need to kill your darlings. When you get your first draft written, you have to start to edit. Look for any questions that are redundant—if you are already getting that information somewhere else, do you *really* need to repeat it? Are there questions you can combine into matrices (see below)? And is everything you have included truly essential? Go back to your RQ and business objective once more. Focus in once more on what you need to know. And then start cutting. It hurts. But it's worth it.

WRITING GOOD QUESTIONS

A survey is only as good as the questions in it; no matter how much planning and preparation you have done, bad survey questions will tank your data and undermine your study. This section will review the basics of writing good questions and—equally important—good responses. We will start with exploring different types of questions, then review basic rules for question writing, and finally move into considerations for responses.

Different Types of Questions

The broadest categories for survey questions are open- versus closed-ended questions. An **open-ended question** is akin to what we did in the qualitative section—questions that have no set answers from which to choose and thus participants can answer any way they want. While this is fabulous for generating information in qualitative studies, you want to use open-ended questions quite sparingly when it comes to quant. The whole beauty of this approach is that you can organize respondents into discrete categories, and that's a heck of a lot harder to do when you have to go in and code a whole range of answers! Sure, there will be times you think it's worth it—maybe you want to get some additional feedback on a rating they give for the store, so the anecdotal information you're getting is used to make sense of their numbers and likely will fit into your existing knowledge. But in general, you want to build your study using **closed-ended questions** that have a set of response options from which participants can choose. This allows for much easier coding and analysis—but it *does* require hard work to ensure that you are writing the best possible questions with the best possible responses.

There are several types of questions to be familiar with within the framework of closed-ended questions. While the list below is by no means exhaustive, it does cover most of the basic question options you'll encounter. For each of these examples, I am using a survey I built in Qualtrics, one of the most popular survey creation and distribution platforms. Whatever program you use, however, you'll likely find templates for each of these question types:

- **Yes/no questions.** Exactly what the name says—respondents can say either "yes" or "no." You might sometimes throw in a "maybe" if you are okay with (or need) the respondents to be a bit wishy-washy on their response, and you likely will want to consider including a "don't know" as well, but it doesn't get more complicated than that.
- **Multiple choice.** You likely are quite familiar with this type of question due to your own experiences with exams in college classes. (Not a fan, necessary evil.) When you have a multiple-choice question, you have a set series of answers from which participants can select. There are two subtypes of multiple-choice questions. Sometimes, you'll want your participants to only be able to select one response; other times, you'll want them to select **all that apply**. Make sure you carefully think through which option is better, since they will give you different information—the top choice versus all acceptable choices. Both can be useful, but know what you need to learn so you make the right selection.
- **Matrix (or battery) questions.** In this type of question, common questions—usually in the form of statements—are bundled together to form one question set. These are then presented in the first row of a table, and the remaining columns are the response options. So, a matrix would look something like figure 10.6.

   The response options usually in the form of what's generally known as a **Likert scale**—a scale that uses variations of the same concept in order to measure the gradations in response. While Likert-type scales can be used outside of matrices, this is the most common usage. You'll want to start with the most negative on the left and then gradually get more positive as you move to the right. Note that the option I am showing you here has four agree/disagree options. Whether you need a "neutral" option in the middle or a "N/A" (not applicable) column at the end are hotly debated by researchers, which we will discuss in more detail in the

How strongly do you agree or disagree with each of the following statements:

	Strongly Disagree	Somewhat Disagree	Somewhat Agree	Strongly Agree
I am a dedicated student.	O	O	O	O
I always complete my assignments on time.	O	O	O	O
I believe in the value of hard work.	O	O	O	O

Figure 10.6   Example of a matrix question.

response option section. But either way, this format allows respondents to quickly answer a range of questions and tend to be particularly helpful for questions related to opinions (agree/disagree) and frequency (often/never). Just make sure that you stick with one number of responses—be consistent. You don't want to use four, then seven, then five. Pick one set and go with it.

- **Rank order.** Ranking questions like the one shown in figure 10.7 allow you to see how participants order options based on certain variables. So, for example, they could rank their preferences for different soft drinks, or fashion brands, or television channels. Anything you want to see in order of preference or relevance, rankings can work.

Please rank each of the following from **most** to **least important** ways your professors can support your online learning.

1 Consistent deadlines

2 Require cameras be turned on during class

3 Offering classes "live" during the scheduled time period

4 Recording lectures for students to watch on their own schedules

5 Hold online office hours

6 Send weekly emails on Monday to outline the week's schedule

Figure 10.7   Example of a rank-order question.

- **Rating sliders.** While ranking gives you the order of preference, you can't tell how much difference there is between the options. Maybe you have two choices that they love and then the next three are much lower—that's great information, but you can't tell it from a ranking. Generating ratings on a sliding scale, by contrast, lets each option be evaluated on its own so that you can tell how each option is evaluated on its own merits. These often look like the example in figure 10.8. These can be challenging on mobile devices, however, so you want to make sure you plan for that when pulling your instrument together.
- **Constant sum.** In this type of question, participants have a certain number of points to allocate, and those points can represent anything you want them to be (dollars, percentages,

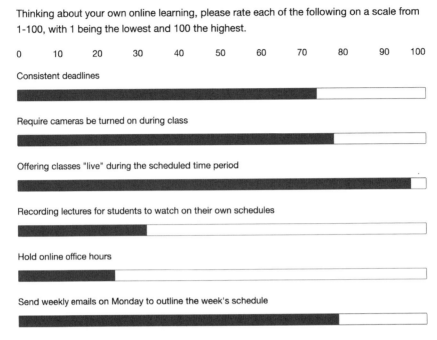

Thinking about your own online learning, please rate each of the following on a scale from 1-100, with 1 being the lowest and 100 the highest.

Figure 10.8   Example of a rating slider; notice how this would be difficult on a mobile device.

etc.). They can then distribute the points across whatever categories you provide. Because there is a cap on how many points can be allotted, this approach gives you a strong indicator of how much value is assigned relative to the other included items. Check out figure 10.9 for an example of how this type of question might look.
• **Semantic differential scales.** In a semantic differential scale, you choose two opposing adjectives (conservative/liberal; heartfelt/unemotional; dark/light) to anchor each end of a rating scale that usually has seven selection points available (see figure 10.10). Participants can then pick the selection point that best represents their perceptions. The challenge with these scales is that you have to find two adjectives to use that truly represent the poles of

Thinking about a typical class, how much of your time (in percentages) do you spend on each of the following activities. Note: Total must add up to 100%.

Reading assigned material (textbook, other readings)	20
Attending class	15
Reviewing notes	15
Working on projects	30
Studying for exams	15
Other course-related activity	5
Total	100

Figure 10.9   Example of a constant-sum question.

How would you describe your learning experience in this course? Click on the button that best represents your experience.

Awful	O	O	O	O	O	O	O	Outstanding
Ineffective	O	O	O	O	O	O	O	Effective
Boring	O	O	O	O	O	O	O	Interesting

Figure 10.10 Example of a semantic differential scale.

the characteristic you are measuring—they need to actually represent the possible range of responses, or the scale does not make sense.

One note of caution: More and more respondents will be taking their surveys on mobile devices and thus have smaller, vertically oriented screens. More complicated or dense question formats may not work as well with those dimensions. It also gets harder to scroll through a ton of questions. As much as possible, make sure you are testing your survey on mobile before going live.

Basic Rules for Writing Questions

If you have ever been on a politician's email list, you likely have seen some wild examples of what are supposed to be survey questions: "How do you rate the job your Representative to Congress is doing? (1) The best!; (2) Excellent; (3) Really great (4) So good." And then nothing else. No other options are available. Clearly, bad or unfavorable feedback is not welcome here. Or, on the flip side, "How interested are you in beating back the other guys and making sure they don't destroy our country? (1) Very interested—let's fight to save our nation!; (2) Not interested at all—I'm too cheap to care!" (Just for the record: While I made the second one up, the first one is all too similar to actual "polls" sent out to supporters as a fundraising tool.) These kinds of questions give *real* research—research intended to understand audiences and provide intelligence—a bad name. In this section, I'll share some basic rules to help ensure you write questions that allow for the generation of quality, meaningful data—even if it's not all good news.

- **Be concise.** The longer the question is, the more likely you are to confuse your respondent. You want to write questions that are easily understood and are not open to wide ranges of interpretation and focusing on being concise helps you do that.
- **Be clear.** The partner to the bullet above, clarity is your best friend during this process. You want to ensure your meaning is straightforward and will be shared by everyone taking the survey. Avoid convoluted language whenever possible.
- **Avoid jargon.** As we saw in the "two-top" example used earlier, we want to be careful to avoid any jargon. If you've done qualitative work, you hopefully have a good sense of what language will make sense and what doesn't. If not, dig back into your secondary research. Talk to your client. Ask around. But make sure jargon doesn't slip in—that ultimately will confuse your participants and undermine your results.
- **Avoid double-barreled questions.** Imagine trying to answer this question: "I prefer to take classes that meet early and in-person." This is a kind of question that you really might see—you might not even see the problem (at least if you are a morning person!). But what if you *aren't* a morning person? What if you want to meet in person but would prefer an afternoon

start? The tricky "and" in there makes it impossible to parse those separate ideas. So when writing questions, make sure you don't bake too much into it—just measure one concept or variable at a time.

- **Avoid biased (and biasing) words or phrases.** Words are powerful, and the words or phrases we choose to use can substantially change the meaning of our questions. Just look at the "language battles" that have taken place over the past few decades; asking someone if they support gay marriage has different connotations than asking if they support marriage equality. It can be all too easy to use language that is decoded by the participants to have political or cultural meaning that can inform their answers. Guard against that happening.

- **Avoid slang.** I know you are already all too aware that this book is lit and off the hook, right? And look! In that one sentence, I have managed to inspire winces and grimaces and quite possibly may have put you off reading the rest of this chapter. (Stick with me, please.) Slang does not work in surveys. It doesn't help you connect to your audience; you just sound like you are trying too hard. So yeah, even if you hear it in the qual, there is rarely a good reason to use slang in your survey. Let's hearken back to the Coombs Rule: Be cool; don't be weird. Slang in surveys? Almost inevitably weird. (Although I do think this book *is* lit, for the record.)

- **Avoid leading questions.** A leading question is one that leads your participants where you want to go—the kind of answer you want them to give. This can be really overt ("How great is the president?") or much more subtle ("How strongly do you agree with this statement: Steele's Pots and Pans are the highest quality cookware around"—by not saying "agree or disagree," you are implying the participant could only agree, and thus you are measuring the amount of agree-ness present). This is also where the word "just" can be a bit tricky: "Would you be willing to buy this jewelry if the price is just $100?" implies the price is low, even though it may not be. Be really careful that your question wording isn't leading your participants in a certain direction.

- **Avoid asking for highly detailed information.** So tell me—how many minutes would you say you spent checking email over the past month? Or on social media? Or doing anything else you do fairly often? That kind of highly detailed information is *so* difficult to calculate that it becomes almost meaningless. Make sure you aren't asking for information that your respondents just can't calculate—that's a surefire way to increase your attrition.

- **Avoid asking for highly personal or potentially embarrassing questions.** Unless you *really* need to know about someone's criminal past or medical history, don't ask. And if you *do* need this information, work to craft questions that are sensitive to potential discomfort. Again, this is a question of ethics—do no harm. And it leads to . . .

- **Only ask relevant questions.** You have limited real estate available in your survey. Use that space wisely. If something isn't relevant, don't ask it. One suggestion from a seasoned researcher: Map each question to how it will be analyzed. This is a great trick to make sure you're only asking questions that will be useful and usable. A reminder: As I wrote earlier in this book, when I was new to my career, my boss affectionately (I think?) told me that I was a kitchen-sink researcher. What he meant was that when given the opportunity to ask questions, I'd throw in everything but the kitchen sink. One of the most important things I learned in my time as a consumer insights researcher was to stop doing that and instead focus on asking the best questions I can to get the most meaningful data possible. Relevance, relevance, relevance—make it your mantra as you start to edit.

I highly recommend looking at examples of survey questions to see what works and what doesn't. I already mentioned the Pew Research Center above, but you can also find some really good material from survey and digital platforms like Survey Monkey, Amazon Mechanical Turk (MTurk), Qualtrics, and Constant Contact. Spend some time playing around on their sites and reading their blogs; they have some fantastic information that will help you develop this craft.

Writing Good Responses

When you are writing your questions, you have to be thinking about your responses—the type of question format you use will determine what your responses look like. That said, it's still important to spend a lot of time thinking about how to craft the best possible response options for your survey. Here are a few rules of thumb:

- **Responses should be mutually exclusive.** This most often applies when you are working with discrete categories that do not overlap—if your response options are **mutually exclusive**, that means a participant can only fit into one. An easy example is looking at how you would ask about ages. Note what's wrong with this question:
  - Which of the following best represents your age?
    - 18–25
    - 25–35
    - 35–45
    - 45–55

  How would someone who is 25 answer this question? Or 35? They can fit into two categories, meaning the categories are not mutually exclusive. To be clear: There may be times when you will have questions where response options will not be mutually exclusive ("select all that apply" questions often will have overlaps, for example), and that is totally okay—just make sure that the question is written appropriately so you get the data you need.
- **Responses should be exhaustive.** Look back at the age question above. How would a 17-year-old answer this? Or someone who is 62? If there is a chance people younger than 18 or older than 55 would be taking this survey, you need to have an option for them. That's what we mean by **exhaustive**—all possible options are included (in other words, you've exhausted the options).
- **Consider even- or odd-numbered scales.** I talked about this subject briefly above, but it bears repeating here. There are two different camps on the debate over offering a middle "neutral" response option and thus having an odd-numbered scale. Researchers on both sides make compelling cases. In my training, we always used even-numbered scales to push people into one category or another. Our thinking was that neutrality doesn't tell us anything and is an "easy out" for participants; even if they are only a scootch more on one side than another, we still want to capture that. Those who advocate for odd-numbered scales, however, believe that the neutral option is necessary to capture a more accurate representation of reality. This is something your research team and/or your client likely will feel strongly about (or at least not be neutral!), so you can follow that lead.
- **Consider if you need an option for "Not Applicable" or "Don't Know."** If you are asking participants about their experience at a local movie theater, you may include a question about the concession stand. There is a solid chance, however, that your respondent didn't go to the concession stand—thus, you need to give them a way to say this is "not applicable" (this is part of being exhaustive). There also may be times they truly don't know—this will help make sure they are only answering things they know about.
- **Make sure your questions match your responses.** Read every question out loud to someone on your team and read the response options to them. Make sure the options you are

giving them make sense for the questions you're asking. You'd be amazed at how often a question is written in a way that only allows for a yes/no answer, but the options are in the form of an agree/disagree matrix: puzzling at best, off-putting (and worthy of attrition) at worst. Reading out loud will help avoid these mishaps.

TREND STUDIES

Most of what I have written about in here is focused on **cross-sectional research**, bespoke surveys that are administered one time to a unique sample of respondents. There are times, however, when researchers want to use the same survey—or at least large sections of it—over time in order to measure change. Called **trend studies**, this type of research is incredibly useful for measuring macro-level changes in your audience—seeing what is becoming more popular and what is fading out. A vice president of research at IHeartRadio, for example, noted that trend studies play a huge role in their efforts to stay ahead of what genres are getting hotter and which are on the downslide. This information helps them determine where to focus their resources in a way that keeps them just ahead of the curve rather than playing catch-up.

Trend studies often involve the same questions asked to different sample; for example, you'd give the same survey to a new sample every six months and then compare data across each survey to measure change. Other times, companies may want to create a **panel** they can use regularly. In panel studies, the same group of people—the same sample—gets the same survey at multiple points over an extended period of time. The advantage is that you can see both macro- and micro-level changes, allowing you to get much more granular in your analysis to see where—and from whom—change is coming. This can be incredibly valuable intel for a business. As you can imagine, however, panel studies are much more expensive and complex to administer than trend studies. Incentives have to be high to minimize attrition, and eventually your participants will become sensitized to the instrument—they will know what to expect, so they are in a sense permanently primed. To help mitigate this, panels will often recruit in waves; if someone is recruited for two years and the target panel size is 2,000 participants at any given point in time, every six months a new set of 600 participants may be recruited to replace the 500 who will be timing out. This extra 100 participants provide a buffer that hopefully will offset those who disappear over the course of their study commitment.

BEST PRACTICES AND KEY TAKEAWAYS

Make no mistake, writing—crafting—good surveys is both highly creative and highly technical, and, boy, can it be fun. And I really, really am not just saying that—this work can be absolutely fascinating, even for those of us who have long considered ourselves math averse. A quality survey instrument not only generates good data but also sets you up for some outstanding data analysis. In our next chapter, we are going to be going over some of the statistical tests you might encounter as researchers as well as the process you'll go through to find—and communicate—your story. Creative thinking and trusting your instincts are essential for your success, so keep the faith—this will all come together.

NOTE

1. https://2020census.gov/en/about-questions.html

KEY TERMS

Attrition: People dropping out/quitting your survey

Baseline: Questions that give you the starting point against which to evaluate change; the first measure that will be used in a benchmarking or tracking study

Benchmarking: Asking a question repeatedly over time to measure change

Closed-ended questions: Questions that have a set of response options from which participants can choose

Cross-sectional research: Research surveys administered one time to a unique sample of respondents

Demographics: The characteristics of the population that often are used to break down large groups into smaller homogeneous subsets, such as race and ethnicity, sex and gender, household income, marital status, and educational achievement

Exhaustive: All possible options are included

Likert scale: A scale that uses variations of the same concept in order to measure the gradations in response

Mask: Writing survey questions and responses in a way that makes it difficult for a participant to identify the true subject of the study

Mutually exclusive: A respondents fit into only one response category

Open-ended question: Questions that have no set answers from which to choose and thus participants can answer freely

Order bias: Introducing bias through the order of the questions and responses

Panel: Pre-recruited respondents who have already been screened and are in an available pool from which you can select

Randomization: Every survey respondent sees response options in a random order; used to reduce or prevent order bias

Rotation: Response options are rotated; used to reduce or prevent order bias

Screener: Questions that determine who is qualified to participate in a research study because they meet the essential criteria

Skip patterns: Ensure your participants are only shown relevant questions; if you answer "yes" to a question, you move onto the next set of questions, but if you answer "no" and thus the next set of questions is irrelevant, you skip down to the next applicable section

Softball questions: Questions that are easy to answer and don't require a huge amount of thought

Tracking: Asking a question repeatedly over time to measure change

Trend studies: Using the same survey or set of questions repeatedly over time to measure change

11

Quantitative Data Analysis and Reporting

You've now finished your data collection—your survey is out of the field and your data reports are ready to review. The culmination of all your preparation and planning is finally here, and you are about to start the final phase of this process: turning data to insight and insight into recommendations. As you picture this, you might find yourself starting to feel overwhelmed. Maybe that itchy feeling is back—you know that this is something that probably won't be as awful as it might sound, but yeah, pages of Excel spreadsheets does not exactly float your boat. Or, for those of you who are solid numbers types (or even those who just really liked what you learned so far in the last couple of chapters and thus now are open to the possibility that maaaaaaybe quant is more appealing/less scary than you had thought coming in), you feel a tingle of anticipation. You are ready to dig in and unlock the mysteries found in these spreadsheets, and you can't wait to get started.

Here's the good news: For those of you eagerly anticipating this experience, you're going to be even more thrilled by what you learn in this chapter. This is chock full of good stuff, including basics on categorizing data (fun!) and different statistical tests you'll be able to run to answer your RQs and address your business objective (even more fun!). For those of you who are still hesitant, that's okay too. My hope is that seeing how this will all come together in the end—and reassuring you again that you don't have to be a statistical expert to make sense of these data and find the story—will lay to rest any lingering doubts you have. While we tend to think of quantitative research as a highly technical and scientific process (which it is), we often forget about the vast amounts of creative and lateral thinking that go into leveraging these data into a meaningful, compelling story. It's incredibly gratifying when your analysis leads to an intelligent, elegant solution to your client's business problem, and this chapter will help you figure out how to do that.

The first part of this chapter is focused on data analysis, including what you need to do to prepare for this process from the earliest stages of survey creation. We then talk about what you as a researcher need to do to make sure your data are accurate before digging into your analysis (even statisticians make mistakes, you know!) and review some basic ways of thinking about and categorizing data. Next, we will review five of the most common statistical tests that are run in consumer insights quantitative research: conjoint analysis, MaxDiff, discrete choice modeling, factor analysis, and cluster analysis. We then wrap up the data analysis section of this chapter by reviewing what this means for your debrief and how to approach your analysis.

The latter part of the chapter centers on presenting these data. As a reminder, the next section of the book—starting in the next chapter!—is where we will share extensive best practices and recommendations for presenting both qualitative and quantitative data. This part is intended to give you an appetizer course, if you will: a brief overview of the most important considerations to bear in mind when you are presenting your data that gets you ready for the main course in section IV. This is particularly useful as you start to sketch out what the final versions of your documents will be, getting you into good habits that will carry through the final presentation.

GOOD PREPARATION, GOOD DATA

As was the case in qualitative research, your goal in this phase of analysis is to find a story—*the* story—that communicates your overarching findings in a way that is compelling, relevant, and memorable. Remember: Your analysis is intended to turn data into insights and insights into recommendations. To do this well, you need to be planning for and anticipating what tests you are going to run while you are still developing your instrument. I cannot stress this enough: You *must* make sure you have the right kinds of questions to run the tests we are going to talk about in here, so you need to make sure you are planning for your analysis while you are developing your instrument. If you don't have the right kinds of data in the right format, you won't be able to do the analysis you need to develop the insights that will drive your story and inform your recommendations.

During their elementary school days, my daughters were taught the "Leader in Me" habits that were developed from Franklin Covey's "7 Habits for Highly Effective People" program. While I certainly did not expect my five-year-old girl to wax enthusiastic about synergizing, I did realize how important it was for kids to learn about Habit 2: Begin with the end in mind.[1] This habit talks about having two acts of creation: the mental and the physical. For our purposes, this means that you first plan for what your analysis will look like—the mental creation of an anticipated outcome—and then you use that vision to craft the physical survey that will allow you to meet that end goal. In the heat of the moment, driven by both your excitement to move forward and the external time pressures that often come with client-based research, it can be tempting to write your survey questions based solely on what you want to learn and just get the survey live to start collecting data. But even if you are staying focused on the RQs and ROs, if you are not thinking about what your analysis will look like once your data are fully collected, you run the risk of total disaster. This is not a place where you can shortcut or move too quickly to get to your survey in the field so you can move onto the next thing. You need to do the first step—the mental creation or envisioning of your eventual analysis—in order to craft a survey that will allow that vision to become a reality. Begin with the end in mind.

ENSURING DATA ACCURACY

As noted throughout this section in an effort to mitigate the automatic shutdown that so many brains experience when "statistics" and "math" are on the horizon, it's worth another reminder: The vast majority of consumer insights researchers never, ever, ever do the data analysis themselves, particularly when your research requires anything more complex than basic reporting of numbers. While my training as a researcher makes me loath to ever speak in absolutes and, thus, I can't bring myself to definitively say it would *never* happen under *any* circumstances, I don't know of any working researchers who also act as statisticians. There will almost always be someone on your team or an external partner you can use to do the first pass at your data, making sure it's all set before they run the tests you need and send the reports to you. That said, it is essential that you understand what is happening in their "black box" so that you can make sure the data are accurately represented. It's not enough to simply accept what they send you; even the best data jockey can make mistakes, and as the person ultimately responsible for what is presented, you need to make sure you're checking and double-checking before moving into your analysis. To do that, there are a few concepts and practices you need to be familiar with.

Descriptive Statistics

One of the greatest lamentations I have from my considerable fear of math and statistics is that for years I wildly underestimated how much I use basic descriptive statistics in my everyday life. Descriptive statistics are used to summarize a lot of data so we can make sense of what we are learning quickly and easily. We do this stuff intuitively. Think about your grades. Your GPA is an average of your grades, right? That's telling you the mean—the average—of all of your grades throughout college. And this stuff still comes in handy outside of academic life. When I'm looking at the bills I pay each month, I figure out which is the most expensive and which is the least—the range. For bills that vary by usage, I look at what I paid over the course of the year and then average those numbers—again, the mean. When planning for the next month's budget (#adulting), I use Excel to list what I am paying out in order from most to least expensive, which then lets me figure out what is in the middle—the median—and, to make sure I didn't double-pay anything, I look to see if any numbers are showing up multiple times— the mode. These techniques aren't scary once you think about how you already use them in practice.

With these examples in mind, here are brief definitions for each concept. For our purposes, imagine we have done a census of people in a graduate-level methods class (that gives us a bigger range than an undergrad class might). When the fifteen students in the course report their ages, we have the following list of values: 21, 22, 22, 22, 25, 26, 26, 30, 30, 30, 30, 32, 36, 48, and 52. We will first examine these in terms of their distribution and then move into the three measures of central tendency: mean, median, and mode.

- **Distribution.** The distribution tells us how often a particular value or range of values is present in our data. This includes the range of values: what is the lowest and the highest number included in your dataset. For our example, the range is 21–52. In addition to the range, you likely will look at **frequency distributions**, or how often each value (or, if you are summarizing into categories, range of values) is included. For example, if we wanted to break this into smaller subsets, we might look at four age categories: 20–25; 26–30; 31–35; 36 and older. If we had those categories, our frequency distribution would look like table 11.1 (as a reminder, the N is the number of people in your sample).

Table 11.1 Frequency Distributions

Age Category	N
20–25	5
26–30	6
31–35	1

- **Mean.** The first measure of central tendency is the **mean**: the average of the values in your dataset, calculated by adding everything up and then dividing by the number of units included. So, to calculate the mean (average) age for students in this class, you'd sum the numbers and then divide by 15. In this case, the sum is 462, so when divided by 15, we get an average age of 30.8.
- **Median.** The second measure of central tendency, the **median** is the value that is the middle of the pack when all of your units are listed in order. In our case, that is 30—when the ages are listed in order, 30 is the eighth number and thus the median. If you have an even number of units in your list and thus there is no true midpoint, you will calculate the median by averaging the two numbers in the middle. The result will be your median. So, for example, if we had a six-digit list—1, 4, 8, 9, 10, and 12—we would select the two midpoint numbers (8 and 9), add them (17), and divide by 2 to get the median: 8.5.
- **Mode.** The final measure of central tendency, the **mode** is the value that occurs most frequently in your dataset. When we look at our list of ages, three values show up multiple times: 22 (three students), 26 (two students), and 30 (four students). This means the mode is 30.

While these are quite basic, these measures are incredibly useful for spot-checking your data and undertaking basic analysis. If you are doing a class project, you likely will be using frequency distributions and the measures of central tendency (particularly the mean) to describe your data and underpin your insights. These also give you a way to make sure what you are seeing makes sense. As we see in our example above, the mean, median, and mode are fairly close: 30.8 (mean), 30 (median), and 30 (mode). Statistical theory tells us this means our data are quite close to being on a normal bell curve (figure 11.1). While a full deep dive into normal distributions is outside the scope of this book, the shorthand takeaway for you is that this is a good thing: The bell curve shows us what we would *expect* our values to look like, and we want the mean, median, and mode to be at the top of that curve.

If you are looking at the mean, median, and mode in your data report and they are looking super off from each other, you might want to recheck your data. While you can (and should) expect some variation, in most cases, the measures of central tendency will be fairly close. One final note: You can do all of this in Excel, which is amazing and incredibly useful. If you need

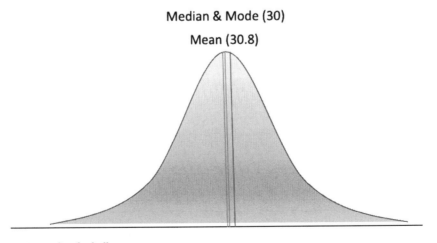

Figure 11.1   Example of a bell curve.

to do this for your analysis, spend some time searching for tips on the interwebs and then play around in there. You'll be blown away by how much you can do with this program.

Weighting

One other area to both anticipate when you collect your data and check when you first get your data report in is the weighting. Because we know samples are not perfect representations of the population, **weighting** helps ensure our data match the population as much as possible. In their summary of different ways weighting can work (a great read for those of you who want to learn more about this), the Pew Research Center gives a clear and succinct explanation of why weighting is used in data analysis:

> Historically, public opinion surveys have relied on the ability to adjust their datasets using a core set of demographics—sex, age, race and ethnicity, educational attainment, and geographic region—to correct any imbalances between the survey sample and the population. These are all variables that are correlated with a broad range of attitudes and behaviors of interest to survey researchers.[2]

Ultimately, weighting means we are either amplifying or reducing the impact or influence of data from some parts of the sample in order to get the balance right in terms of matching the target audience. As the Pew Center notes, this typically is tied to demographic variables, often using the U.S. Census as a reference for what representations look like in the general population. For some client work, however, you may want to use their existing knowledge of their industries and/or competitive landscapes for your weighting and include variables like regional representation (in the United States, often broken into Northeast, Midwest, South, and West).

While weighting is an essential tool, it is a place where data can go awry. You need to ensure your sample is sufficiently robust to do the weighting in a way that maintains your data integrity; you can't amplify 10 respondents to be equally weighted to 100 in a different category. Make sure you are looking at the Ns for each category to ensure they are sufficiently large to do this type of work without undermining your results.

Checking on What Happens in the "Black Box"

While you don't have to be the one doing it, you *do* want to be familiar with the different ways data are examined and manipulated or adjusted when the data experts and statisticians are working their magic in the black box. This basic knowledge will help you in the mental stage of your data prep and survey creation as well as when doing the quality checks needed to ensure data accuracy as you move into analysis. Again, I am giving you very broad definitions here, but I encourage those of you interested in this to dig in and learn more. It's really fascinating stuff.

- **The data file.** Once all of your survey data are collected, a data file is created that contains all of your respondent information. This file usually is in a format that makes it suited for use in data analysis software, such as SPSS, SAS, Stata, or Excel. This file is filled with **raw data** that will then be organized, summarized, and run through appropriate tests to eventually get your report.
- **Metadata**. The metadata in your report give you the categories or headers to help organize your data and make sure it is all properly categorized and coded. This is where you can look

at the header given to a certain variable (EDUCATION, for example—and I'm not yelling at you, these are just usually in all caps), get a description of what that means (Highest level of education achieved), and then what each value represents (1 = high school diploma or lower; 2 = some college; 3 = college degree; 4 = advanced degree).

- **Coding and recoding variables.** When doing this initial work with the data file, your statistician will code and recode variables to make them useful. For example, if you collected birth year, this will be coded into age categories that can then be used more intuitively in analysis.
- **Deleting respondents.** Inevitably, there will be some respondents who clearly rushed through the survey and thus did not provide useful answers; for example, they might have just clicked "neutral" for all responses on matrix questions, or they stopped answering after the first few items in the survey. Because you don't want these data to undermine the validity of the rest of your dataset, these respondents' data should be deleted.
- **Missing data.** While a participant who dropped out early is easy to just delete, there will be times when someone just skipped a question or two. You can approach this in a couple of different ways. First, some prefer to not represent the missing data as missing, and instead just have a lower N for that variable. Other times, you may want to code the missing data as actually missing and thus keep your N constant for your entire survey. The choice you make here will affect your interpretation since it can change your percentages by a considerable amount. Make sure you think through which approach is better and work with your statistician to ensure you get the most accurate representation possible.
- **Do a solid "gut check."** Finally, when you get your data file, do a gut check to see if your data pass the proverbial smell test. Scientific? Not really. Good practice? Absolutely. Make sure that everything you are seeing in your data file makes sense based on what you already know. If your data are wildly inconsistent with what you learned in other phases of research, your client's previous research studies, or just common sense, take a deeper look. It's likely something is off that needs to be corrected.

It's helpful during this process to remember that the statisticians and data experts you are working with are there to be your partners. Ask questions. Learn from their expertise. Get their opinions on how to best approach your survey and make sure you're getting what you need. These are excellent teammates to have. These relationships are invaluable, and make sure you are truly working together to craft the best possible instrument and report.

STATISTICAL MODELS FOR THE NON-STATISTICIAN

Now that we have reviewed the basics of statistical analysis and data weighting, we are ready to dig into five of the most commonly used statistical models in consumer insights research. As I briefly review each of these, I am going to focus on the purpose—*why* you would use it and what information it provides—and what kinds of data are needed to do this analysis. If a specific question type needed, I will show an example (some of which may be familiar from chapter 10!). While this is not an exhaustive list, the five types of statistical models I am reviewing in here—conjoint analysis, maximum-difference scaling (MaxDiff), discrete choice modeling, factor analysis, and cluster analysis—are ones you are likely to encounter in consumer insights research. This section will give you a basic understanding of what they are, what they do, and when you want to use them.

Conjoint Analysis

One of the most commonly used techniques in consumer insights research, conjoint analysis is used to simulate real-world situations in order to really understand priorities and preferences in terms of the trade-offs consumers make. To do this, survey questions are crafted using realistic decision-making scenarios that then ask consumers pick options in relation to each other, thereby indicating how much value they place on each item or attribute. This is particularly useful when conducting research on new product attributes that might be brought to market and figuring out how much pricing flexibility there is around it. Or you might use conjoint analysis if you are trying to figure out a messaging strategy that is intended to increase price flexibility—when presented with a range of options, what are consumers willing to pay more for? And what are nonstarters?

Imagine you are running research for a movie theater that is considering changing its concessions model and want to understand how this could bear out with ticket prices. In this scenario, a conjoint analysis could be run to determine how receptive your audience is to different items, including concessions, beverage options (including adding in alcoholic beverages), types of movies, movie times, special deals, and so on. The options seemingly are endless, so this kind of research can help inform decision-making by better understanding which options are most appealing to your audience—and how much they are willing to pay. While there will always be variables that can't be anticipated, particularly in-the-moment events that will affect your results (a pandemic, for example!), this gives you a lot of flexibility in terms of assessing what is possible.

When creating survey questions for a conjoint analysis, researchers often will present this as "would you rather" scenarios (more than a drinking game, folks!) and then have respondents pick their preferred choice. You generally want to focus on about five attributes to make sure you can get the best possible data and not overwhelm (or underwhelm) the process. These are presented as a unit and the different combinations are switched out. Typically, you would start with an explanation of what you are doing: *As we begin preparations remodel our movie theaters, we are considering a range of options for our offerings. We would like your help in identifying your preferences for these offerings. There are six possible combinations presented. Please consider each one independently.* You then introduce the evaluation question and scale: *Based on this option, how likely are you to attend the movies at least once a month once theaters reopen? [Very likely/somewhat likely/not very likely/not likely at all]*.

Each option would then be presented individually with all attribute categories represented:

TICKET PRICE: $10 (adult)
MOVIE START TIME: 7:00 PM–10:00 PM
FOOD ORDERING: Ordered via app from seat
FOOD DELIVERY: Delivered to seat
BEVERAGE OPTIONS: Alcohol available
• Very likely to attend at least once a month
• Somewhat likely to attend at least once a month
• Not very likely to attend at least once a month
• Not likely at all to attend at least once a month

You can then rotate through each option to test out different combinations (food ordered via app and picked up at the counter, food order at counter and delivered to seat, etc.). Results will help you understand which features or attributes are more (and less) important to your target audience when making complex decisions.

Maximum-Difference Scaling (MaxDiff)

While conjoint can tell us what combination of factors are most appealing to our consumers, MaxDiff (also colloquially called the Best-Worst Test) gives a bit more insight into how important or preferred each of those attributes is to our audience. Instead of presenting different combinations of attributes considered and evaluated as total packages, MaxDiff measures introduce three to five different attributes. Respondents are asked to pick the one that is *most* compelling or preferred (the best) as well as the one that is *least* compelling or preferred (the worst). To continue our movie theater example, you might see something like table 11.2:

Table 11.2   Maximum-Difference Scaling (MaxDiff)

Of the following four features, please select the one that is the most *important to you and the one that is the* least *important to you.*

Most Important		Least Important
▨	**Beverages:** Alcohol can be purchased and served at the theater.	▨
▨	**Food delivery:** Food can be delivered to my seat.	▨
▨	**Food ordering:** I can order food from an app rather than go to the counter.	▨
▨	**Movie times:** All movies start no later than 10:00 PM.	▨

These attributes and others will be rotated and evaluated in different combinations to see what rises to the top and what options are never picked. The patterns identified in your data analysis will reveal the relative importance of each attribute, which is extremely useful when you are making recommendations to meet your client's business objective. (Side note: This question type can be created in Qualtrics or other survey platforms; it was not included in the last chapter because it is only used in MaxDiff.)

This test isn't limited to testing new product attributes or offerings. MaxDiff can be useful for understanding the concepts, terms, and perceptions most associated with your brand (and your competitors) as well as audience levels of satisfaction. For those who are going to be working in branding and advertising, MaxDiff can be an incredibly valuable tool. This approach is often used to test slogans, logos, and branded content, as well as testing and messaging and copy.

Discrete Choice Modeling

So, we now know conjoint analysis will help understand how compelling different combinations of attributes are for consumers and MaxDiff will help uncover preferences based on the best and worst options. But there are times when you want to be able to make decisions based on less idealized circumstances; after all, in the real world, there are trade-offs that have to be made, right? Maybe you want to order food from an app *and* have your drinks delivered to your seat at the movies—but is that worth a higher ticket price? Or would you rather have rock-bottom ticket prices but have to spend a ton of time in line waiting to order and then waiting on your food? That's where discrete choice modeling comes to play. This approach allows researchers to study specific levels of benefits across several attribute areas by exploring the value equations and trade-offs your consumers are willing to make when presented with discrete (or distinct) alternatives.

To do this, you create a master set of options across key attributes (again, usually limited to about three to five attributes). Within each, you'll have different options. For example, ticket prices can be at $7, $10, and $15; food ordering will happen at the counter, via kiosk in the lobby, or via an app from anywhere; food delivery can be at counter pickup, delivered to your seat, or not available, and so on. As you present each combination, respondents have to pick the one that they find most appealing; in other words, you can't have the lowest price *and* the highest levels of service as your preferred option. You have to pick your priorities. By running these various combinations and exploring the data they generate, we can better understand and predict audience preference for their in-theater experience—including how much they are willing to pay.

While conjoint, MaxDiff, and discrete choice modeling are closely related to each other, we are now shifting gears a bit. The last two statistical approaches we are reviewing in this chapter—factor analysis and cluster analysis—focus less on having consumers pick between and among choices. Instead, these two approaches seek to understand how variables and other measures fit together, whether through examining underlying relationships (factor analysis) or grouping around key variables (cluster analysis).

Factor Analysis

As researchers, we often want to understand the underlying relationships between and among variables in order to identify the dimensions that matter to our audience. We also want to make our data as manageable as possible, which can be tricky when we have an abundance of information from our matrix questions. This approach helps address both of these concerns. Factor analysis is used to condense or reduce large sets of observable variables—the answers to certain questions in your survey—to a much smaller set of **factors** (or, in academic terms, latent constructs) that show how these concepts relate and hang together. You can think of these factors as "super-variables" that represent a summary of individual data points collected in your survey. These factors—the super-variables—are used to explain variance from the average result for your variables. In other words, they are used to explain how much one factor (a collection of variables) influences your results.

For example, imagine you are doing research on handbag purchasing for a luxury brand in order to understand the most compelling motivations to purchase. You do a survey with 1,000 women who purchase luxury handbags (operationalized as an average cost of $200 or more per bag) at least once a year. Your survey includes a wide range of matrix questions using Likert-type scales, and you wind up with about 100 individual variables from those batteries. Analyzing and reporting the individual results of those 100 individual variables can be extraordinarily cumbersome. Running a factor analysis on your data could reveal three "super-variable" factors: product quality, brand exclusivity, and aspirational value. These factors can then be used to explain the variance within your data in a much more manageable and meaningful way than you would get by individually reporting on each.

If you are planning to do factor analysis, you will need to make sure you have a sufficient number of matrix questions that address similar concepts in different ways. You likely will do this across different matrices and even different sections of your survey; in our handbag example, exclusivity is relevant as a psychographic measure ("I want to stand out from the crowd"; "My appearance is indicative of who I am"), a category measure ("My handbag is the best way to show my individual style"; "You have to pay more to get exactly what you want"; "I am willing to pay more for something no one else has"), and a brand measure ("Fount handbags speak to my individual style"; "I love the design of Fount handbags"; "Fount handbags are like nothing else on the market"). While these specific questions could be spread across your survey, the factor analysis would pull them together into the same category to show how they work as a unit—the "brand exclusivity" super-variable.

Cluster Analysis

While factor analysis identifies the underlying dimensions that connect your data into super-variables, **cluster analysis** is intended to see how the various data points pull together into natural groupings (the "clusters" for which this is named) to form distinct entities that are relatively homogeneous or alike. In other words, instead of trying to uncover the connections between and among variables to understand consumer behavior or brand perceptions, cluster analysis is generally used to form groupings that can be used to segment or differentiate the audience into overarching "types." As you might expect, this form of analysis often is the backbone in audience segmentation studies that brands use to identify their primary and secondary audiences, helping them understand what natural groups exist in their audience and how those groups perceive and engage with their category and brand. It can also be used to look at brand or product positioning, however, to help identify gaps in the market and thus white space opportunities.

To create your clusters, you will start with selecting initial variables on which your clusters will be developed. These variables should be picked based on your existing knowledge of the audience as well as your RQs, but you also may want to take a quick look at frequency distributions to see if anything jumps out as particularly relevant or differentiating. If you know you need to either develop audience segmentations or look at positioning of brands or products, you must talk with your statistician at the start of your quantitative work so you have the right questions on your survey and they can plan for the statistical clustering procedures they plan to employ. Unlike the other approaches included in this section, there is no one test to use for cluster analysis—there are a range of different approaches that can be used, depending on the data and what you need to do with it. Once data are in, you'll also work with them to test out different iterations of clusters based on different combinations of questions in order to determine the best possible clusters to address your research needs.

Typically, we'd only want a maximum of five clusters total in our final data analysis. Again, these clusters are based on key variables—points of differentiation that help explain the differences among groups in a way that is relevant to your research question. In other words, if you are developing clusters based on the handbag scenario detailed above, you would not want to cluster on "everyday low prices" as a variable since that is not an area of focus. Once you have your clusters that are statistically sound and appropriately differentiated, you can then interpret relevant data to develop characterizations of each segment to inform your analysis and eventually tell your story. If you are doing this for an audience segmentation study, this is the foundation of consumer archetypes that become representative of different consumer groups in your audience: "The Diva" is driven by fashion and style; "The Smart Shopper" looks for deals and steals and will never pay full price for anything; "The Maven" wants only the highest quality material and is willing to pay more, and so on. Using these archetypes, you can then recommend primary and secondary audiences for your client to target and help them truly understand the cluster in terms of motivations, perceptions, behaviors, psychographics, and demographics. Even better: The variables used in your cluster analysis often can be used to create a "typing tool" to identify members of your target cluster, helping you find the right people for your future research projects.

Now that you have your statistical tests clear and your survey data have been collected with these tests in mind, you need to think about how you communicate what you need to your statistician—how do you make sure you get the right data used for your tests, that all data are cleaned and weighted appropriately, and that your report is derived based on the criteria you need for your analysis. Phew. While this may seem a bit overwhelming, with the prep work you did to make sure your survey instrument was sound and connected to your future analysis—by starting with the end in mind—you can quickly and easily put together instructions that will help ensure you are ready to launch analysis as soon as the data are processed and ready.

DATA REPORTS AND BANNERS

To make sure you get the data you need in your report, you will put together a processing request sheet for your statistician to use. Remember that this person likely is working on running data for a ton of different projects, so they are not going to necessarily have the time or capacity to be guiding your thinking on this or guessing what might work best. The processing request sheet will clearly communicate what you need in terms of organizing your data in **banners**, or specific versions of reports that are focused on one variable or measure. These can be created in Word, although Excel can be more useful since you can more easily create tables that are connected so changes are made consistently across the document. All examples in this section come from the same study. We will be reviewing three tabs: banners, weights, and custom tables.

As the example in figure 11.2 demonstrates, you might have a banner for all respondents, then banners for gender (male and female), age brackets, age/gender combinations, and so on. Each of these banners will give your research team a different way to break down and think through the data, based on different ways of looking at your audience. Note that the "Definition" column—Column C—gives specific instructions for which questions should be used to create each banner.

The second tab of our processing request file (figure 11.3) gives instructions for weighting data. As you can see, this sample is being weighted in terms of age (equal weight to the three age categories), gender (weighting male respondents more heavily than female respondents), race (mapping to U.S. Census information on race and ethnicity representation in the United States), and region (with the South weighted most heavily and Northeast weighted the least). As you can see in the orange bar at the bottom of the sheet (line 22), weighting is based on the 2,000 completed responses.

Our final tab (figure 11.4) identifies specific tables that need to be run for our analysis. As you can see, Column A—Question Number—gives specific instructions on which question should be used, and the second column (B) defines how data should be organized. The use of "top box" or "top two boxes" is a common approach to quantitative data analysis. Remember that our goal is to translate our data into insight and insight into recommendations. Often, summing the top or bottom two boxes and presenting those data as a unit helps tell that story more easily. Think about it in terms of actual numbers. There are times when you want to tease out

Category Name	Banner Name	Definition
	All	
GENDER	Female	QGENDER=C2
	Male	QGENDER=C1
AGE 1	18-29	QAUD1=C1
	30-44	QAUD1=C2
	45-54	QAUD1=C3
QUADS	Males <35	QAUD2=C3
	Males 35+	QAUD2=C4
	Females <35	QAUD2=C1
	Females 35+	QAUD2=C2
ETHNICITY	Caucasian	QCODERACE=C1
	Af-Am	QCODERACE=C2
	Hispanic	QCODERACE=C3
	Asian / Other	QCODERACE=C4
DISCOVERY VIEWERSHIP	Core	QVIEWERCODE=C1
	Casual	QVIEWERCODE=C2
	Potential	QVIEWERCODE=C3
	Lapsed	QVIEWERCODE2=C1
CORE VIEWER TYPE	Lifestyle Core	QVIEWERCODE3=C1
	Auto Core	QVIEWERCODE3=C2
ITV	TB	QWATCH_c = C1
	T2B	QWATCH_c = C1 OR C2
	B2B	QWATCH_c = C4 OR C5
CH MORE/LESS	More	QMORELESS=C1
	Same	QMORELESS=C2
	Less	QMORELESS=C3
POLITICS	Conservative	QPOLITIC= C5-C7
	Moderate	QPOLITIC= C4
	Liberal	QPOLITIC= C1-C3

Category Name	Banner Name	Definition
	All	
HHI	<$70k HH Income	QINCOME=ANY(C1-C3)
	$70k+ HH Income	QINCOME=ANY(C4-C6)
PARENT	Parent	QPARENT=C1
	Non-Parent	QPARENT=C2
EDUCATION	College Degree	QEDUCATION = C4, C5
	High School Degree	QEDUCATION = C1, C2, C3
EMPLOYMENT	Full time	QEMPLOY=C1
	Part time	QEMPLOY=C2
	Not Working	QEMPLOY=C3
GENRE VIEWERSHIP	Comedy	QGENREVIEW_a = ANY (C1, C2)
	Drama	QGENREVIEW_b = ANY (C1, C2)
	News	QGENREVIEW_c = ANY (C1, C2)
	Unscripted Reality	QGENREVIEW_d = ANY (C1, C2)
	Sports	QGENREVIEW_e = ANY (C1, C2)
	Talent/Competition	QGENREVIEW_f = ANY (C1, C2)
NETWORK VIEWERSHIP	A&E	QNETWORKS_a=C1-3
	Animal Planet	QNETWORKS_b=C1-3
	History Channel	QNETWORKS_d=C1-3
	National Geographic	QNETWORKS_e=C1-3
	Netflix	QNETWORKS_f=C1-3
	Paramount Network	QNETWORKS_g=C1-3
	Science Channel	QNETWORKS_h=C1-3
	Travel Channel	QNETWORKS_i=C1-3
	TruTV	QNETWORKS_j=C1-3
REGION	Northeast	QREGION = C1
	Midwest	QREGION = C2
	South	QREGION = C3
	West	QREGION = C4

Figure 11.2   Example of a banner-processing request, used to request specific data reports ("banners") from the data processing team.

Audience	Definition	Weight	Comments
QAGE			
18-29	QAUD1=C1	33.00%	
30-44	QAUD1=C2	34.00%	
45-54	QAUD1=C3	33.00%	
QGENDER			
Male	QGENDER=C1	67.00%	
Female	QGENDER=C2	33.00%	
QRACE			
White/Caucasian/Oth	QCODERACE = C1 OR C4	70.00%	
Af-Am	QCODERACE = C2	14.00%	
Hispanic	QCODERACE = C3	16.00%	
QREGION			
Northeast	QREGION = C1	17.00%	
Midwest	QREGION = C2	21.00%	
South	QREGION = C3	38.00%	
West	QREGION = C4	24.00%	
Please weight to n=2000 completes			

Figure 11.3   Example of how data categories would be weighted after data collection to better represent the characteristics of the target population.

Question Number	Base Definition
QGENRE	Top Box Summary (C1)
	Top 2 Box Summary (C1-C2)
QNETWORKS	Daily (C1)
	T2B (C1-C2)
	Viewer (C1-C3)
QBENEFITS	Top Box Summary (C1)
	Top 2 Box Summary (C1-C2)
	Bottom 2 Box Summary (C3-
QAFFINITY	Top Box Summary (C1)
	Top 2 Box Summary (C1-C2)
	Bottom 2 Box Summary (C3-
QMOMENTUM	Top Box Summary (C1)
	Top 2 Box Summary (C1-C2)
	Bottom 2 Box Summary (C3-
QWATCH	Top Box Summary (C1)
	Top 2 Box Summary (C1-C2)
	Bottom 2 Box Summary (C4-
QRECOMMENDATION	Recommend (C9-C11)
	Not recommend (C1-C3)
QNETBENEFITS	Top Box Summary (C1)
	Top 2 Box Summary (C1-C2)
	Bottom 2 Box Summary (C3-

Question Number	Base Definition
QSHOWAFFINITY	Top Box Summary (C1)
	Top 2 Box Summary (C1-C2)
	Bottom 2 Box Summary (C3-C4)
QNEWFOCUS	More (C1)
	No Effect (C2)
	Less (C3)
QTOPICINTEREST	Top Box Summary (C1)
	Top 2 Box Summary (C1-C2)
	Bottom 2 Box Summary (C4-C5)
QTOPICRANK	Top Rank (C1)
	Top 3 Rank (C1-3)
	Top 5 Rank (C1-C5)
QTOPICMOMENTUM	More (C1)
	Enough (C2)
	Too Many (C3)
QNEWTOPICMOMENTUM	More (C1)
	Enough (C2)
	Too Many (C3)
QNEWTOPICFIT	Top Box Summary (C1)
	Top 2 Box Summary (C1-C2)
	Bottom 2 Box Summary (C3-C4)

Figure 11.4 Example of the types of custom tables that can be requested to aid in data analysis.

the difference between the 32 percent who strongly agreed with a statement and the 24 percent who somewhat agreed, but other times, saying "56 percent agreed" with your statement is more meaningful—this shows that the majority agreed, rather than the weaker plurality around "strongly" as an individual measure.

Each of the custom tables requested in this section are asked for due to the anticipated results based on what is already known about the audience or the RQs. It is useful to have this list as complete as possible when you submit your processing request to your statistician, but you usually can go back to ask for more customized tables as needed if something else emerges during your debrief.

After your survey is completed in the field, the data report is sent to your statistician and they do the cleaning and weighting we discussed above, then go in and create your requested banners. Once those are sent to you, it's time to get busy. After an initial check to make sure everything looks copacetic, you're ready to dig in and start your analysis. One cautionary note: Because they are just giant spreadsheets or Word docs filled with data in seemingly endless columns, banners can be quite overwhelming at first. When you get them, take a breath and spend a little time just getting a sense of what's there. I like to print out the ones I think are particularly important and start highlighting and circling. Working with paper works better for my brain, although others prefer to be able to search and sort on digital files. Whichever way works better for you, go with it. But don't be afraid of the numbers. Remember: Your job is to look for the patterns—the meaning—in the data. You already know your audience—this is just adding another layer to your understanding and expertise.

DEBRIEFING AND DATA ANALYSIS

If you've already done a qualitative debrief, this process should be fairly familiar to you. While your data will look quite different, the experience of debriefing should not be wildly different. Maybe you won't have a room full of collages and other materials created in qualitative creative exercises (if you are even meeting in person!), but you'll still have a Leader Linda,

Relief Ryan, Idea Ingrid, Collaborative Carl, and Negative Nancy around to make sure you're making progress on **transforming data into insight and insight into meaningful recommendations**. The main difference is that quantitative data analysis can be grounded in either inductive (as was the case in qual) or **deductive reasoning**, meaning you start with a **hypothesis**—a prediction about what you will find in your data—and then look for your data to support that supposition. Deductive reasoning is particularly applicable when you have already completed your qualitative phase of research and thus have a pretty good sense of what is going on; you're starting from an informed perspective, so you know what to look for. That doesn't mean you won't find surprises in your data—you often do—but you don't go in cold. You let your expectations help guide your analysis much more directly than you do in qual.

Preparing for Your Debrief

Before you go into your debrief, you want to make sure you have spent some quality time poring over your banners and custom tables. You want to know what data are there and start to think about what they mean, both in the context of existing qualitative research (if you did that phase of research) and on their own. You need to block off time to do this in advance of your team's debrief; you never want to go in cold, no matter how casual or preliminary the meeting seems. As I mentioned earlier, I am a paper person—I like to have printouts that I can mark up with notes and questions and ideas, and then I have tons of little Post-It notes as tabs and markers and reminders throughout the stack of banners. Others have different approaches, and you will figure out what works for you as you go through your own process. But the key reminder here stands true, no matter how you approach this: You *must* spend time getting to know the data and thinking about what is in there before you go into your team's debrief.

Debriefing

Assuming everyone on your team comes in prepared, your debrief should start fairly easily and run fairly smoothly. You may find yourself needing two debriefs—the first to take an initial pass at the data and then, after your data have been refined, conducting your deeper analysis in part two. As was the case in qual, push and pull on the data. See how different data connect in interesting ways. And again—look for the overarching story that will tie your data together and ensure it all makes sense. You never, ever want to just present data to your client and let them figure out the story. That's your job. If you are doing your job well, you are transcending basic data reporting and instead serving as an interpreter, a translator, and a storyteller. You need to do that analysis and the legwork to derive meaning from your data and ensure that what you find answers the RQs and addresses the business objective guiding your research.

To help ensure this result, you should start your debrief by reminding all participants about what the RQ and client objectives are. If you are building off another phase of research, consider reminding the team about what that report found and how it informed this study. As you go through initial ideas that emerge, keep a list that everyone can see, using either a whiteboard or a flip chart in person or digital versions in chat boxes or Google Docs if online. Focus on generating some initial big ideas that can evolve into insights, and then see what data are there to support those ideas—*and* what data contradict them. And once you get to the point where you think you're closing in on some meaningful insights, think about how they hang together—do these connect? Do they flow? If not, how come? Is there another way to think about or define them that better supports an overarching story?

Remember that your job is to find and tell that story in a meaningful way because that is the best approach for your client to be able to use what you find to make good decisions grounded in consumer insights. This means you don't need to present every single data point; if your client wants those data for some reason, you can share them as an appendix. But your focus is to look for the patterns in the data that add up to something more. Something bigger. You want to integrate and synthesize your data so that you have multiple data points supporting the same insight. And if something doesn't work? Just don't use it. That does *not* mean that you ignore contrary data; if you're doing your analysis well, you'll examine those data and use them to iterate or shape your story to make it more accurate and yet still compelling.

These debriefs take time, so you want to be patient. Don't try to rush this process. Good data analysis requires both active thinking and solid periods when ideas just marinate in the back of your mind. When you're struggling to figure out a connection, think about going for a walk. I logged an awful lot of miles on the mean streets of New York, walking some (or, in particularly desperate times, all) of the commute between my office in Tribeca and my apartment on the Upper West Side as I worked through some issue with the data where things weren't *quite* making sense, although I knew we were on a good path. Give yourself permission to breathe and set your data to the side while you work on other things. If you do this, you are much more likely to come up with compelling insights, supported by your data, that help your client meet their business goals.

REPORTING QUANTITATIVE RESEARCH

In chapter 8, we talked about the topline research report—the interim deliverable you share with your client to update them on what progress you are making, what you've learned, and where you are going next. If your project requires quantitative research happen as the first phase, you'll use that same topline approach to report out what you've learned and what you anticipate for your second phase of research, so go check that section again for advice. Or, if you are wrapping up your research project, you'll move into the final report—and the next two chapters will be setting you up for success! But before we move on, I do want to spend some time talking about best practices in reporting quantitative data.

Remember that your charge—your mission—as a researcher is to ensure that your work can be understood by your client's colleagues far outside of the actual research team. You need to make sure that you are including enough information to reassure them of your credibility, without overwhelming them with data. This is a delicate balance. But one of the places we often fall short is by not making clear where our data come from and what is actually being said. With that in mind, here are a few rules of thumb:

- **Always include mandatory information.** Whenever you present any quantitative data, you always need to include the question wording, response options, and the total number of responses. You can put these in a text box at the bottom of the slide if you are doing a PowerPoint deck or in a caption for the figure in a written report. Just make sure it's clear where you are getting your information so readers can evaluate the credibility.
- **Make sure numbers are clear.** Some default chart-making programs do not automatically include the numbers (percentages or the true N, depending on what you are showing) on the charts. This information is necessary to ensure you are clearly communicating your data. If they aren't there by default, add them.

- **Check your math.** This may feel like a no-brainer, but you need to make sure things add up—and if they don't, you need to explain why. (Refer back to our earlier discussion on how you code/account for missing data for a common explanation.)
- **Check your numbers.** It is terrifyingly easy to transpose numbers when you are writing a report; you've got a ton of data in front of you, and you just read something wrong. Double and triple check *everything*. Have teammates help as well to get fresh eyes. You never want to find mistakes once your deck is in front of the client. Make sure you are completely buttoned up.
- **Use the right kinds of charts to best tell your story.** We are going to spend more time on charts in chapter 13 (unlucky for some), but know that not every chart is appropriate for every kind of data. Make sure you are really thinking about what your chart is communicating. Spend time playing around with different versions so you are telling the clearest, most intuitive story possible with your data.
- **Know your audience.** This is a drumbeat that will continue throughout the next section, but I cannot stress it enough—know your audience. Present your data in a way that will make sense to them. Don't get overly technical on your slides—make sure you are presenting data in a way that will make sense to nonexpert readers (some of whom may share the stats-induced itchiness common among creative types).

Finally, you likely will be thinking about recommendations while you are doing this analysis; after all, you want to see how these different pieces fit. As we noted in the qualitative data analysis chapter, remember that your recommendations must meet three criteria: (1) they must be *relevant*; (2) they must be *actionable*; and (3) they must clearly be *grounded in your data and insights*.

BEST PRACTICES AND KEY TAKEAWAYS

Hopefully, you have all stuck with me and are now feeling much more confident about conducting quantitative research, including the creation of a survey all the way through to analysis. If you are still feeling overwhelmed, remember that you do not have to be a sole expert here; research is a team exercise, and you will have more seasoned pros around to help you navigate this process. But from my perspective, the most important takeaway I want you to have from this chapter is that this work *is* creative. It's not just processing numbers and spitting out data. Our clients aren't looking for pages of numbers. They need someone to help them understand what the data say and translate that to a meaningful story. That is what we bring to the table. This process truly is *fun*. When you get into your banners and they start to make sense—you start to see the patterns emerge and realize what the story might just be—it's a truly gratifying experience.

As you are working with your data, you need to remember to give yourself the time and space to do this well. Quantitative data analysis can't happen on a whim. You need to immerse yourself in your data. This is an active process, both mentally and physically. Spend time marking up your banners, whether on paper copies or digital. Draw pictures for yourself to test out different ways they might connect. Keep a notebook that you have with you for when inspiration strikes—then, when you feel like you keep running into the same brick wall, you can go back and look at what ideas were sparked. Don't be afraid to be wrong. Experiment. Play. See what happens.

And with that note, we are wrapping up the methods part of this textbook. Hopefully, by now you are comfortable with both qualitative and quantitative research. You know that you always need to keep the RQs and business objective front of mind during your research project, and you are all too aware that our job as researchers is to turn data into insight and insight into meaningful recommendations. You have excellent data, and your story is compelling and relevant. But the last part of this process—the final act, if you will—is ensuring that all of this brilliance is clearly, concisely, and compellingly communicated to your client. And with that, we move into section IV: reporting findings.

NOTES

1. https://www.franklincovey.com/the-7-habits/habit-2/
2. https://www.pewresearch.org/methods/2018/01/26/how-different-weighting-methods-work/

KEY TERMS

Banners: Specific versions of data reports that are focused on one variable or measure

Deductive reasoning: Analysis wherein you start with a prediction about what you will find in your data and then look for your data to support that supposition

Factors: Constructs that represent a summary of individual data points collected in a survey

Metadata: Categories or headers in your reports to help organize your data and make sure it is all properly categorized and coded

Raw data: Data that have not yet been cleaned, organized, or summarized for reporting

12

Writing Your Report

Congratulations—you've made it through a rather intense introduction to consumer insights research! You've now learned about working with your client, secondary research, being ethical—and how to do both qualitative *and* quantitative methods. If you've been doing data collection, you're now sitting on a treasure trove of information, and hopefully your efforts at analysis have been fruitful and you have turned data to insight and insight into recommendations. You are, officially, a researcher. Feels good, right?

But, alas! The job is not *quite* done. Before we can move on, you need to spend some time on the last phase of your project: presenting your research. Most of the time, you will be putting together a written **deliverable**, the material you leave behind as the final product for your research project. Usually, this is in the form of either a Word document or, more often, a PowerPoint deck—and at times, you'll do both. You'll then take this work and present it to your client, giving you a chance to shine as you talk through what you've done, what you've learned, and what you recommend. This also gives them an opportunity to ask questions and probe more into your insights and recommendations, getting the context and clarification they need to move forward with your results.

In this final section of the book, we will dig into each of these areas. This chapter is focused on how to organize and write your deliverables, including executive summaries, memos, full-scale reports, and PowerPoint decks. Chapter 13 is centered on making everything look fabulous, including best practices in visual design and recommendations for how to tell your story with visuals as well as words. Chapter 14 is chock full of recommendations for your in-person (or online) presentation, including a wide range of best practices gleaned from my years presenting to clients, presenting to colleagues and students as an academic, and watching hundreds of students do their first-ever client presentations in my classes. While I love presenting, I was still terrified the first few (hundred) times I had to present in front of clients. Heck, I still get nervous now before the first day of classes, and I've been doing this for years! But with the right preparation and confidence boosters, you'll be able to come across as confident and competent—even if you feel like a complete mess.

As we move into this last section, remember that good researchers approach projects holistically. While this book is, by necessity, broken into discrete sections focused on preparation, data collection and analysis, and presentation, you should be thinking about your final report from the beginning. When you are in the field collecting qualitative data, think about the images that serve as data that can bring your ideas to life in the final deck. Make notes of really powerful or evocative quotes—including who said them, the context, and when (it's amazing what you'll forget over the course of a research project!). When you have your quant banners in hand, make sure you are marking the data points that you think are most effective at telling your story. It can be tempting to just put these things to the side and then figure it out later. Don't. Seriously—don't. To go back to Habit 2 discussed in the last chapter, beginning with the end in mind is a great strategy to take here. You'll save yourself a ton of time and effort if you have a running list to reference when putting your final materials together.

As we go through this chapter, some (and maybe most?) of what I share might sound a bit familiar. And it's true—much of this has been covered earlier in various places throughout the book. But this final push—the written deliverable and your presentation—is your last and best opportunity to blow your client away with the work you did. No matter how fantastic your data, no matter how brilliant your insights, if your final deliverables are weak, you likely won't be asked back for future projects. In fact, all that time, energy, and effort you put into your project might just be wasted. If what you leave behind isn't compelling, clear, and relevant, your recommendations likely won't be taken seriously, particularly with more senior executives and those outside of your direct client relationship. It's imperative that you knock it out of the proverbial park in this final phase of your client project. This section will help you do that.

GOAL AND PURPOSE

The final written deliverable—the focus of this chapter—is what you leave behind with your client and their team to share what you've learned and what you recommend. Remember that most of the people who need to know what this research has uncovered—the product developers, show runners, ad copywriters, brand managers, corporate executives, and so on—won't be in the room when you're doing research, and they might not even be in the room when you present. Your final written deliverables, from long-form writing to a more visually oriented deck, need to stand alone to communicate what you've learned. And, no pressure, but they need to do that in a way that is persuasive, useful, and has a high "stickiness" factor—it needs to stay with them long after their initial read in a way that lets your research actually inform decision-making. For that to happen, your final report needs to:

- **Be highly credible.** Your report needs to reinforce that the work you have done is rigorous and credible. It needs to communicate your expertise and that your insights and recommendations truly are driven by consumer data, not your own agendas or preexisting beliefs.
- **Be carefully written and proofread.** Credibility absolutely is undermined if your final deliverables are riddled with typos and errors. Sure, mistakes happen—I am sure you have found some in this book, even though it has been proofread roughly a million times by multiple people. But typos and data errors will undermine your credibility and make people question your professionalism. Do everything you can to eliminate them.
- **Be polished.** Formatting matters. Appearance matters. Everything needs to look really, really good. Most research teams will have a standard template they use that includes all necessary logos and design elements, so you'll be able to build off of that. If you don't have one handy, spend time looking for a template that will work. Make sure you are using high-quality

images and that you are organizing your information in a way that is easy to process and understand. (And again, proofread.)

- **Tell a compelling story.** Even if you've hit the target on these first three bullets, you really are just meeting the industry table stakes. To make sure you have the stickiness factor you need to succeed, you need to tell a compelling story. Remember, you are acting as a translator, interpreter, and storyteller. You have to knit the pieces of your work together to ensure all of the elements hang together. Without your story, it gets much harder to have your big ideas stick.

- **Offer actionable, relevant recommendations.** This last one is a doozy, and we will be digging more into what this means later in the chapter. While all of what we do as researchers matters, this part—the quality of your recommendations—is what separates the top tier from the also-rans. This is your chance to show how what you learned can be applied in practice, and having thoughtful, feasible recommendations can make all the difference in maximizing the lasting impact of your research project. And if you've done your job well, these recommendations should feel like they have a high "duh" factor—based on everything you've learned, these definitely are the way to go.

- **Always keep your audience in mind.** As you are writing, think about who will be reading this—and what they will be using it for. Your job is to make sure this report works *for them*; if you write it in a way that won't make sense or meet their needs, you haven't done your job well. So think about what your audience will want in terms of data—how much is too much? Too little? You want to be Goldilocks—juuuuust right. The same applies for fancy design elements and clever wordplay. Some clients love it and appreciate a deliverable that keeps it light and easily understood, while others might feel the flash undermines the substance. Know your client, know your audience, and craft a deliverable that works for them.

With these criteria in mind, let's move into how you make that happen. We will first talk about how you organize your thoughts as you develop the story, and then we will review how you tell the story in your written deliverables. Finally, we will review different forms of written deliverables that you are likely to encounter in the future.

DEVELOP YOUR "ELEVATOR PITCH"

As you get started with your writing, it is important that you have your story crystallized into an **elevator pitch** that sums up your story in a compelling and concise way. Elevator pitches force you to get your big ideas condensed into a few powerful sentences. The idea is that you imagine you are waiting for an elevator with someone who has huge decision-making power. In the time of your elevator ride together, you need to be able to sell them on your big idea. You won't have forever, so you need to be fast and persuasive. For example, if you were doing research for an NFL team on their clothing options for women fans, your story might look something like this:

> *Women already are fans of the team, and they are tired of being treated as if they are all Janies-come-lately who are just there for the men in their lives. They want clothes that let them be part of the fan community—true members, not "girlie" members who only wear blinged-out pink and low-cut crop tops. They want to represent their fandom—their football family—in a way that feels authentic and true and recognizes that these women are truly welcomed and recognized by your*

team. Team merch that recognizes the balance between being women and being true fans will help them achieve this goal.

This elevator pitch hits all the key parts: How women fans have felt in the past, how the available merch has contributed to that (pink and bedazzled), and what they want—to feel welcomed and recognized as true fans. This is a quick summary that can have impact, and this crystallization of the story will help your clients remember it as well, maximizing both the usefulness and the stickiness of your deliverable.

The beauty of this exercise is it requires you to think through the core of what your story needs to communicate—you have to summarize and synthesize, and that forces you to craft and polish your story until it shines. But you really have to think of this as something that can be communicated during an elevator ride—30 seconds, max (no New York skyscrapers for this exercise!). Summarizing your story in a punchy, compelling sentence or two will help focus your efforts and ensure that each ensuing insight is written in a way that connects to that story.

ORGANIZING YOUR THOUGHTS

Once you have your story crystallized into an elevator pitch, you're ready to move into your outline. As is the case any time you are trying to effectively communicate a story, a good research presentation requires that you pay close attention to how you organize and structure your work. The biggest mistake novice researchers can make is to jump right into the writing without taking the proper time to prepare. In this section, we will review some best practices for preparing your outline, integrating insights into themes, making sure you've planned sufficient signposts and transitions to guide your reader or audience, and the importance of coming back to your story.

Preparing Your Outline

When it comes to preparing to produce your deliverables (and really, at most other times as well), the greatest simple tool in a researcher's toolbox is the outline. This lovely, elegant little list often has been relegated to the dustbin. Instead of starting with a thoughtful, well-crafted outline, we move right into writing the report or structuring the deck. But our writing reflects our thinking. If you just jump right in and don't take the time to start with an outline, you'll wind up with something that likely is not as clear nor compelling as it could and should be. Starting with an outline lets you test your arguments and establish how the elements connect—the knitting together we talked about earlier. You'll want to do several passes on your outline, following a fairly simple process. First, list out the major bullets—the sections you need to include in your report. You'll start with key words or concepts that communicate what each section should include, and then with future passes you'll add in more detail, including quotes and specific data points you'll want to include.

At the top of your outline, start with what you need to include in the first section—often a summary of your RQs and client objectives, the methods employed (including both data collection and analysis as relevant, the number of participants/respondents in your samples, etc. —check out figure 12.1 for what this might look like in your final deck), the timing of your research, and then, if needed or useful, a brief reminder about the type of project you're working on (television concept testing, ad campaign, etc.). This will represent the first section of

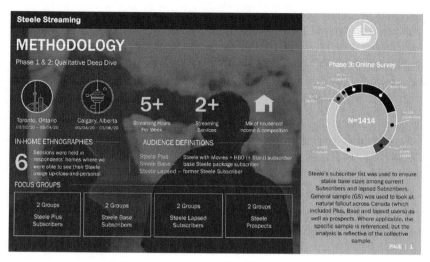

Figure 12.1 Example of a methods slide in a PowerPoint deck.

your report, which serves to give the lay of the land and ground your findings and recommendations in terms of the work you actually did. If you have this information all pulled together in here, you can then easily shape everything into a client-ready methods summary.

Once this is done, you'll move into the body—your findings section—and then your recommendations.

Integrate and Synthesize Insights into Themes

The insights you've generated through your analysis have power and meaning. While they sometimes can stand alone, you'll often find that different insights translate into broader **themes**. Themes help you take your insights and craft them into something that explains and connects to your story. Focusing on themes—a literary device since we are now focused on writing our findings in a compelling and persuasive manner—is a good reminder you that you can't just data dump. Always remember that you need to present your work in a way that will make sense to those who will see and use your research, even if they were not directly involved in your research project. Through this process, you'll often be surprised at the ways your insights connect together and can be presented as integrated ideas—this becomes another level of analysis and refinement. In these cases, those synthesized concepts become the themes that are built out in your presentation.

Themes also let you streamline your presentation and encourage an intuitive flow, rather than presenting insights one by one as discrete items. For example, in the women's football merch example given during the elevator pitch, you might have separate insights from the women about the past clothing options ("*Wearing Team Colors Matters*," meaning the clothes available made us feel like they had no idea who we are, nor did they care to have us represent the team in the appropriate colors) and the team's outreach to women ("*They Think We're All Newbies*," meaning they act like we are all brand new to football and don't know what a quarterback is). These two insights can be combined into a theme: *Football Doesn't Value Us.* Each insight can then be explored in the context of that overall theme, strengthening the clarity of your findings and the stickiness of your report.

Plan Your Signposting

When we think about how to effectively communicate with audiences, we need to remember the importance of signposting. **Signposts** are verbal signals that help orient your reader and keep them on track with your argument; words like "however" when you are countering a previous statement or "consequently" indicating the directional relationship between the two statements you are connecting. As the fabulous Academic Skills Centre at the University of Birmingham in the United Kingdom advises, "Your essay is a journey through your argument or discussion. Your paragraphs are stepping stones in that journey. Signposts help to guide the reader through. They indicate what will happen, remind them of where they are at key points along the way, and indicate the direction your essay is going to head in next."[1]

While this advice is written specifically for university-level essays (and thus chock full of potentially helpful information for those of you taking writing-intensive classes, so check out the source!) I love a good metaphor, and the stepping stones imagery works really well here. You are helping navigate what can be overwhelming—a fast-rushing river that can be intimidating or inspire a sense of foreboding. Remember that your client's colleagues often are as research averse as you were before starting this course; you want to eliminate any barriers to them understanding and buying in to what you are doing. By making your work as easy to read and understand as possible, you are vastly increasing the odds that they will stick with you through your recommendations and your research will have a lasting impact.

Bake in Transitions

The final step in writing the body of your outline is to make sure you have baked in your transitions. Your essay needs to flow and feel like a natural progression is occurring; transitions will help you do that. This often comes along with the signposting process. If you are ensuring you have signposted the direction your work is going, the transitions typically emerge fairly naturally. It is worth taking some time to make sure they do, however. Nothing in your final deliverable, whether a written document or a visually oriented PowerPoint, should feel jarring. Everything needs to feel organic and integrated. The story—the backbone of what you are doing—provides a fantastic structure for this, but you need to make sure your transitions between and among ideas are clear when you are presenting your work.

An extra benefit from this: If you are finding it difficult to write your transitions between your themes, you might just have a problem with your story—and if your story isn't working, you need to figure out why. Go back a few steps in your analysis. Revisit your data. Talk it through with your team. Figure out *why* this isn't working and brainstorm ideas about how to rectify the gaps or uncertainties. No matter how perfectly the pieces seem to fit before you put them to paper (tangible or digital), it's unfortunately common to uncover issues when you are actually building it out for your deliverable. Hopefully, some time spent with your data—going back to your qualitative materials and your banners, as well as the notes you've taken throughout the process—will let you see the solution fairly quickly.

Flesh Out Your Recommendations

As noted throughout this book, to be meaningful, your recommendations need to meet three criteria: (1) they must be *relevant*; (2) they must be *actionable*; and (3) they must clearly be *grounded in your data and insights.* Putting your recommendations into your outline helps ensure that your themes—your findings—actually build to the recommendations and make sure they are clearly tied together. Remember that no new data should be presented in this section; all needs to be introduced earlier in your report. By fully fleshing these recommendations out in the outline, you can make sure you have properly laid the groundwork for your report—and eventually, you'll be able to pull together something like the slide in figure 12.2.

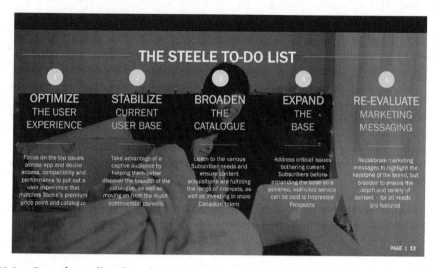

Figure 12.2   From the outline through to the final presentation, remember that recommendations must be relevant and actionable.

Always Come Back to Your Story

Before you declare your outline is set and ready to go, take at least one more pass and make sure that each point connects to your overarching story. Go back to that elevator pitch. Confirm that each theme and idea is related to that story and helps elucidate it—make it clearer and contextualized—for your audience. If you need to tweak or iterate, this is the place to do it. Once you get more into the writing and creation of your report or deck, it becomes much harder to figure out where things aren't working and why. Each of the strategies introduced above—the elevator pitch, the signposting, baking in transitions, and fleshing out your recommendations—will help ensure that you have a sound, solid story that is driven by insights and supported by your data. These will also help ensure your recommendations feel organic based on what the story is telling your client; by the end of your report, this should all feel fully intuitive. A good outline will make sure that happens.

TELLING A STORY

We've talked a ton (endlessly, some of you might feel!) about telling a story through your research deliverables. Now we are at the best part (they're all the best part) of the process: exploring what that actually means and how you do it. While much of what I will share in here might feel redundant for those of you who have taken a number of writing courses, remember that our orientation is different from much of what you'll experience in academic writing. When you are doing *this* writing, you are doing it for clients. Professionals. Professionals who are busy and need to know that they can trust you and what you report. And finally—perhaps most important—professionals who need to know they can trust you because they are planning to invest large sums of money in their business, based on your recommendations, to address their business objective. No pressure, right? But it bears repeating: The stakes in consumer insights research can be really, really high. Your client needs to have a clear understanding of what you learned and how you learned it. And you, as an ethical researcher, need to make absolutely sure that everything you are communicating is both intelligible and accurate. The practices we discuss in this section will help ensure you do that.

Keep the Story Moving

Part of making sure your report effectively communicates your findings and recommendations is ensuring that you keep the story moving. Don't belabor points that you have already made. Your clients are busy and their time is limited. Even those there during your in-person presentation likely will have mobile phones and smart watches beeping at them with urgent emails and messages while you are speaking. Think about your own experience in classes. How often do you get to just give material—even really important material—your full attention? Most likely, during the time you are reading this chapter, you'll have multiple alerts dinging to remind you of deadlines, meetings, or incoming communication that needs to be dealt with urgently. Friends will be calling or texting to set up plans. Your professors are sending reminders about upcoming exams. With all of this going on, it can be quite challenging to stay focused and really pay attention. What helps? Getting through material efficiently. Keep the story moving forward. Keep the narrative flowing. That doesn't mean shortcutting data or foregoing clarity; you still need to make a strong case. But remember that time is limited and valuable. Use it wisely. If you can keep the story progressing in a compelling way, the beeps and blinks will be easier to ignore.

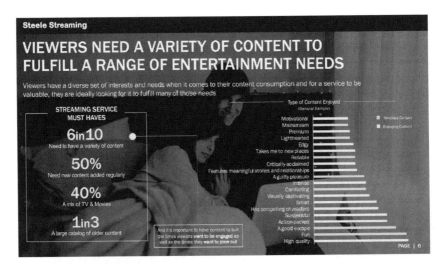

Figure 12.3   As this slide shows, the headline makes clear the theme to advance the story; the remainder of the slide supports that headline.

Figure 12.4 The secondary sources covered in chapter 3 often offer white papers for free downloads on their sites, which provide fabulous examples for what these can (and should) look like.

Share Data Strategically

One area where research reports often stall out is through the oversharing of data. Remember that your job is to translate and interpret the data—you are the one giving the meaning so your client doesn't have to figure it out for themselves. Check out figure 12.4 for a great example of how this works. To make this work, you need to be thoughtful and strategic in the data you choose to share when writing your report. Data should be **illustrative**, illustrating or adding dimension to the points that you are making in your headlines (the themes).

Data provide color and credibility; the context is up to you. It can be tempting to overshare data; after all, that's what you've spent all this time collecting, right? But I cannot stress this enough: For most people, data are boring. A snooze. A one-way ticket to Boresville, a suburb of Checkedoutland. But if used sparingly and effectively, data suddenly become the gold-leaf illustrations in medieval Bibles. They are beautiful and engaging, and they serve to help your story make sense in the context of the research deliverable *and* increases its future stickiness and utility. After all, it's much easier to remember that 72 percent of your audience feel a certain way when you don't have to try to remember twenty other percentages as well, right? You can give your clients an appendix or supplemental report with all of the data they want (usually only the quant banners), but the focus when writing a report is on centering data that support and illustrate your story and themes.

The other part of the strategic sharing of data to remember: You always have to make sure you are crystal clear about where these data come from. There should be no mystery about what you are sharing. Your readers need to know where each data points come from. That means you give relevant context for quotes; if gender or age are germane, share those, or maybe employment status or profession if that is what matters for your specific project. If it's quant data, share the Ns and percentages as well as the question asked and response options. Nothing should be unclear, since a lack of clarity often can be interpreted as hiding something—and even if it's not seen as malicious, it can still create uncertainty around your credibility. So be transparent about where your data come from, but don't let them overwhelm your story.

Focus on Your Flow

Think about the best thing you're read recently—it can be fiction or nonfiction, short-form or long. When you were reading it, did you have a hard time putting it down? Did you want to keep going to the next page to see what happens next? Chances are good that you did—that's what good narrative writing will do. And that should be your goal when writing your client's deliverable. You want them to *want* to keep going—to see what happens next. And you do that by focusing on your flow. Your story needs to build as you move through the report, with each section leading to the next. Your themes connect to your overarching story and your recommendations make complete sense based on everything you've already established. The flow works, and it gives your report the supercharged impact you want.

If you've spent the recommended time and effort on your outline, the flow should already be in place before you start writing. But if you didn't, I cannot stress enough how important it is that you look carefully at your report to make sure the flow is there. Have other people read it, particularly people not on your research team who wouldn't have the insider knowledge you do about what happened and how you got to where you are. The flow may seem clear to you, but to an outsider, things may not quite connect. Good flow makes for a good report. And good hockey hair.

Stay Focused

The last point in this section certainly is not the least. It can be really tempting to throw in some additional information or insight into your report; after all, you have the space to do it, and maybe they'd want to know? I completely get it. My kitchen-sink researcher tendencies didn't stop with instrument development; I'd be tempted during report writing, too. But resist. Remember your story. Keep a laser focus on building that story throughout your deliverable, and don't get distracted by other pieces that are fun or interesting, but ultimately not relevant to said story. Keep going back to your RQs and client objective. If you've done your job, your story offers the answers to those guardrails. Anything that doesn't fit organically into your story likely doesn't need to be included. As you already know, you have limited time to make your case before you lose your audience. You need to use that time as wisely as possible. Staying focused will make sure you do.

REPORT SECTIONS

Most reports would follow a fairly consistent structure in terms of how sections are ordered and organized. While these are not absolute, they provide a good overview of what needs to be included. You will see the connections between this structure and the outline; if all goes to plan, you should be able to transition smoothly from the outline to your report. Here are the instructions I give my students each semester as they prepare for their final presentations. Again, your client may want something different, but I have found this summary provides an excellent starting point:

- **Cover slide or header** with relevant information (project name, dates, etc.)
- **RO/RQs**
- **Methods**
  - Methods of data collection (interviews, focus groups, surveys, etc.) for all phases of your research
  - N for each method
    - Include necessary and relevant information for each sample, including any subcategories that were included in your analysis (women/men; age brackets; etc.)

○ Any other relevant information to help explain the work you did
- **Findings**, organized by **theme**
  ○ These should *not* be presented RQ by RQ at this point—instead, take a more analytical approach
  ○ Start with your "elevator pitch" for what the story tying your research together is
  ○ Each theme generally would get its own slide or section
    - Use quotes and materials from both phases of research to illustrate your points
    - Remember that each theme should be tied to your story and connect to the insights derived from your work
  ○ Depending on your client preferences, you may want to then add additional slides addressing each RQ specifically
- **Recommendations**
  ○ No new data or findings can be presented in this section
  ○ As a reminder, all recommendations must be relevant, actionable, and grounded in your data/insights
  ○ The recommendations must make sense when considered in the context of your findings section. Think of your findings section as laying the groundwork for these recommendations; they should not come out of nowhere. This should feel like a natural outgrowth of what was learned through your research and presented earlier in the report.

So again, while this may not work for every scenario, I have found that this works the vast majority of the time with just some potential tweaks to tailor to your individual scenario.

REPORT FORMATS

As is the case with so many things in consumer insights research, there is no one "right" way to present your findings. Some clients have specific preferences for what they want: long or short, visually oriented or text based; inundated with data versus "data-lite." Some clients will give you very specific parameters in which they want to work—this is particularly common for brands or organizations that use a range of vendors in their research and want to have consistency when sharing reports within their companies. In this section, I will cover five of the most common report formats: executive summaries, memos, long-form reports, PowerPoint deck, and white papers. Think of these as broad introductions to these formats. When you are actually working on client projects, this introduction should give you a leg up in anticipating needs and making sense of what they are looking for so you can hit a home run. Either way, you will want to make sure you are checking in with your internal team and your client so you don't inadvertently take your report in the wrong direction.

- **Executive summaries.** The defining characteristic of executive summaries in this context is that they are *short*. Straightforward and to the point, an executive summary would hit the main points and not include a lot of context or data. Clients who prefer this type of communication often don't have the time to wade through the full report but want to have a concise, accurate representation of what was learned. This summary typically would partner with a longer-form report, but they should be treated as two separate documents. The executive summary should stand alone so that those who don't have the time nor inclination to read the full report will still be able to read and understand your research. These are typically under ten pages and have a minimal number of charts.

- **Memos.** A newer form of report, memos are particularly popular among clients in the technology sector. In practice, memos are quite similar to a full report or an executive summary; some can be as short as five pages, while others can go north of forty. These memos have a more casual tone, although they are still highly professional documents.
- **Long-form reports.** While long-form reports may seem like the stodgy old dude of the research report world, they still hold a valuable space in consumer insights research. A long-form report is the most comprehensive and thorough of our options. It will cover all sections in great detail and will likely have an appendix where quantitative data can be presented in full.
- **PowerPoint decks and supplements.** PowerPoint decks are the most common approach to report deliverables in consumer insights research, and much of our time in chapter 13 will be spent reviewing how to make these look pretty. As we have seen through the examples shown in this chapter, writing an effective deck is a work of art. You need to craft efficient headlines that pack a lot of information into few words. You don't want to overwhelm with words, so you need to really think about how to make your case in short, powerful statements rather than full explanations. Because decks often make more sense when given a presentation voiceover (hello, chapter 14!), some researchers will offer a written supplement as well. This often will be about ten to fifteen pages, and it gives more depth and nuance to what each slide says, as well as additional data to illustrate the points.
- **White papers.** While the other formats in this section almost always are considered proprietary and thus kept confidential to help businesses make informed decisions, white papers are intended for public use.

  Companies often will use these to demonstrate thought leadership in their industry or to provide evidence of why their approach is more effective than their competitors, as seen in figure 12.4. They also can provide an excellent opportunity to generate promising client leads by collecting contact information in exchange for the free download, as in figure 12.5.

  White papers often are produced by or on behalf of industry organizations to benefit their members and the public, such as reporting findings from an industry-wide survey on harassment in the workplace. Because these are public, they are freely available on websites and via search engines.

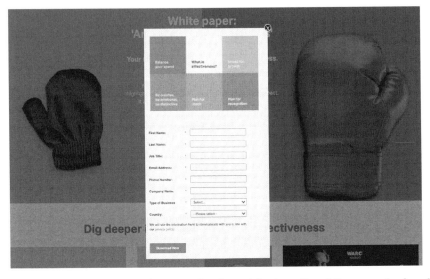

Figure 12.5   Companies and organizations are often incentivized to offer white papers for free download because they can collect contact information for future customer leads.

BEST PRACTICES AND KEY TAKEAWAYS

After all of the work you have done to collect relevant data and develop brilliant insights, you want to make sure that your report helps make all of that clear to your client. This is your chance to shine—to give them a deliverable that is highly compelling and persuasive with a strong "stickiness" factor. All of this starts with a strong outline. Take the time to really marshal your thoughts and make sense of what you've learned. Sift and sort what emerged during your analysis until you can tell a compelling story. And that story—the backbone of your report—is what will stick. That's the element that will help your client remember the other pieces, since the connections become more powerful and potent when tied to an overarching story.

As you write your report, make sure you save time to develop a strong visual presentation. Even basic Word documents need to look nice, and it is important that you bake time into your schedule to ensure you can do the formatting you need to make your final deliverables look polished and professional. Remember that these deliverables are what is left standing when you are done with your work; if you have a powerful, compelling deliverable that stays useful for your client, they are much more likely to want to ask you back.

NOTE

1. https://intranet.birmingham.ac.uk/as/libraryservices/library/asc/documents/public/Short-Guide
-Signposting.pdf

KEY TERMS

Deliverable: The material a researcher leaves behind with the client as the final product

Elevator pitch: A short paragraph sums up a research story in a compelling and concise way

Illustrative: Using data to illustrate or add dimension to the points that you are making in your headlines (the themes)

Signposts: Verbal signals that help orient readers to keep them on track with your argument

Themes: Constructs of related consumer insights that help shape and support an overarching story

13

Developing (and Designing) Your Deliverable

Think about the last billboard that caught your eye. Or a poster that really struck you. Or a textbook that made everything clear and easily understandable (cough, cough). More immediately: Look around the room you're in. What examples do you have of design that speaks to you? Material that strikes you as appealing and/or informative? What grabs your attention? As you likely already know, design is incredibly powerful. Design—good design, hopefully, but bad design as well—is sufficiently evocative to break through the clutter of all the various items competing for your attention and often inspires you feel something. And for our purposes, design can be a remarkably useful tool for helping communicate to your client that your work is professional, credible, and rigorous. A well-designed deliverable is essential for your success in consumer insights research, and this chapter will give you the basics to do that.

Think of this chapter as the BFF of chapter 12. In that chapter, we covered how you take your analysis and pull together the structure and written components of your final deliverable. One of the important (out of the SO MANY IMPORTANT) things noted in there is that you really have to think about both the usefulness and the "stickiness" of what you are presenting. It's not enough to just have good information; you need to be able to present your information in a way that will appeal to your client and their organization and stick with them enough to help ensure they successfully meet their business goals. To do that, you need to make sure your deliverable is professional, polished, and—well—*pretty*. That's not just a word I used because I love any chance to alliterate (although I totally do). It really matters that your deliverable looks good. Think of "pretty" as defined as broadly as possible—it doesn't mean girly or frilly, but visually appealing, graphically interesting, and easily understood. Going back to the brainstorming exercise that opened this chapter, the look of the deliverable—its prettiness—helps ensure it will be on your easy recall list. If you can pull off these three components when presenting your story, you have the best possible shot for your work to stick—and hopefully, that means they will come back to you again in the future. So, as always, the question is: How do we do that?

To help reach that goal, this chapter is divided into three parts. First, we briefly will review the basics of developing your deliverable that we covered in the last chapter but highlighting the ways you need to think visually about these. After that, we will review the various formats a visually oriented deliverable might take, including a PowerPoint deck, newsletters, dashboards, and infographics. Finally, we will review the basics of good design, including broad principles for designing your deliverable and then specifically for presenting data. To be clear, this chapter will not teach you how to go into the different programs and actually build your work—that's far outside of the scope of this textbook, and you may be asked to work in different programs at different points in your academic life and professional career. But if you follow the design principles outlined here, you'll be able to put together a credible, competent deliverable that represents you, your data, and your story beautifully.

DESIGNING YOUR DELIVERABLE

No matter what format your report is taking, you want to make sure that you are following the structure outlined in the previous chapter. In case you skimmed (which, if you are reading a chapter a week, you probably did since you are now getting to the end of the term and likely are quite tired of reading even though this book obviously is hilarious and quite interesting), this section is going to address some of the same concepts and briefly elaborate on the visual requirements for each. When reading this, feel free to jump back and forth between the last chapter and this one, and when you actually are working on a deliverable, look through both chapters as needed. These practices are ones that will serve you well in almost any research-based situation. So when you are pulling your deliverable together, don't forget to look at these parameters.

Make Sure Your Story Is Clear

The story is the backbone of what you are presenting. Everything that comes after must be tied to your story, including your themes and insights. The recommendations you proffer should make complete sense and have a high "duh" factor, based on what the story says. But stories can be tricky to tell through your deliverable, particularly ones like PowerPoint decks that don't have much space for text. So what does this mean visually? There are a few ways to approach this that can work. When you're pulling your deliverable together, think about which of these approaches will work best for your deliverable format, your client, and your story. Or play around with different ideas you have for how to present your story clearly and succinctly. You may come up with something new and innovative that works exactly the way you need it to for your report, your project, and your client—just make sure the story is presented early and stands out from the other text.

Text-Based Programs

When writing in Word or other text-heavy formats, use text boxes to offset your story. This usually means writing it as a narrative paragraph, perhaps bolding the key terms you want to really stand out to your client. Depending on how much real estate you have, you can consider having this text box include very short versions of your insights and recommendations. Figure 13.1 offers an example using the "women football fans" story we identified in chapter 12.

This approach helps your client and their broader team get a quick and easy understanding of what they need to take away from your report without having to spend too much time, energy, or effort figuring it out. Remember that these people are *busy*—they often don't have tons of time to pore over your report and figure out what matters on their own. Providing this story early is a solid reassurance that they are dealing with professionals who understand

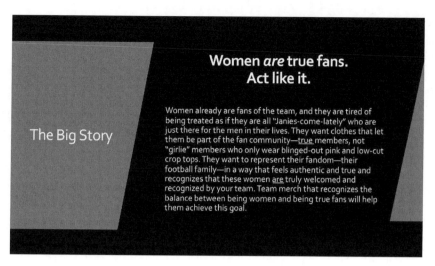

Figure 13.1   Example of a text box in Word to summarize the story.

they are busy and have limited resources (mental and temporal) available. Sharing the story clearly in the early part of your deliverable will go a long way in making sure they keep reading.

Design Programs

When using PowerPoint, Keynote, or InDesign (or really any program with more visual possibilities than Word), you'll have a little more creative flexibility with how you present your story.

On the slide shown in figure 13.2, for example, the headline is supported by a range of colorful data illustrating three key points: Subscribers are open to adding more services, consumers are reaching a tipping point on content fatigue, and the opportunity to try something new is

Figure 13.2   When properly utilized, visually oriented programs like PowerPoint provide a powerful platform for creating compelling and effective presentations.

essential for adoption. There is a ton of information on this slide, but the visual nature of PowerPoint (and some stellar design work) makes it clear and easy to understand. The overarching theme—the importance of "for me" content—is clear, and the information shown supports that premise. The slide format makes this easy to understand at a glance, rather than having to wade through large swaths of text to get to the big idea. Remember that clients are busy; for some, the opportunity to get this quick fix is preferable to the deeper, lengthier analyses found in most text-based deliverables.

Make Signposts Clear

The signposts (or "stepping stones," as the quote from the University of Birmingham in the previous chapter called them) are essential for helping your audience make sense of what you are sharing. You want to clearly identify each section that you are covering, using effective headlines, visual breaks (spacing, color bar, etc.), and/or white space to visually represent progress through the report and separation of ideas. This is really, really important when you are pulling your deliverable together. Your signposts will help your audience make sense of the different ideas that you are presenting, and you can use visual design to help make this as clear as possible.

Headlines

I cannot stress enough how important it is that you think of headlines as something to be crafted to signpost important material and demonstrate progress through your deliverable rather than placeholders relevant only to that particular slide. Headlines, whether on a new slide in your PowerPoint deck or emblazoned on a page in your white paper, are incredibly useful for making your story clear, as we see in figure 13.3. Think of it this way: The headline is what your audience needs to know, and the body beneath it just gives more context and explanation. While all of that matters, the headline gives direction for what to look for, why it matters, and how to interpret what you see.

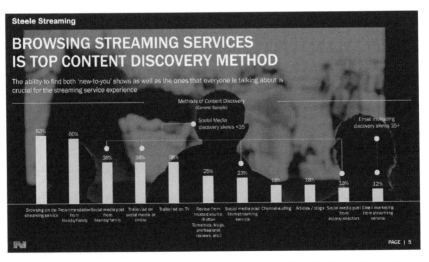

Figure 13.3   A good headline communicates the main theme or insight; the body of the slide includes an illustrative data point.

Remember, your job as the researcher is to do the heavy lifting of finding meaning in the data; headlines distill that meaning into manageable "bites" that make your work easier for your clients to understand and digest. (Nothing like a good human biology metaphor to make this clear!)

Consistency

Consistency in how you structure and format your deliverable is essential for helping ensure your audience can find their way through the document easily. This may seem like a no-brainer but trust me—it's something that can be surprisingly difficult to employ when you are scrambling to get everything done on deadline. But think about how much easier it is to read and make sense of something when you can look and automatically know what you're looking at without having to think about what goes where. This is why your professors ask you to use certain style guides and media outlets spend so much time figuring out their design template. It's a useful shortcut so your audience doesn't have to waste time figuring out where they are; your consistency helps them orient to new sections and concepts without having to engage in conscious thought.

Later in this chapter, we will give specific suggestions for how to format and present both qualitative and quantitative data, but this is another area where consistency is essential. For example, if you are presenting quant data in a table that goes from the lowest value to the highest, you'll want to follow that same model every time. Using the same colors for different brands or audience segments across all charts and figures helps the reader keep track of what data connect under certain headers. Again, this consistency will take the mental load off your audience so they can focus on what *really* matters: what you've uncovered about the audience and how it will help them address their business questions.

Metaphors Matter

Finally, don't forget the power of the metaphor. By giving your readers a powerful metaphor to latch onto, you'll be able to help maximize both the utility and the stickiness of your story. Think about some of the examples I shared earlier in this book: a student feeling like she's just moving from treadmill to treadmill and never being in a place to actually make progress toward her degree. The shoe-buying experience feeling like a tightrope for those who don't like shopping for footwear, so building in "platforms" for them to rest throughout their shoe-buying experience will help them move through the purchase funnel. These powerful metaphors are ones that will stick with the audience long after the research project has been completed, and they offer incredibly useful **heuristics**, or mental shortcuts that make recall easier, for your client.

In this same vein, it can be useful to think about names and titles as metaphor proxies. If you are doing a segmentation analysis and identifying target audiences for your client, you'll want to create names that are sufficiently evocative of that segment's core and relevant characteristics to ensure your client knows *exactly* who that person is when making business and creative decisions. For example, a client in the fashion industry might want to target "The Diva." Without knowing much about the research, you probably can envision what "The Diva" would be—her style, her look, her personality. From a business perspective, having "The Diva" be so easily visualized means you can keep this **archetype** as a guiding light when you are buying merchandise, refining your in-store layout, and developing your marketing and branding materials. This name is short, clear, and evocative, and it has real meaning for those who need to understand this audience to make the best possible decisions for their company and brand.

While this section elaborated on concepts introduced in chapter 12 to connect the visual elements to them, it's important to also think about the ways visual content can be presented. In the next section, we will review some of the main formats for visually oriented deliverables. One of these—PowerPoint decks—was covered in the previous chapter, but we will cover it here too since it's one of the most common forms of visual deliverable.

DELIVERABLE FORMATS

As was the case with report formats covered in chapter 12, the options contained here are not exhaustive. You'll likely come across different options in your future research experience, and you may come up with your own. These do cover the most common options, however, and hopefully will give you a solid grounding for how to think about ways you can create visually compelling deliverables for your client. As a reminder, these are not mutually exclusive; you may want to create an infographic as a takeaway for the full report, or one of these options may be paired with an executive summary (discussed in chapter 12). You'll also want to check in with your client to see if they have a template they'd like you to follow or if they expect a certain type or combination of deliverables—this will save you headaches and an awful lot of time down the road. Even if they don't, as always, you'll want to think about your client, their needs, and how you can best present your work in a way that will maximize utility and stickiness. Don't be afraid to think about how you can pull elements of these together as well; these deliverables can be a fantastic opportunity to get creative!

- **Infographics.**[1] A well-designed infographic can offer a compelling way to share data in a fun, creative, and (relatively) concise format (see figure 13.4 for an example). As the popular online design site Canva.com notes, infographics are a way to "make data beautiful—and easy to digest."[2]

  If you search around online for infographics, you'll likely come across some that require scrolling. Lots and lots of scrolling. Too much scrolling, one might say. (Me. I say it.) Remember that you want to use infographics to help communicate your story cleanly and clearly. If your infographic is longer than a page, it gets much harder to keep track of what is being reported and how the story fits together even when you're on a computer; imagine the disaster this is on mobile devices! While sites like Canva make it super easy to create your own visually compelling and fun infographics, you want to make sure that you're not carried away with the ease of creating complex visuals. If your deliverable is not presented in a way that maximizes utility and stickiness, you are not doing your job the best way you can.[3]

- **Dashboards.**[4] As we see in figure 13.5, dashboards are a useful tool for collecting and collating data that will be updated regularly. Rather than having data from just one source, dashboards often pull together a range of information to provide a one-stop shop of sorts for marketers, executives, and other decision-makers. By having everything collected in one dashboard, they can more easily access information needed to understand their current situation and make data-driven decisions.

  While you won't often be creating a dashboard as a consumer insights researcher, you may find yourself tasked with generating data that will fill in key areas. For example, your brand managers may need to be updated on awareness and consideration each month, and those data likely would come from brand tracking surveys for which the research team would be responsible. You'll need to be familiar with the dashboard to make sure you're collecting the right data and presenting it in a way that lets it slot in seamlessly.

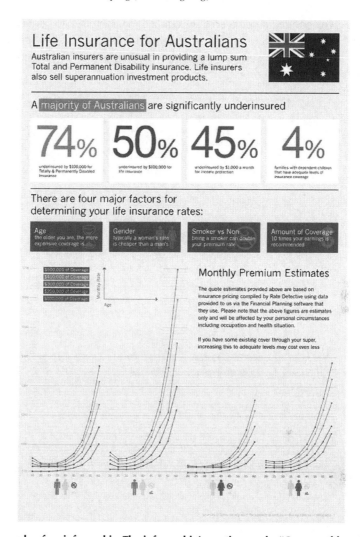

Figure 13.4 Example of an infographic. The infographic's caption reads, "Our monthly rates for life insurance depend on many factors, but most predominately gender, age, whether you smoke, and the amount of coverage you desire are key. A quick comparison of life insurance with the charts below can tell you if you are paying more than the industry average for your coverage, and what you can do to reduce your rates."
Source: Kirie Mukai for Guardian Insurance Company, Australia (http://www.guardianinsurance.com.au/Life-Insurance.aspx)

- **Newsletters.** Much like dashboards, newsletters aren't as common a format as others we have covered in the last chapter and this one. That said, you might find that some clients like this format: a bit newsier and more journalistically oriented than some of our other options. The newsletter is a tried-and-true form of internal communication within organizations, so this would be most appropriate when you're crafting research findings either as the internal research team or as the person responsible for disseminating research results. This would most likely be an add-on or supplement to the main research deliverable, intended to share high-level findings, key datapoints, and basic recommendations.
- **PowerPoint decks.** While we talked about PowerPoint decks in the last chapter, they really are the bread and butter of research presentations. These decks offer flexibility in terms of

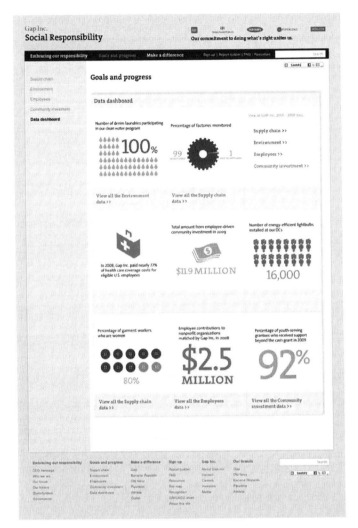

Figure 13.5   Example of a dashboard used to manage a range of relevant data. *Source:* Bryan Zug for Gap Inc.

balancing text and visuals, and they often are the best option for sharing your story in a fairly deep manner without completely overwhelming your audience with text. The size and format also make it really easy to print and bind these, making it easier to use them as reference tools (good for being both useful and sticky!).The deck is particularly practical when you are presenting quantitative data; both the horizontal aspect ratio (which makes information easier to digest) and the ability to easily add in text boxes and graphics makes this format ideally suited for presentations.

In the next section, we will get into some of the best practices for presenting data, so I won't go into that much here. However, I do want to caution you that it can be really easy to make your data look amateurish and unprofessional if you don't take the time to really craft your slides. PowerPoint giveth and it taketh away; it's the industry standard and can produce high-quality products, but it can also be tricky (and tiresome) to get all of your text boxes aligned, ensure your charts are readable, the font doesn't adjust to a size more appropriate for field mice than people, and so on. You need to plan your work to make sure you have enough time to get this right.

No matter the format, you need to make sure you are putting together a deliverable that looks professional and polished. If you do decide to go into this field (or anywhere you'll be working with visuals in InDesign, Word, or PowerPoint), I highly encourage you to take a LinkedIn Learning course or some equivalent to learn how to do this well. It's worth it, in terms of both helping you produce a professional deliverable more quickly and ensuring you are equipped to create a quality deck. And for that, you will need to learn some design basics.

DESIGN BASICS (VERY, VERY BASICS)

Hopefully, by now we have built up sufficient trust that you'll believe me when I tell you that I have zero artistic ability. Stick figures test my abilities. I am proud of myself if I can draw a passable tree. So please believe me when I say: Good design does *not* require artistic ability. Sure, it's helpful to have a good eye, and you hopefully will find yourself with a designer on your team who can help ensure what you put together looks fabulous. But even without those advantages, it is more than possible to put together a deliverable that is professional, polished, and—yes—pretty. The remainder of this chapter focuses on giving you some basic rules and guidelines to follow when you're designing your deliverable. As recommended in previous chapters, if you aren't required to do a project for this class, I encourage you to take some time and independently put together a range of visually compelling pseudo-deliverables. Find some publicly available data (e.g., the results of a political survey) and create an infographic, a PowerPoint deck, and an executive summary. For this exercise, it doesn't matter as much what the story is—you can really even use some "dummy" data that you made up. But having some practice on the technical aspects of putting deliverables together and creating meaningful charts and graphics will help everything in this chapter make a bit more sense and give you a leg up when you're actually charged with putting these together.

As noted in the previous chapter, it's possible (and maybe even likely) that your team will have a PowerPoint, Word, or InDesign template that you'll use to craft your visually oriented deliverable. Other times, you may need to start from scratch; if you do, you'll want to use a template that is branded with your information (including your company's or team's name and logo, if available). PowerPoint has some basic templates that you can adjust and personalize in order to have your work be clearly identifiable and recognizable. If that's the path you take, make sure you choose a template that is clean and easily navigable—you don't want one that looks too generic or too busy. You also don't want to use a template that others might use as well; make sure you adapt it enough to differentiate your work visually from others they might see. Remember that you don't have to be a full-on graphic designer to make this work, although certainly it is useful to have a designer on your team. If you follow the basic principles of design thinking covered in this chapter, you'll be able to put something together that represents you and your work beautifully. So now, with those disclaimers in place, let's get into the good stuff.

Designing Your Deliverable

At the end of this chapter, I'm going to give you a few resources you can use to help you get more information about how to create beautifully designed deliverables. For now, however, we are going to focus on four "Design Musts" that you should always bear in mind when crafting your visually oriented work: readability, hierarchy, consistency, and effective use of contrast and color.

Readability

If you want your deliverable to be both useful and sticky—the two factors that lead to success—you have to ensure that whatever you put together is, at is core, highly (and easily) readable. This covers a range of concerns. Think about how your audience will be engaging with your deliverable. If you're writing an executive summary, your client will have time to sit, read, and digest what you have to say. A PowerPoint deck, however, likely will involve a face-to-face presentation, whether online or in person. In that case, you need to greatly reduce your text and think more about what can be seen and understood from those who might only have a few minutes of exposure to each individual slide (even if you are going to leave digital and physical copies of your deck behind). Also, remember that the typical college student has young eyes, and you are much better suited to seeing tiny print than oldies (like me!). Keep your font sizes reasonably sized to ensure readability, particularly when dealing with data and complex ideas that need to be fully comprehended. I generally recommend not going below a font size of eleven in a text-based document or ten in the smallest subhead in a PowerPoint, but you will want to check this with your client and your team.

Finally, you'll want to make sure that you are avoiding clutter and using **white space** wisely. (Interesting note: "White space" is just a term for space that doesn't have design elements or text boxes and thus is strategically left blank; this also sometimes is known as "negative space.") It can be tempting to pack as much as possible into your presentation, filling up available space on your slides. When you do that, however, you're just creating walls of information with sentence after sentence, crammed on a slide. Sure, those slides are just chock full of informational goodness. But can you read it? Do you *want* to read it? Probably not. Think about professors you've had who insist on packing their slides with text that they often just read back to you anyway. Is that interesting? Do you remember what it says? Again, probably not. But if you have a well-designed slide that uses negative space effectively (like the example in figure 13.6), you'll be able to ensure you communicate what you need to communicate in an easily readable (and thus understandable) manner.

Hierarchy

Graphic designer Norman Mallard shared a good rule of thumb for effective presentation of information: When you're putting each page or slide together, you want to direct the eye where you want it to go. This is done through an effective use of **hierarchy,** or using visual cues to show what is most important—what you want your audience to look at first—versus what can come later. The size, prominence, and location of your various items will guide the viewer's eye where you want it to go. Make your headlines stand out. After all, they are the core of what you are trying to share in each area. The remaining content will be illustrative, as we discussed in chapter 12, so you can make that smaller. If you are sharing multiple data points that have a specific order needed to tell your story (e.g., 67 percent of audience members are aware of your show, but only 32 percent watch it regularly), think about how you can structure the charts or graphs to demonstrate this. For Western audiences who read left to right, you'll

Figure 13.6   Example of the effective use of white space in a presentation.

want to put the first point they need to know in the "correct" space—either on top or on the left. Again, you want to reduce any extra mental energy your clients have to spend figuring out what you mean; you want all of their attention and energy invested in your story. The use of hierarchy can do that.

Consistency

While this topic briefly was addressed earlier, it's important enough to repeat here: Consistency is essential when you're designing your visual presentation. Use the same fonts throughout your deck or document (after, of course, making sure they are readable). Use consistent punctuation; if you're putting periods at the end of first-level bullets, do it throughout your text. If you have a border on your chart, do it throughout your data visuals. If you're capitalizing the first letter of all words in the headline, you guessed it—keep doing that throughout the piece. This type of consistency is a fabulous way to reiterate the professionalism and polish of your deliverable, since it makes your work easy to follow. Some places to check and double-check for consistency include:

- Headlines (capitalizations, font size, punctuation)
- Charts and graphs (fonts, labels, data order [smallest to largest, etc.], presenting percentages or numbers, data scale)
- Qualitative quotes (formatting, font size, punctuation, identifiers)
- Tables (internal lines, capitalizations within text, internal labels ["%" or "$"])
- Photos (shape, borders/frames, cropping, etc.)
- Captions (font size, information given, etc.)
- Citations if using other people's work (grammatical style, information contained, formatting)

This certainly isn't an exhaustive list, but these tend to be where many of us trip up when pulling our deliverables together. While you'll want to carefully proofread no matter what, it never hurts to take a few extra minutes to make sure these areas are consistent.

Effective Use of Color and Contrast

If you are building your deliverable from scratch, you'll want to make sure you carefully consider the colors you use. Consider the two website homepages shown in figure 13.7. Think about the ethos, if you will, of the client you're representing. If it's an outdoors brand (like Fin, Feathers, and Fur), you'll likely want to go with earthier, more natural or neutral colors, and a brown accent color would not be amiss. That same brown, however, might look quite out of place if you're working on a project for Comedy Central, a channel heavily associated with its yellow logo on a black background and considered "cooler" and more subversive.

The brand characteristics of your client should always be considered and reflected in your design. This does not mean you have to tie yourself to the colors used in their branding, but it *does* mean that you should ensure the colors you select fit with both the client's ethos and the subject of your study. For example, if you have a brand heavily associated with men and you're doing a study to examine the opportunity for broadening their target audience to better incorporate women, you can use colors to help subtly communicate the purpose of your study. Be careful that you don't fall into essentialist traps, however; as we learned through the NFL example shared in chapter 12, you don't want to metaphorically "pink it and shrink it" by using hot pink to show this study is on "the ladies." Instead, you can use color and your overall design to set the stage for what your study is—maybe lighten the team colors, for example, or use gradients to show that this deliverable is shifting the "normal" perception of what is expected in NFL viewership.

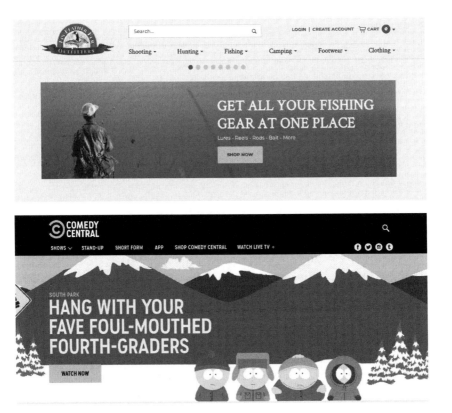

Figure 13.7   As these two websites show, color can be used as cues for who the target audience is.

When picking your color scheme, you also want to think about how your deliverable will look in whichever medium is used. More times that I care to remember, students' presentations were unreadable when shown through the projector because they used too light a color on a white background. It might look fabulous on a computer screen, but it does not connote professionalism when your report is practically unreadable when your client is watching your presentation. Likewise, dark (not black) backgrounds can be fantastic on a big screen, but they often don't print as nicely as a light background. If your client wants a paper copy of the deck, this also makes it challenging to write notes on important points while they are watching your presentation. Make sure you're anticipating and planning for your ultimate form of delivery and select your colors accordingly. And, of course, test everything in advance to make sure your template or color scheme works in all formats before you move forward with building out the entire deliverable.

Finally, consider how you can use **contrast** to help tell your story. While learning about color theory falls far outside the scope of this chapter, it's useful to understand how colors work together to create a compelling visual design. For example, check out the graphic below from Canva.com (figure 13.8).[5]

By using lighter and darker shades of the same colors, you can create contrast that helps ensure you're calling attention to what matters most in your story and guiding your reader though your work. You also can use contrasting colors (remember the color wheel from elementary school? Still relevant!) or similar color schemes to create the contrast you want to craft your deliverable.

One final note before we move onto creating data visualizations: Make sure you bake enough time into your workflow to really develop a solid design for your deliverables. Again, this is the ultimate leave-behind for your client; this is *the thing* that will most inform the ways they remember you and your work. Don't try to fast track this process, and *definitely* do not try to wing it in the waning days before your deadline. The best research in the world won't be a success if your deliverable falls short. Proceed accordingly.

01. Contrast with Dark and Light Colors

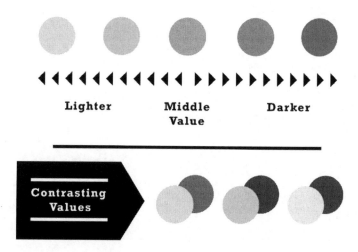

Figure 13.8   Color contrast chart by Canva.com.

PRESENTING DATA

There are so many incredible resources out there to teach you about data visualization. This is not one of them. And to be honest, most of what the "data viz" experts talk about are techniques used for much more sophisticated statistical work than what your average consumer insights research project would cover. As such, in this section, we will focus on the most common forms of data presentation used in applied research, both quantitative (charts and graphs, tables, and axis mapping) and qualitative (quotes and creative exercises). We will then review some guidelines to follow to ensure you are presenting your data clearly and ethically.

Forms of Data Presentation

Great research design usually involves taking great care to figure out the best way to visualize your data. You want these to make both the data and the meaning clear to your audience, and that means you need to think about how to most effectively meet both of those targets. We will review a number of approaches below, but as you get started, take a look at the slide in figure 13.9.

This slide uses a ton of different data visualization approaches—yet because they are clearly captioned and laid out and color is used to tease out differences, it's easy to understand what the meaning is. This is a fabulous example of how you can make your data look good by using the right kind of chart or graph and making sure that you are focused on design.

Charts and Graphs

Charts and graphs are used when you are presenting visualizations of basic statistical information, usually to allow for comparison within or across data points. The type of chart or graph you use are determined by the kind of data you have and what you are trying to show. Typically, consumer insights studies would use a combination of pie charts, bar charts (vertical or horizontal), and line graphs.

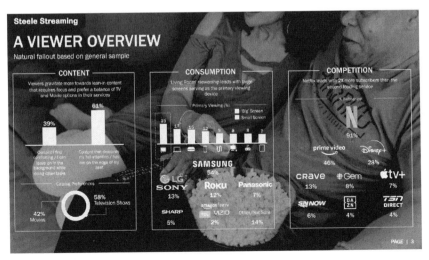

Figure 13.9   This slide shows a range of data visualization approaches, including bar charts and pie charts.

- **Pie charts.** One of the most immediately recognizable types of data presentation is the trusty pie chart. These charts are useful when you want to show the parts of a whole, or the breakdown of a total number (usually 100 percent). So, for example, if you are trying to show days of exercise for your population (women, 45 and older), you could use a pie chart to demonstrate this.
- **Bar charts.** While pie charts show how a total number is broken down into constituent parts, bar charts are used to compare data points. Vertical bar charts (also called "column charts" or "column graphs") are particularly useful for showing comparisons over time, since they follow an intuitive progression across the bottom axis. The horizontal bar chart typically is used when presenting data points with longer headers; for example, the statements used in a matrix question (per chapter 10). This option is also useful if you need to show negative numbers, such as showing how far off the average a particular subpopulation is.
- **Line graphs.** Line graphs are incredibly useful for visualizing the progression of data across variables, such as the number of students enrolled in a major over time or the completion times for exams. Because they are demonstrating the relative associations between data points, however, line graphs can *only* be used when the bottom axis (the *x* axis) is representing data that are continuous, meaning you can put them in a meaningful order (typically lowest to highest).

Axis Mapping

Sometimes, you'll want to be able to show what a broader landscape looks like—how your audience segments or competitors map out in relation to each other, based on relevant criteria. To do this, you'll develop a map based on **axes** (the plural form of "axis," used to refer to the lines). Pronounced "axe-eze," these charts allow you to visualize how variables are spread out across two key axes: value (high to low), credibility (high to low), etc.

These can be derived through statistical analyses, but sometimes you'll want to do a qualitative representation based on what you learned throughout your research. Just make clear to your client which approach you are taking so they are fully informed about how the map was derived. Figure 13.10 offers a really good example of how this would work in your presentation deck.

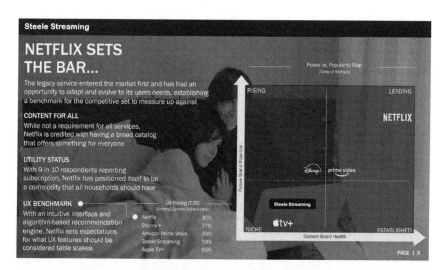

Figure 13.10   As this slide shows, relevant axes can be used to differentiate among competitive brands on key criteria.

Qualitative Quotes

The final form of data presentation we will review shifts away from quantitative data and instead centers on qualitative quotes. As you now well know (hooray for section II!), qualitative data still are data—just in word form rather than numbers—and, as such, are essential tools for illustrating your themes and telling your story.

When you are using quotes in your deliverable, you'll want to make sure you are consistently formatting what these look like in a way that makes clear you are using words that came directly from your participants (often called **verbatims**). If you are editing out "ums" or other placeholder words, you need to make sure you tell your client. I am fairly agnostic on this process; I typically will do whatever works best for the project and the client. Just be consistent. And, if necessary, make sure you're presenting this in a way that is kind to and respectful of your participants. If you have a young participant who uses "like" more than seems humanly possible, you have to weigh the value of the full, direct quote versus editing out the "likes" to keep the meaning clear without opening the participant up to mockery. For example, read these two quotes:

- "I was, like, super into the game. It was, like, really cool and, like, the levels were like wicked hard."
- "I was super into the game. It was really cool and the levels were wicked hard."

While the first quote might actually be the verbatim—the direct quote—the excessive use of "like" makes the meaning harder to parse and the participant could be perceived as particularly inarticulate. As long as your client knows that you "lightly edited for clarity" and that is made clear in your deliverable, you remain in good ethical standing.

The other ethical piece you want to bear in mind when presenting qualitative quotes is that you need to protect the confidentiality of your participants. Rather than using real names, you can use relevant identifiers (often age, gender, or category [user/consumer, grade, etc.]), as shown in figure 13.11. This helps add context to the quote that is useful for your client and their team, particularly those who were farther away from the actual research process. Finally, it is

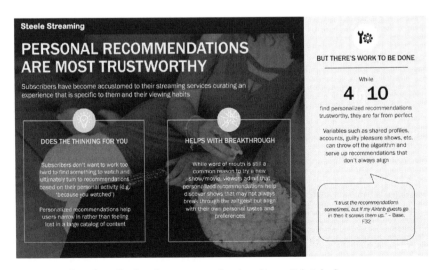

Figure 13.11   Examples of qualitative data presentation in a PowerPoint deck.

essential that you never, ever make the claim that qualitative data "proved" anything. Qualitative research is directional, not absolute. While these data are incredibly useful for providing depth and color, you need to be super careful to not overstate how universal qual findings are. So instead of using "proved," consider "indicates" or "demonstrates" to better reflect the nature of qualitative methods.

Creative Exercises

If you used creative exercises (per chapter 7) in your qualitative research, you likely have some artifacts that will help add visual interest and evidence in your deliverable. These can be quite powerful, and I have found clients appreciate the glimpse into the "purer" data to help make sense of your findings. If you are adding photos or scans of these artifacts, make sure you clearly explain where they come from and what the creative exercise was. This doesn't have to be a huge deal—it can be a text box at the bottom of the page or a footnote—but you need to offer the necessary context to explain what it is and why it was created to help make clear why it matters. Finally, be sure you crop or block out any names that might be visible to protect the confidentiality of your participants.

Guidelines for Presenting Data

When you are presenting data, you always want to make sure your audience is super clear about what they are seeing and where the data came from. For quantitative data, this means:

- Including the N for each question (the total number of respondents)
- Labeling each bar or pie section with the relevant number or percentage
- Providing the question wording and response options (often in a text box at the bottom of the page)

Even if you are focusing on just the top or bottom two boxes (very and somewhat likely, for example, combined into one number), your chart should show the numbers for each response. You can use a text box to show the total.

You also want to make sure you are carefully proofreading all charts and graphs to make sure the data you are providing are accurate. It is all too easy to transpose a number or mix something up when creating your charts; spend time proofing to make sure you are 100 percent correct in what you are putting forward. While mistakes are human, it's never a good look to have significant errors in the data you are presenting. Proofread. And if something doesn't add up properly—for example, maybe your percentages don't total to 100 due to rounding—anticipate questions about that and explain why. Again, text boxes are your friend. Throw a line in at the bottom of the page explaining why. Just make sure it doesn't look like a mistake.

To help facilitate your own creation of data visualizations, here are some useful tools:

- **Canva.com**: Not only does Canva have a solid infographics creator, but it also has an incredibly useful tool for creating charts. Easy to use and manipulate, the Canva app can be a lifesaver.
- **Excel**: While we tend to think of Excel as spreadsheet central, it has also some fairly robust chart-making tools. While I find their Help feature to be less than ideal, there is a ton of information available on the Internet on how to make this work. This applies to the Google Sheets as well.

- **Qualtrics and Survey Monkey**: These survey platforms have also some pretty useful chart-making tools available internally. If your data are already in there, this might be the most efficient solution for you to use.

BEST PRACTICES AND KEY TAKEAWAYS

Your deliverable is the single most important document you'll create during your research process, since it is the one thing that will be left behind to (hopefully) have an impact. The principles introduced in this chapter will give you a solid start to creating something worth sharing, and I encourage you to start practicing now—even if you don't have a real project, just mock something up. The more time you spend playing with data and presentation software, the easier this will be. It can be scary to get started, but trust me: it will be worth it.

As you continue to develop your skills as a researcher, you'll soon become more comfortable with understanding what *really* needs to be included in your deliverable. You'll learn to read your client and their organization, helping you craft documents and decks that are both useful and highly sticky. Just remember that you need to do the work in chapter 12 first—developing your story, working out your insights and frames, and really nailing both why your findings matter and what they can do with what you learned—before you jump to the design. Good design without good information is empty. Think of this step as when you take on the role of a jeweler. You already have the gem there, but now your task is to cut it and polish it to make it shine.

One final note: As you create your deliverables in any format, keep ethics front and center. Treat your participants with respect, including avoiding any mockery (whether intentional or not) and protecting their confidentiality. You also want to treat your client with respect. Present your findings honestly and fairly, but be strategic. While your job is to tell them the good *and* the bad, remember that no one wants to listen when they are feeling beat up and defeated. This is when a compliment sandwich can come in handy. Lead with the good so that can cushion and contextualize the bad. Frame problems as opportunities. Craft recommendations that will help fix the issues identified in your research. And, as always, if you are using someone else's data, *cite it.* Give credit where credit is due. This includes any forms of secondary research you might have in your deliverable. Never be afraid to share credit. That's a mark of a confident, qualified, ethical researcher.

In some instances, the deliverable will be sent with no presentation element included. The client will represent what you learned to their team, and your job is done once the deliverable is in hand. Most of the time, however, you'll have some sort of formal or informal presentation to share what you learned with your client organization. And for that, you need to be prepared. Our next chapter—the last one (#tears)—focuses on how to put together a top-notch presentation to show off both your work and you. This really is your time to shine, and developing professional presentation skills will benefit you far outside of this class.

NOTES

1. https://www.canva.com/learn/best-infographics/
2. https://www.canva.com/create/infographics/
3. https://search.creativecommons.org/photos/f9ec0181-f022-4a8a-a30c-e485f732a29e
4. https://search.creativecommons.org/photos/ec8c96bd-7890-48b5-bffb-5c930467559a
5. https://www.canva.com/learn/contrasting-colors/

KEY TERMS

Archetype: A prototypical example of a person or concept
Heuristics: Mental shortcuts that make recall easier
White space: Open areas that are strategically left blank and free from design elements or text; this sometimes is also known as "negative space"

14

The Client Presentation

I can still remember my first formal presentation in front of clients when I was a baby researcher. While I wish I could tell you that I went in with complete confidence and a strong sense of my own skill as a researcher and communicator, that's not exactly what happened. Mostly, I remember being terrified that I would trip. Or puke. Or just blank out and have no idea how to talk. During our practice runs in the office, on the flight to our client's office, while prepping the client's conference room and waiting for the team to join us—every step of the way, I was so, so nervous. Even though I knew we had done a great job and that the client would be super happy, I just genuinely felt like I had no idea how to be a professional doing a presentation to people who made real-life business decisions with real-life financial consequences. I was just a mouthy kid from Akron (long before LeBron made that cool), and I was convinced that they immediately would see me as the fraud that I feared I was. I imagined executives in fancy business suits deriding my lack of knowledge about their business and the broader industry. I pictured old bald men mocking our data and calling me out on a minute point for which I'd be unprepared. Every horror story I'd heard or read (or imagined) went through my mind.

Then the doors opened. The high-profile executives in fancy business suits streamed in, but—and this is when I started to have an inkling I might be wrong—they smiled at me. They welcomed us and told us how much they'd been anticipating our presentation. As we started, we had their full attention—and we kept it the entire time. Far from my nightmare scenarios, this was a receptive crowd, and they *loved* what we did. Their questions were smart and insightful, and I was relieved that I actually knew how to answer them. New RQs and ideas bubbled up during the discussion, and the CEO made clear we would be the team to follow those paths on their behalf. We talked long after the meeting was scheduled to end, and once we finally wrapped up our point person on the client side was overjoyed. Our presentation— our project—had been a hit, and the work we did wound up leading their company to great success.

Over the course of my career as both a researcher and a professor, I've learned some really effective strategies for presenting research. The students I've taught have commented on how much they learned from presenting in our class, and I have pulled together those suggestions and recommendations into this final chapter to help you do the same. Before we get into that, however, I want to make very clear that some of the students who wound up excelling at presenting were not the most comfortable and enthusiastic at the start. You don't have to be a natural entertainer or jokester to be an effective presenter; in fact, some of the most compelling presenters I know are ones who are quieter, often deliberate and thoughtful in their approach. And I think it's always good to remember that *everyone* is nervous when they first start presenting, particularly when you're in a high-stakes field like consumer insights research. I still can't believe sometimes that I presented research findings and debated recommendations with C-level executives from some of the biggest companies and brands in the United States. But I did. And they listened, and they trusted me and my team to help them make good decisions. Eventually, I figured out that I *am* good at this, and trust me—you can be too.

This chapter is divided into four parts, first covering the goal and purpose of presenting research and then reviewing strategies for preparation, the presentation, and post-presentation. At the end of that, I'll wrap up the book and send you off with parting thoughts and words of wisdom. And I implore you to please keep this in mind as you read this chapter: Trust the process. You may not buy everything I write in here, but I truly believe that every one of you has the potential to be an excellent presenter. Give these techniques a go, whether in this class or another. And have faith that you *can* do this and do it really well.

GOAL AND PURPOSE

While it may seem obvious, it's worth taking a few minutes to think through the goals and purpose of presenting research. As we discussed in the last chapter, your deliverable is the last tangible result of the research you have done. The presentation, however, is where that deliverable comes to life. This is the place where you can make sure your points are all clear and that your story resonates with your clients. Think back (way, way back) to chapter 2 which focused on working with clients. In that chapter, we reviewed a number of principles that should guide your interactions with those for whom you are conducting research. As a refresher, you'll want to keep all of these in mind so that you set your presentation off on the best possible foot.

- **Look professional.** Research companies often are, much to my delight, fairly causal places. But if you're going to be in front of your clients, you want to look your best. Get a sense of what the standard of dress is where you are presenting and plan to go a level up (unless it's full business wear, in which case you want to be on par with your audience). This serves two purposes: first, it communicates professionalism to your client, but it can also help you fight off feelings of imposter syndrome. Whether you are presenting online or in person, dress to impress.
- **Be confident and humble.** Confidence is hugely important, and we'll talk in later sections of this chapter about how you can prepare yourself so that confidence is completely warranted. But no matter the situation, remember to use body language that communicates confidence. Sit up straight. Shake hands with authority (assuming that's a thing again post-COVID). Try to avoid uptalk, which makes it sound like you're asking rather than stating. Make eye contact. And *smile*. It's remarkable how much a smile can do to convince the world you know what you're doing. Just make sure your confidence doesn't read as arrogance. You want to make sure you are coming across as an expert, not a know-it-all. Which leads to our last point.
- **Remember *you* are the expert on the audience and your research.** Your client chose your company and you to do this research because you're eminently qualified, and you've done

a fabulous job. Your presentation probably has been vetted by your primary point person at your organization, and most likely various representatives from your client organization attended at least some qualitative field work. If you've done your job well, you've been building buy-in for you and this research project since the RFP many moons ago. So when you are in the conference room and presenting, remember that you are there because you are an expert—*the* expert—on the audience and this research project. You are there to be the audience's seat at the table, so to speak. Advocate for them. Speak for them. Don't be so intimidated that you are afraid to defend your research and your understanding of the audience if challenged. You know your stuff, and again, this is why you're in the room.

Clearly, if you want to achieve these goals during your presentation, you need to be absolutely prepared when you walk into the room. Armed with your beautifully structured and designed deliverable, proper preparation will allow you to hit a home run during this final stage of your research project.

PREPARATION

Good preparation is essential to presentation success. When you are planning your workback schedule, make sure you have at least a couple of days built in between the completion of the deliverable and your presentation. This also means running through a mock presentation before you declare your presentation complete; it's amazing how many snags you'll notice—missing datapoints needed to solidify your insight or theme, missing words or typos, a weak transition that needs strengthened—when you run through it out loud in true presentation mode. Then, once the deliverable is rock solid, you can send it to your client, get printing underway if needed, and start your presentation prep. And when you do that, you need to keep three things in mind: know your audience, know your material, and make sure you internalize your information.

Know Your Audience

A common theme in this book is to know your audience, and this is no exception. As you go into the presentation, you likely have a sense from your deliverable prep what kind of audience will be in the room. Do they like jokes and a light-hearted style, or is a more serious presentation more appropriate? Do they want you to go into detail on charts and graphs, or is it better to just hit the highlights and move on? (It's almost always better to just hit the highlights and move on.) Make sure you clarify these expectations in advance so you can meet—or hopefully exceed—their expectations.

Both during your prep and your presentation, you also want to keep time limits in mind. The people in this room are there to learn what you have to say because it is going to help them answer a business question, so it follows that they are probably really, really busy. You can't just go over because you have so much to say. Know the time limits and abide by them. Don't spend so much time on the upfront pieces (RQs, methods, etc.) that you don't have time to get to the stuff that really matters to them: the findings and recommendations. Plan your time and use it wisely, and make sure you have a way to watch the clock to ensure you don't take too long.

Know Your Material

Any presentation success is grounded in knowing your material backward and forward. You need to know what is coming up and why. By now, the RQs and business objective driving your project should be second nature. You need to make sure you are completely clear on what methods you fielded and where, along with relevant Ns for any quantitative work (including relevant subsamples). You should be able to recite your elevator pitch in your sleep because you know it so well, and you need to be completely familiar with your deliverable.

Particularly when you are still a presentation newbie, you might want to write a script to help guide you through the key points that you need to cover. That's totally fine, particularly if you have some stage fright when you are going to be up in front of people. That said, you *never, ever, ever want to read a script in front of your clients*. Never. Ever. Like, Taylor Swift's anticipatory rejection of her treacherous ex levels of never ever. This includes notes. Nope. Nada. A script or notecards are fine when you are practicing, but you need to leave those in your office. When you are presenting live, there is an expectation that you know this so well you don't need notes. You've lived this. You have been immersed in it. And that needs to come through during your presentation. While you might want to bring a binder with additional banners or data in case you need them for questions, anything that is in your main deliverable needs to be metaphorically tattooed on your brain. If you are going to be perceived as the expert you are, you need to know your material cold. And that means internalizing your talking points so that it feels natural and organic rather than scripted and stilted.

Internalizing

We talked quite a bit about internalizing earlier in the book, particularly in the qualitative chapters. The same principle applies here. You want to think through and really bake what you are going to say—that's an essential part of being prepared. So write a draft script, including all of the key points you need to make sure you're including. Know the signposts so you can easily navigate through your deliverable. Practice your transitions so the story and presentation flow. Put all of the major points that you definitely need to know in bold so they stand out. Once you have the right script, practice it as much as you need to until you've learned the material cold. And then once you know the material, put the script to the side and practice until you sound completely natural.

One suggestion, particularly for those of you more comfortable with presenting: Rather than writing a full script, just do an outline with the parts that would be bolded above. Anything you want to be sure you say makes it in, and then you can freestyle between them during your practice. This is a great strategy for avoiding any chance of sounding like you have memorized a script rather than speaking from the heart. You can keep the outline handy, perhaps handing it to a colleague who is listening to you practice to make sure you hit the key points accurately. By doing this, you'll have the confidence that comes with preparation without the risk of over-reliance on a script.

Finally, if this is your first time presenting to this group or team, don't hesitate to ask your main client (your point person) for advice on how to best meet their expectations. Every organization has its own internal culture, so having this information in advance will give you the best chance to know to hit the mark during your big event.

DURING THE PRESENTATION

After months of preparation, you finally are in the room (real or virtual). You're looking at your clients' faces, hoping and praying that you don't suddenly have to go to the bathroom or become desperately thirsty. Everyone is seated around the table (again, real or virtual), ready to get started. You've done your preparation and are ready to launch. Take a deep breath, smile, and get ready to go.

When starting any presentation, it's essential that you set expectations in the room (sometimes called "leveling expectations" in corporate speak). Introduce yourself and your team, and, particularly if this is a client that has not done much research in the past, briefly explain your roles. Give an estimate for how long the presentation will last. Depending on your team and your client's preferences, establish whether questions should be asked during the presentation (more common) or saved to the end (a bit rarer). If possible, make sure everyone who wants a paper or digital copy has access to one. Then it's time to get started. Since you're prepared, this hopefully will go swimmingly. But no matter how prepared you are, there are some general tips you should follow to ensure your success:

- **Make eye contact.** When we get nervous, we have a tendency to stop making eye contact. Don't do that. While you don't want to be weird (welcome back to the Coombs Rule!), you do want to make sure you are projecting confidence. Eye contact is a great way to do this.
- **Watch your body language.** When presenting, make sure you are conscious of your body language. Crossing our arms in front of our chests communicates being closed off and fidgeting or rocking back and forth are distracting to viewers. Stand steady and still, using motion only deliberately to make a point or better connect with your audience. This also applies when you aren't the one talking. If a teammate is presenting, you want to demonstrate attentiveness and engagement. So you still don't want to fidget or (God forbid) check your phone. Pay attention and stay engaged the whole time.
- **Pay attention to the staging.** If you are presenting in front of a big screen, you'll want to make sure you're not blocking any important data or information. If you are taking turns with teammates, make sure the person talking is not on the edges. And have a plan for how to advance through slides or pages—if you don't have a remote clicker, know who is going to advance forward and have a cue for when to make the move.
- **Watch the clock.** This was briefly addressed above, but it bears repeating: You need to carefully watch the clock during your presentation. I highly recommend not doing that by using your phone if at all possible; it's really distracting for both you and your audience when you're picking up or poking at your phone to get the time to show up, and when alerts come it can be difficult to tune them out and maintain your flow. If you can wear a watch, that's typically a subtler way to do a quick check. If necessary, ask out loud how you're doing on time. Someone on your team or your client can give you that information and a cue as to whether you need to hurry up or if things are going okay.
- **Read the room.** Finally, you'll want to make sure you are paying attention to the emotional state of the room throughout your presentation. If your audience members are showing signs of getting bored, consider moving forward more quickly and cutting out extraneous bits. (Bonus: This is much easier to do when you've internalized the presentation!) On the flip side, if there is something that clearly is sparking, think about pausing to ask if they want to learn more about it or have an interim discussion. Don't be afraid to ask as well. If you are sensing they want more or less detail, you can always tell your audience you're doing

a "temperature check" to see how you should proceed. This is a good way to ensure you're hitting the mark for your audience. This technique also works if you're doing an online presentation via a platform like Zoom or Microsoft Teams. If you can't see their faces, just ask for feedback—it's a much better approach than just not realizing that you've lost your audience's attention or they have questions about what you're saying.

Once you have made your way through the deliverable, you're ready to move into one of the most dynamic and exciting parts of the job: the question and answer session with your client and their team. This is where some of the most interesting and lively discussions happen, and you often will be asked to share your thoughts and insights on ideas they have been kicking around that are relevant to your project. This also gives your audience a chance to ask about clarifications to your presentation and for more information on topics that sparked a particular interest, which is where the aforementioned binder full of banners can come in handy.

To prepare for the Q&A, you'll want to do a few practice sessions with your teammates. Brainstorm the questions that are likely to come up, or even ask your client if they have any areas they think will be particularly of interest or relevant to the broader organization. Think about who is best suited to answer in different areas; for example, one of you may focus on the quant while someone else is the main respondent for qual, and a third person may take the lead on answering queries on recommendations. The more you can come across as polished and professional in the Q&A session, the better off you'll be in the long run. And, like always, your odds of success are greatly increased with proper preparation.

WRAPPING UP THE PROJECT

As your post-presentation discussion is wrapping up, you'll want to make sure you are on the same page with your client on what, if anything, comes next. During the Q&A, you might offer to dig more into the data to address something that came up; you want to put that on your list. Or you might need to better explain a particular area that was not as clear as you had hoped or anticipated. In the best-case scenario, your client wants to talk about future research ideas that emerged from the presentation and the ensuing discussion. You need to have someone on your team who is in charge of taking notes on all of these items, creating a master list that you can then review with your client before taking your leave. This is usually the project manager, but the task can really be assigned to anyone. Then, once you are back in the office, you make sure that you follow up on each item on that list as quickly as you can.

Back in the Office

A day or two after wrap-up, I recommend sending a quick note to your client as a general follow-up delineating all action items discussed and the associated timeline, including anything you need to send them and vice versa. If there is anything you promised that is ready to go, include it here as well. Any anticipated materials that will take a bit longer should be noted along with an estimated date for sending (and then make a note on your calendar so you don't drop the ball!). Once everything is in, you'll also want to send a specific thank-you email to your client. It's never a bad idea to end a relationship on an upbeat note, and this is likely to leave a positive impression. To be clear, this does not need to be an elaborate message; short and sweet are your guiding sentiments here. But this is a fantastic way to close the loop with your client, make sure they don't have any lingering questions, and leave the door open for future communication.

BEST PRACTICES AND KEY TAKEAWAYS

As this chapter makes clear, the best way to ensure you have an excellent presentation experience is to prepare, prepare, prepare. Internalize your key talking points so you sound natural and can pivot if needed based on questions asked or discussions that arise. And, of course, have confidence that you are an expert. *The* expert. You know of what you speak, and you have earned your place in that room. Remember that everyone is nervous when they start presenting, but spending time getting comfortable with the material will ensure you are ready to rock when you are in the room with your client organization.

FINAL THOUGHTS

Hopefully, this textbook has served the purpose outlined in chapter 1: to help you learn how to successfully design, conduct, and analyze consumer insights research—and do it well. And hopefully you are now on board with my position that consumer insights research is, in fact, quite fun. I can truly say I loved my job, and my former students who have gone into this field (many of whom contributed thoughts, recommendations, and insights to this book!) have found this field to be rewarding and intellectually gratifying. For those of you who are thinking a career in consumer insights research might be for you, I highly recommend getting as much experience as you can doing this kind of work. Design and conduct small, scrappy research projects with organizations in your orbit, whether it's a student group or a small business that needs some help. Ask the administration and/or faculty in your school if they have topics they'd like researched and volunteer your services. Look for internships that have keywords like "research," "consumer insights," "account planning," or "strategic insights." And when you're ready to move into the job market, figure out which organizations have research departments that appeal to you. Even if you can't get in right away, getting your foot in the door through other roles and departments gives you the chance to later demonstrate your own expertise and hopefully get your dream role sooner rather than later.

Learning about consumer insights research is important even for those of you who have no intention of ever doing this as your primary job. Understanding audiences is at the core of any success in media industries. If you have insight into your audience and their wants and needs, you are much better positioned to create content that will break through the clutter, whether you're making television shows and films or working in persuasive industries like advertising or public relations. The tools and skills reviewed in this text are relevant even if you *don't* go into research specifically; almost all of you will engage with consumer insights research in some way in your careers. So when you engage with research, remember what you learned in here. Check out the RQs and business objectives that guided the research. Review the methods and consider if the claims made can be justified by the ways data were collected. Critically examine the themes and insights presented, and consider if the ensuing recommendations have the "duh" factor that is an indicator of a successful project. What you have learned in here prepares you to do this sort of analytical examination, and this will help ensure you use those research findings wisely.

Finally, whenever you are conducting research, don't forget the core principle of this book: consumer insights research is focused **on translating data into insight** and **insight into meaningful recommendations**. Our role is far outside of data collection. We have the great good luck to be able to represent the audience at the table, acting as the bridge between their wants and needs and the client's business. It's all too easy for businesses to get caught up in their own expectations and preferences, leaving the audience without a meaningful voice. In this book, we've shared some examples of that happening, which can lead to disaster. The best way to ensure your company is growing and succeeding, whether you're testing the development of a hot new app, developing a marketing plan a classic breakfast food that has been lagging on the market, or adapting a best-selling novel into a blockbuster film, is to have a sense of what your audience wants and how to talk to them in a way that is compelling and effective. The work consumer insights researchers do is an invaluable part of the business world, and I hope you get to experience the joys of this work in your future careers.

Glossary

A/B testing: A type of testing used to compare audience responses to two iterations or options of the same ad or product (option A versus option B).

Abstraction: Taking concrete data and pulling them out of their immediate context to help find connections and derive meaning.

Academic research: Research conducted in academic environments, often with little money but a lot of time; findings are public and usually published in scholarly journals or monographs.

Applied research: Research intended to answer specific business questions; produce relevant insights that can lead to action.

Anonymity: A participant *cannot* be associated with their data; zero identifying information has been collected and it is impossible to connect the participant with their responses.

Anthropomorphize brands: Bringing brands to "life" in the minds of the consumer to generate insight into perceptions of brands on a wide range of criteria, including how relatable, personable, and appealing they really are.

Archetype: A prototypical example of a person or concept.

Artifacts: Materials produced as a result of creative exercises, such as collages, drawings, and fill-in-the-blank results; these are useful during your analysis and presentation stages of research by offering visuals to add interest and depth.

Attrition: Recruited participants drop out of study and do not complete their commitment (also called "mortality").

Autonomy: An ethical principle stating that researchers must respect the rights, values, and decisions of participants and allow for self-determination; also known as "respect for persons."

Banners: Specific versions of data reports that are focused on one variable or measure.

Baseline: Questions that give you the starting point against which to evaluate change; the first measure that will be used in a benchmarking or tracking study.

Behavioral variables: Measure what we actually *do*, such as time spent engaging with media, frequency of shopping trips or time spent in stores, and money spent on a particular category.

Belmont Report: Published in 1979, this report identified three basic ethical principles that must be followed: respect for persons, beneficence, and justice.

Benchmarking: Asking a question repeatedly over time to measure change.

Beneficence: An ethical principle stating that research must "do good"; this principle is often considered in conjunction with *nonmaleficence*.

Bias: When you find what you want or expect to find rather than truly understanding the audience's perspective.

Bracketing: As a strategy to reduce bias, researchers identify existing biases and beliefs—what you *think* will be learned and why—before research starts.

Business objective: The overarching business-wide goals that drives a research project; consumer insights research usually is only one of multiple approaches happening concurrently to address the business challenges.

Census: Research that includes every member of the population as a participant.

Clarifying interviews: Brief (around 5 minutes max) question and answer sessions that typically happen during an observational experience.

Clearinghouse question: Asked at the end of each research incident, this question gives your participants a chance to share any ideas or information they want to share that didn't come up during questioning.

Closed-ended questions: Questions that have a set of response options from which participants can choose.

Confidentiality: A promise to participants that while you *could* connect someone to their responses, you promise that you won't do so.

Consumer insights research: Research focused on helping clients better understand their consumers or audiences.

Convenience sample: A nonprobability sampling approach wherein respondents are recruited because they are easy to access/find.

Coombs Rule: Be cool; don't be weird.

Correlation: A statistical measure of the relationships between and among variables.

Cost per incidence (CPI): The cost to find individual participants for your research study, based on incidence in the general population.

Cross-sectional research: Research surveys administered one time to a unique sample of respondents.

Data: Material you use to uncover relevant information for your research, including words, numbers, and visuals.

Debrief: A lengthy meeting where a research team works through the data to generate insight and develop the story.

Decks: The industry term for PowerPoint or other forms of slide presentations.

Deductive reasoning: Analysis wherein you start with a prediction about what you will find in your data and then look for your data to support that supposition.

Deliverables: The final written product given to your client typically summarizing the research conducted, findings generated, and recommendations for moving forward.

Demographics: The characteristics of the population that often are used to break down large groups into smaller homogeneous subsets, such as race and ethnicity, sex and gender, household income, marital status, and educational achievement.

Dyads: Research with two participants paired up.

Earned media: Media coverage that is sparked by a company's efforts to get coverage, usually through some form of public relations or publicity campaign.

Elevator pitch: A short paragraph sums up a research story in a compelling and concise way.

Ethics: Researchers have an obligation to do what is *right*, not just following the letter of the law; ethics are about your behavior, not your morals—it's not just about *knowing* right from wrong but also about *doing* the right thing in any given situation.

Ethnographies: Research that uses the context—the surrounding environment—to add richness and relevance to the discussion; abbreviated as "ethnos."

Exhaustive: All possible options are included.

Expert interviews: Interviews with authorities (including opinion leaders) in whatever your study is about.

Extrapolation: Generalizing the results from research with a representative sample to the population as a whole.

Factors: Constructs that represent a summary of individual data points collected in a survey.

Field notes: A record of everything you remember a qualitative research experience, including what was said, anything that stood out, things you want to remember; these also serve as a first level of analysis by including ideas sparked and thoughts on guide iteration.

Focus groups: A research method that provides an opportunity to use group dynamics and conversations to your advantage; the group format allows for a multiplicity of voices and perspectives.

Funnel: Structuring a guide to start with broad, general questions and then move toward specifics.

Guide: The set of questions and instructions used to frame the discussion in qualitative research (in academic research, used interchangeably with "instrument" or "protocol").

Header: The top of the qualitative guide/protocol with mandatory information (study title, date, etc.).

Heuristics: Mental shortcuts that make recall easier.

Hypothesis: A proposed model for the relationships between and among variables.

Incentives: What you offer to persuade (or incentivize) someone to participate in your research, sometimes based on FMV.

Incidence: How easy or hard it is to find qualified respondents for your study from the general population.

Illustrative: Using data to illustrate or add dimension to the points that you are making in your headlines (the themes).

In-depth interviews (IDIs): Long-form interviews that typically last anywhere from one to two hours; ideal for making sense of deeper questions, developing strong insights, and centering individual responses without the risk of group think that comes with focus groups.

Inductive reasoning: An analytic process that starts with data and, through abstraction, leads to the identification of key themes and insights that will help advance understanding of RQs.

Informed consent: Persons, as much as they are capable, get to decide whether they want to participate in the research based on sufficient information and sufficient understanding; participation must be voluntary.

Insight: A deeper, clearer understanding that transcends individual data points.

In situ: Research that happens "in the situation"; associated with ethnographies.

Institutional Review Board: An administrative body established to review proposed research projects within an institution in order to ensure all human-subjects research is conducted ethically.

Internalize: Learning the guide thoroughly in order to maximize flexibility and flow.

Iterative: Not set in stone; can change over time to respond to what is learned.

Jot notes: Quick notes taken in the midst of the qualitative research experience.

Justice: An ethical principle stating people who are equals should be treated equally.

Lifestyle variables: Often are closely tied to psychographics, these variables are focused on shared interests or experiences that would help inform our attitudes and beliefs, such as being a parent or deeply religious.

Likert scale: A scale that uses variations of the same concept in order to measure the gradations in response.

Mall intercepts: A recruitment technique used in nonprobability samples wherein participants are recruited in malls or other public spaces.

Mandatories: "Must-haves" are for your research proposal, often including expectations and formatting for your proposed budget, estimated timelines, your relevant experience and references, and any potential constraints on your end.

Mask: Writing survey questions and responses in a way that makes it difficult for a participant to identify the true subject of the study.

Member checks: Checking the team's initial analysis with participants, allowing for feedback and providing an opportunity to dig more into what participants have to say from an informed perspective.

Metadata: Categories or headers in your reports to help organize your data and make sure it is all properly categorized and coded.

Moderator: Research team member leading a focus group or other qualitative research.

Mortality: Recruited participants drop out of study and do not complete their commitment (also called "attrition").

Mutually exclusive: A respondents fit into only one response category.

N: The N is the total number of participants in your study; if you are using subsets, or smaller homogeneous groups within your total population, you use a small "n" to denote that number.

Negative cases: Experiences reported by your participants that fall outside your story.

Nonmaleficence: An ethical principle stating that research must "do no harm"; this principle often is considered in conjunction with *beneficence*.

Nonprobability samples: Samples that do not follow rigorous scientific sampling procedures and thus the results cannot be generalized to the population.

Nonpublic sources: Secondary material with limited access.

Occam's Razor (also spelled "Ockham's"): The simplest explanation is usually the right one.

Open-ended question: Questions that have no set answers from which to choose and thus participants can answer freely.

Operationalization: Establishing clearly articulated definitions for key concepts and variables.

Order bias: Introducing bias through the order of the questions and responses.

Owned media: Media controlled by a company, such as its own website and digital presence.

Paid media: Media coverage that is paid for by the company or brand, such as advertising messages.

Panel: Pre-recruited respondents who have already been screened and are in an available pool from which you can select.

Participant observation: In this method, you are in the space where the action happens (meeting room, sports stadium, concert venue, movie theater, etc.) as an observer.

Periodicity: Something about the way your sampling frame list is organized makes it more likely one unit on that list will be selected than another.

Pilot test: Thoroughly testing research instruments with members of your target audience in advance to ensure your questions make sense, your language is clear, and you are not priming your respondents.

Primary research: Research that you are conducting to answer specific questions your client has, usually to inform a business decision.

Priming: Revealing information that changes the way participants respond to later questions.

Probability samples: Samples that meet rigorous scientific statistical procedures so findings can be extrapolated to the population.

Probes: Digging in deeper to participants' responses in specific directions to find out more and learn what's underneath.

Projectives: Exercises that require participants project brands or products into an imaginary situation.

Proprietary: Research that is confidential and "owned" by the paying client; usually not released publicly unless it is through a white paper or press release.

Proprietary resources: A type of nonpublic sources, proprietary secondary resources are data collected by a company with the purpose of sharing data only with subscribers or other paid audiences.

Public: Anyone who wants to access the report and/or the data behind the findings can do upon request.

Public sources: Secondary research sources that can be accessed by anyone who wants to find it, typically including governmental or nonprofit research databases that provide raw data as well as analysis.

Psychographics: Variables centered on psychological characteristics, such as attitudes and beliefs, preferences, and aspirations.

Qualitative research: Research grounded in words and nonnumerical data, such as interviews and focus groups.

Quantitative research: Research centered on numbers and statistics; in consumer insights research, most commonly through surveys.

Randomization: Every survey respondent sees response options in a random order; used to reduce or prevent order bias.

Raw data: Data that have not yet been cleaned, organized, or summarized for reporting.

Reactivity: The very act of observing changes the behavior itself.

Recruiters (qualitative): Often are associated with fieldwork facilities, qualitative recruiters have expert knowledge of their geographic area and help consumer insights researchers find participants for their research projects.

Recruiters (quantitative): Companies that specialize in finding respondents for survey research.

Redundancy: No new information or data are being generated on certain topics; in academic research, this is also called "saturation."

Reflexivity: The critical examination of your research and your role in it.

Request for Proposals (RFP): A document created by a company or organization to solicit proposed research plans and establish study parameters.

Research: The act of trying to discover something.

Research design: A specific plan of action for what a research team will do, when, and with how many participants.

Research objective (RO): The research-specific component intended to address the overarching business goals driving a research project.

Research questions (RQs): The "big picture" questions that provide a framework for your research project.

Respect for persons: An ethical principle stating that researchers must respect the rights, values, and decisions of participants and allow for self-determination; also known as "autonomy."

Rigor: Holding ourselves as researchers to the highest of standards and doing things the *right* way rather than the easiest.

Rotation: Response options are rotated; used to reduce or prevent order bias.

Sampling frame: A list of every member of a population.

Scales: A series of related questions that use the same set of answer options.

Screeners: A series of close-ended questions crafted to identify people who fit your defined criteria for your research project.

Secondary research: Research that exists outside and independent of your research project.

Shop-along: The specific activity researchers engage in with; for example, you can do in clothing or grocery stores.

Signposts: Verbal signals that help orient readers to keep them on track with your argument.

Skip patterns: Ensure your participants are only shown relevant questions; if you answer "yes" to a question, you move onto the next set of questions, but if you answer "no" and thus the next set of questions is irrelevant, you skip down to the next applicable section.

Snowball sampling: A nonprobability sampling approach used with hard-to-find populations; once you find a respondent who fits your criteria, you ask for recommendations and assistance with recruiting.

Softball questions: Questions that require little thought and are easy to answer; used to make participants more comfortable as they start their qualitative research experience.

Standardization: All questions are asked the same way and in the same order.

Stimulus: Materials or ideas brought into a research experience with the intention of generating responses from participants.

Stratum: Also known as a segment or subsample in your total sample, a stratum (plural: strata) is a way of looking at one part of a population as defined by the researcher.

Survey research: Research that uses standardized questions to collect information from participants; the most common form of quantitative research in consumer insights research.

Timetable: A summary table at the top of a qualitative instrument to give direction on how long each section of the guide is expected to take.

Themes: Constructs of related consumer insights that help shape and support an overarching story.

Through line: The connection that links insights generated in research.

Topline: An interim presentation that comes mid way through a research project or after each phase of research.

Tracking: Asking a question repeatedly over time to measure change.

Trend studies: Using the same survey or set of questions repeatedly over time to measure change.

Triangulate: Using multiple methods to help address limitations of others.

Variables: Factors researchers are interested in investigating that can vary across participants—in other words, the concepts or characteristics that matter most to our research.

Volunteer sample: A nonprobability sampling approach wherein interested people voluntarily go to your poll and take it.

White space: Open areas that are strategically left blank and free from design elements or text; this also sometimes is known as "negative space."

References

Bryanzug. (n.d.). *Zug portfolio – gap inc – data dashboard – flat* [Infographic]. Creative commons. https://search.creativecommons.org/photos/ec8c96bd-7890-48b5-bffb-5c930467559a

Canva. (2021). *Infographics.* https://www.canva.com/create/infographics/

Claritas. (2020). *Prizim Premier.* https://claritas.com/prizm-premier/

Franklin Covey. (2020). *Habit 2: Begin with the end in mind.* https://www.franklincovey.com/the-7 -habits/habit-2/

Google. (2020). *Google trends.* https://trends.google.com/trends/?geo=US

ICC & ESOMAR. (2016). *ICC and ESOMAR international code on market, opinion and social research and data analytics.* https://www.esomar.org/uploads/pdf/professional-standards/ICCESOMAR_Code _English_.pdf

Insights Association. (2019, April). *IA code of standards and ethics for marketing research and data analytics.* https://www.insightsassociation.org/issues-policies/insights-association-code-standards -and-ethics-market-research-and-data-analytics-0

Insinfo. (n.d.). *Life insurance for Australians* [Infographic]. Creative commons. https://search.creative-commons.org/photos/f9ec0181-f022-4a8a-a30c-e485f732a29e

Kliever, J. (n.d.). *Designing with contrast: 20 tips from a designer.* Canva. https://www.canva.com/learn /contrasting-colors/

Library Services Academic Skills Centre. (2015). *A short guide to signposting in essays.* University of Birmingham. https://intranet.birmingham.ac.uk/as/libraryservices/library/asc/documents/public/Short -Guide-Signposting.pdf

Marks, R., & Jones, N. (2020, February). *Collecting and tabulating ethnicity and race responses in the 2020 census.* United States Census Bureau. https://www2.census.gov/about/training-workshops/2020 /2020-02-19-pop-presentation.pdf

Mercer, A., Lau, A., & Kennedy, C. (2018, January 26). *How different weighting methods work.* Pew Research Center. https://www.pewresearch.org/methods/2018/01/26/how-different-weighting-meth-ods-work/

Mintel Group Ltd. (2020). *About mintel.* https://www.mintel.com/about-mintel

MRI-Simmons. (2020). *About.* https://www.mrisimmons.com/about/

Thomas, J. (n.d.). *40 of the best infographics to inspire you.* Canva. https://www.canva.com/learn/best -infographics/

U.S. Department of Health and Human Services. (2020). *The Belmont Report.* https://www.hhs.gov/ohrp /regulations-and-policy/belmont-report/read-the-belmont-report/index.html

United States Census Bureau. (2020). *Census academy.* https://www.census.gov/data/academy.html

United States Census Bureau. (2020). *Quarterly services survey overview.* https://www.census.gov/services/qss/about_the_surveys.html

United States Census Bureau. (2020). *Questions asked on the form.* https://2020census.gov/en/about-questions.html

WARC. (2020). *About Core WARC.* https://www.warc.com/about-core-warc

Wunderman Thompson. (2020). *Intelligence.* https://intelligence.wundermanthompson.com/

Index

Page references for figures and tables are italicized.

abstraction, 98
A/B testing, 106
academic research: confidence level, 116–19, *118*; defined, 4; ethics, 42–43, *43*, 126; hypotheses, 21, 110; quantitative research design and considerations, 119–20; redundancy, 97; reliability, 120; scales, replication/confirmation of, 120; surveys, 126; validity, 119–20
academic resources, 30–31
Academic Skills Centre at the University of Birmingham, 166
action words, 22
ad, Doritos, 1
adaptability, 54, 76
agency theory, 40–41
American Community Survey, 34
Annual Business Survey, 34
Annual Social and Economic Supplement, 34
Annual Survey of Manufacturers, 34
anonymity, 47–48
anthropomorphizing brands, 85–86, 89
appearance, personal, 14, 15, 72, 196
applied research, defined, 4
applied research ethics. *See* ethics
archetypes, 152–53, 179
arrogance, 15, 70
artifacts, 86
attrition, 6, 128
audience: for client presentation, 197; qualitative data analysis/reporting and, 158; report writing and, 163; sizing, 107; target, 5–6; understanding, 201
audience/market analytics, 32

authority, obedience to, 40–41
autonomy, 43, 60
axes, 189
axis mapping, 189

background, in RFP, 16
banners, 153, *154*
bar charts, *188*, 189
baseline questions, 130
battery questions, 134–35, *135*
"begin with the end in mind," 144, 153, 162
behavioral variables, 5
behaviors, 125, 129
Belmont Report, *43*, 43–44
benchmarking questions, 130
beneficence, 43–44
Best-Worst Test. *See* maximum-difference scaling
bias: bracketing to mitigate, 63; order, 129; as researcher influence, 55; words or phrases, 138
big picture, focus on, 21
Boaty McBoatface, 115
body language, 15, 73, 199
bracketing, 63
brainstorming, 100, 125–26
brand information, 130
"brand parties," 89
brands, anthropomorphizing, 85–86, 89
"buddy groups," 61
budget, 18, 22–23, *24*
business objectives, 16, 20, 21, 63
buy-in, client, 30

Canva.com, 180, *187*, 191

card sorts, 92
category information, in surveys, 129–30
causation *versus* correlation, 109–10
census, 33–34, 111, 132, *133*
Census Academy, 34
Centers for Disease Control, 34
centralized information/data, 31
charts, 158, *188*, 188–89
CIA's World Factbook, 34
clarifying interviews, 57
Claritas PRIZM, 32
clearinghouse questions, 68, 79
clear questions, 137
client name/contact info, in RFP, 16
clients: buy-in by, 30; communicating with,
    124–25; ethics and, 41; focus groups and, 77;
    needs of, 19–20; positive feedback for, 101;
    prioritizing, 8; thanking, 200–201; types, 13
clients, presenting to: about, 195–96; audience,
    knowing, 197; best practices and key
    takeaways, 201; body language, 199;
    expectations, setting, 199; eye contact, 199;
    goal and purpose, 196–97; internalizing,
    198; material, knowing, 198; preparation for,
    197–98; question-and-answer session, 200;
    reading the room, 199–200; staging, 199;
    time constraints, 199; wrapping up project,
    200–201
clients, working with: about, 13–14; best
    practices, general, 14–15; best practices
    and key takeaways, 24; budgets, 22–23, *24*;
    business objectives, 20; needs, understanding,
    19–20; pitching new business, 18–19; research
    objectives, 20; research questions, 20–22;
    RFPs, 16–18, *17*; starting work, 16–23, *17*, *24*;
    terms, key, 25; traits and skills needed, 13–14
closed-ended questions, 134–37, *135–37*
clothing: professional, 14, 72; women's football
    fan, 163–64, 165
cluster analysis, 152–53
cluster sampling, 114
cockiness, 15, 70
code of conduct, Insights Association, 44–45, 47
coding/recoding variables, 148
Collaborative Carl (debrief role), 99
Collaborative Institutional Training Initiative, 42
collages, 83, 87–88, *88*
color, in deliverables, *186*, 186–87
community college students, 83, *84*
comparisons, 108
competitor information, 130

"compliment sandwich," 102–3
concepts, operationalizing, 125
concise questions, 137
confidence, 14–15, 70, 87, 196
confidence interval. *See* margin of error
confidence level, 116–19, *118*
confidentiality, 47–48
conflict management, 7
conjoint analysis, 149–50
consent, informed, 43, 45–47, *46*, 68–69
consistency, 179, 185
constant-sum questions, 135–36, *136*
consumer archetypes, 152–53, 179
consumer insights research: about, 2, 202;
    defined, 3; focus of, 1, 3; mantra, 1, *2. See
    also specific topics*
contrast, in deliverables, 187, *187*
convenience samples, 115
Coombs Rule: about, 69–70; in client
    presentation, 199; in focus groups, 76; in
    interviews, 72; in qualitative data analysis and
    reporting, 96; in surveys, 138
correlation *versus* causation, 109–10
cost per incidence (CPI), 5–6, 23
cover slide, 170
creating lists and organizing data, 85, 91, *92*
creative exercises: about, 83–84;
    anthropomorphizing brands, 85–86, 89; best
    practices, general, 84–87; best practices and
    key takeaways, 93; card sorts, 92; collage,
    83, 87–88, *88*; creating lists and organizing
    data, 85, 91, *92*; data, generating, 84–86; data,
    presenting, 191; digital, 87; drawings and
    storytelling, 88–89; fill-in-the-blank, 89–90,
    90; goal of, 86; instruments and, 69; "magic
    wand" exercise, 90–91; "marketing exec"
    exercise, 92–93; practicing, 87; process, 86;
    "selling," 86–87; terms, key, 94
credibility, 162
cross-sectional research, 140
Current Population Survey, 34
custom tables, 153, 155, *155*

dashboards, 180, *182*
data: accuracy, ensuring, 144–48, *146*; axis
    mapping, 189; bar charts, *188*, 189;
    centralized, 31; charts and graphs, *188*,
    188–89; creative exercises, 191; creative
    exercises for generating, 84–86; in debriefing,
    101; defined, 3; illustrative, 169; line graphs,
    189; manipulation of, 147–48; missing, 148;

organizing, 85, 91, *92*; pie charts, *188*, 189; presenting, *188*, 188–92, *189*, *190*; qualitative quotes, *190*, 190–91; raw, 147; sharing strategically, 169; weighting, 147, 153, *154*

data analysis, planning, 124. *See also* qualitative data analysis and reporting; quantitative data analysis and reporting

data collection. *See* qualitative data collection; quantitative data collection

data.gov, 34

data jockeys, 105

data reports and banners, 153–55, *154–55*

debrief: brainstorming, 100; data, coming back to, 101; defined, 95; ethics and, 101; online, 100; physical space for, 100; preparing for, 156; qualitative data analysis and reporting, 98–101; quantitative data analysis and reporting, 155–57; roles in, 99; through line, looking for, 101

Decennial Census. *See* U.S. Census

decks, 19, 102, *165*, 172, 181–82

deductive reasoning, 156

deliverables: about, 175–76; axis mapping, 189; bar charts, *188*, 189; best practices and key takeaways, 192; charts and graphs, *188*, 188–89; color and contrast, *186*, 186–87, *187*; consistency, 179, 185; creative exercises, 191; dashboards, 180, *182*; data presentation, *188*, 188–92, *189*, *190*; defined, 161; design basics, 183–87; designing, 176–80; formats, 180–83, *181*, *182*; hierarchy, 184–85; infographics, 180, *181*; line graphs, 189; metaphors, 179; newsletters, 181; pie charts, *188*, 189; PowerPoint decks, 102, *165*, 172, 181–82; qualitative quotes, *190*, 190–91; readability, 184, *185*; as RFP component, 16, 18; signposts, *178*, 178–79; story, clear, 176–78, *177*; terms, key, 193. *See also* report writing

demographics: defined, 5; ethics and, 131; questions about, 130–32, *131*, *133*

descriptive statistics, 145–47, *146*

design programs, 177–78

difficult participants, 77–79

digital creative exercises, 87

discrete choice modeling, 150–51

discussions, maintaining, 76–77

disproportionate stratified sample, 113

distribution, 145

"don't know" response option, 139

Doritos ad, 1

double-barreled questions, 137–38

drawings, 88–89

dyads, 61

earned media, 37

editing surveys, 133

elevator pitches, 163–64

embarrassing questions, 138

emotions, reading, 199–200

errors, 116, 162

ethics: about, 39–40; academic research, 42–43, *43*; anonymity, 47; autonomy, 43, 60; beneficence, 43–44; best practices and key takeaways, 50; clients and, 41; confidentiality, 47–48; debriefing, 101; demographic questions, 131; focus groups, 74–75; importance of, 39, 40–41; informed consent, 43, 45–47, *46*; IA code of conduct, 44–45, 47; instruments, writing, 68–69; justice, 44; online research, 49; participant observation, 60; participants and, 41–42; plagiarism, avoiding, 49–50; principles, key, 43–44; privacy laws and legal implications, 48; qualitative quotes, 190–91; researcher and, 42; research team and, 42; respect for persons, 43, 60; surveys, 126, 131; terms, key, 52

ethnicity questions, 132

ethnographies: about, 57–58; in-home, *58*, 59; in situ, 58, *59*, 73–74; online, 58–59, 74; shop-alongs, 58

even-numbered scales, 139

Excel, 191

executive summaries, 102, 171

exhaustive responses, 139

exit polls, 114

expectations, setting, 79, 199

expert interviews, 57

experts, researchers as, 196–97

extrapolating results, 107

eye contact, 78, 199

factor analysis, 151–52

factors, defined, 151

Fair Market Value, 23

Federal Communication Commission, 34–35

Federal Election Commission, 34

fee proposal, project, *24*

fidgeting, 199

field notes, 96

field qualitative data collection: about, 71–72; ethnographies, 73–74; focus groups, 74–79; interviews, 72–73. *See also* qualitative data collection

field trips, 85–86, 89
fieldwork, 96–97
fill-in-the-blank exercise, 89–90, *90*
findings, 23, 171
FiveThirtyEight, 36
flexibility, 54, 76, 108
flow, 125, 169–70
focused, staying, 170
focus groups: about, *60*, 60–61; clients and, 77; difficult participants, managing, 77–79; discussion, maintaining good, 76–77; ethics and, 74–75; flexibility/adaptability in, 76; ground rules, 75; group dynamics, 76; moderator, 74; online, 61; private collection methods, 76–77; relationships, building, 76; respect, 76; starting the group, 74–76; time, watching, 76; wrapping up, 79
Food and Drug Administration, 34
frequency distributions, 145, *145*
funnel, 67–68, 128
fun of consumer insights research, 2, 8–9, 55

generalization, 107
Georgetown Law Library, *48*
Golden Rule, 40, 50
Google Alert, 36
Google Trends, *36*, 36–37
government resources, 33–35
graphs, *188*, 188–89
grocery store, research in, 73–74
ground rules, 7, 75
group dynamics, 76
guides: internalizing, 72–73; iterative, 66, 69; writing, 66–69, *67*
"gut check," 148

handbag study, 151–52
headers, 66, 170
headlines, *178*, 178–79
healthy eating research in kitchen, 73, 74
"Here It Goes Again" video, 83, *84*
heuristics, 179
hierarchy, 184–85
Hispanic origins, 132
hubris, 15
humility, 15, 196
hypotheses, 21, 110, 156

IA. *See* Insights Association
iced tea survey, 127–28, 129
Idea Ingrid (debrief role), 99

ideas: accurate representation of, 49–50; pushing and pulling, 100
iHeartRadio, 102, 140
illustrative data, 169
imposter syndrome, 14–15
incentives, 6, 23
incidence, 108
in-depth interviews, 57
inductive reasoning, 98
infographics, 180, *181*
informed consent, 43, 45–47, *46*, 68–69
in-home ethnographies, *58*, 59
Insights Association (IA), 44–45, 47
in situ ethnographies, 58, *59*, 73–74
Institutional Review Boards (IRBs), 42
instruments: internalizing, 72–73; iterative, 66, 69; writing, 66–69, *67*
internal client materials, 30
internalizing, 72–73, 198
international students, 50
interpreter role, 102
interviews: body language in, 73; clarifying, 57; expert, 57; in-depth, 57; internalizing guide for, 72–73; online, 56–57, 73; participants, centering, 72; rigor, ensuring, 63
investigation, open, 54–55
IRBs. *See* Institutional Review Boards
Israeli-American relations, 85–86
iterative guides, 66, 69

jargon, 123, 137
jewelry, 72
Johnson, Dwayne "The Rock," 109
jot notes, 96
justice, 44

kitchen-sink researchers, 21, 138, 170

language in informed consent forms, 46–47
laws, privacy, 48
Lawson, David, 69
Leader Linda (debrief role), 99
leading questions, 138
lifestyle variables, 5
"like," as filler, 190
Likert scale, 134–35, *135*
line graphs, 189
lists, creating, 85, 91, *92*
long-form reports, 172

"magic wand" exercise, 90–91

mall intercepts, 115
mantra, consumer insights research, 1, *2*
margin of error, 116–19, *118*
"marketing exec" exercise, 92–93
market research emergencies (MREs), 4
masking, 127
matrix questions, 134–35, *135*
maximum-difference scaling (MaxDiff), 150
McCarthy, Melissa, *60*
mean, 145, 146, *146*
measurement error, 116
media: coverage/content, 36–37; earned, 37; owned, 28–29, 30, 37; paid, 30, 37
median, 145, 146, *146*
member checks, 97
memos, 172
metadata, 147–48
metaphors, 179
methods: as report section, *165*, 170–71; as RFP section, 16; triangulating, 62. *See also* qualitative methods
microphones, muting, 80
Milgram Experiment, 40–41, 44
Mintel, 31
mirrors, two-way, 75
mobile devices, 135, *136*
mode, 145, 146, *146*
modeling, discrete choice, 150–51
moderators, 63, 65, 74. *See also* focus groups
mortality, 6. *See also* attrition
movie theater study, 149–51, *150*
MREs. *See* market research emergencies
MRI-Simmons, 31
multiple-choice questions, 134
mutually exclusive responses, 139

n (subsets of total population), 6, 113
N (total number of participants in study), 6, 112, 113
National Commission for the Protection of Human Subjects of Biomedical and Behavioral Research, *43*, 43–44
needs, understanding/assessing, 19–20
negative cases, 98
Negative Nancy (debrief role), 99
negative space, 184, *185*
nervous tics, 15
neutral context, 56
newsletters, 181
Nielsen Company, 32, 114
nonmaleficence, 43

nonprobability sampling, 114–16
nonpublic sources, 29, 30–32
"not applicable" response option, 139
notes: client presentation and, 198; field, 96; jot, 96; in qualitative data collection, 70–71, 80; rigor and, 62
notice, verbal, to difficult participants, 78

obedience to authority, 40–41
objectives: business, 16, 20, 21, 63; research, 6, 16, 20, 21, 170
observation, participant, 59–60
Occam's Razor, 110
odd-numbered scales, 139
OK Go video, 83, *84*
online research: in budget, 23; debrief, 100; ethics in, 49; ethnographies, 58–59, 74; focus groups, 61; interviews, 56–57, 73; qualitative data collection, 79–80; qualitative methods, 61–62
open-ended questions, 134
open investigation, 54–55
operationalizing, 109, 125
order bias, 129
outliers, 100
outlines, 69, 164–65, 198
overhead, 23
owned media, 28–29, 30, 37

paid media, 30, 37
panels, 124, 140
participant observation, 59–60
participants: centering, 72; difficult, 77–79; ethics and, 41–42; prioritizing, 8
perceptions, 129
periodicity, 112–13
personalization, 108
personal questions, 138
Pew Research Center, 35, *35*, 132, 138, 147
pie charts, *188*, 189
pilot testing, 108, 125
pitching new business, 18–19
plagiarism, avoiding, 49–50
planning: for qualitative data analysis and reporting, 124; for quantitative data analysis and reporting, 144; for research design, 5–7
plus/minus lists, 91, *92*
point person, on client staff, 19
polls, exit, 114
population: defining, 124; extrapolating results to, 107; target, 123

Population Estimates Program, 34
positive attitude, 8
possibility, remaining open to, 21
PowerPoint decks, 19, 102, *165*, 172, 181–82
presentation to clients. *See* clients, presenting to
primary research, 27
priming: defined, 108; qualitative data collection
    and, 68; survey writing and, 126, 127, 129
privacy laws, 48
probability sampling, 112–14, *113*, *114*
probes, 69
problems, solving internally, 7–8
processing request sheets, 153
project fee proposal, *24*
projectives, 85, 87–88, 89, 98
project name/title, in RFP, 16
proofreading, 18, 162
proportionate stratified sample, 113, *114*
proposal, project fee, *24*
proposal requirements/mandatories, in RFP, 18
proprietary research, 4
proprietary resources, 31
psychographics, 5
public research, 4
public sources: defined, 29; government
    resources, 33–35; media coverage and content,
    36–37; other publicly available datasets and
    reports, 35–36

qualitative data analysis and reporting: about,
    95–96; best practices, general: during fielding,
    96–97; best practices, general: post-collection
    data analysis, 97–101; best practices and key
    takeaways, 103; debrief, 98–101; terms, key,
    104; topline research reports, 98, 101–3
qualitative data collection: about, 65–66;
    best practices and key takeaways, 80–81;
    ethnographies, 73–74; in the field, 71–79;
    focus groups, 74–79; instruments, writing,
    66–69, *67*; interviews, 72–73; online, 73, 74,
    79–80; recording, 70–71; terms, key, 82
qualitative methods: ethics and, 60;
    ethnographies, 57–59, *58*, *59*; focus groups,
    60, 60–61; interviews, 56–57; online methods,
    56–57, 58–59, 61–62; participant observation,
    59–60
qualitative quotes, *190*, 190–91
qualitative research: defined, 4; quantitative
    research *versus*, 106, 108
qualitative research design and considerations:
    about, 53–54; benefits of qualitative research,

54–55; best practices and key takeaways, 63;
    ethics and, 60; ethnographies, 57–59, *58*, *59*;
    focus groups, *60*, 60–61; importance of, 103;
    interviews, 56–57; limitations of qualitative
    research, 55–56; online methods, 56–57,
    58–59, 61–62; participant observation, 59–60;
    qualitative methods, 56–62, *58*, *59*, *60*; rigor,
    ensuring, 62–63; terms, key, 64
Qualtrics, 124, 134, 139, 150, 192
quantitative data analysis and reporting: about,
    143–44; best practices and key takeaways,
    158–59; data accuracy, ensuring, 144–48,
    146; data reports and banners, 153–55,
    154–55; debriefing and data analysis, 155–57;
    descriptive statistics, 145–47, *146*; planning
    for, 144; reporting quantitative research,
    157–58; statistical models, 148–53, *150*; story,
    telling, 156–57, 158; terms, key, 160; topline
    research reports, 157
quantitative data collection: about, 123–24; best
    practices, general, 124–25; best practices and
    takeaways, 140; clients, communicating with,
    124–25; concepts, operationalizing, 125; data
    analysis, planning for, 124; ethics and, 126,
    131; flow, focusing on, 125; piloting, 125;
    population, defining, 124; questions, writing,
    133–40, *135*, *136*, *137*; responses, writing,
    139–40; surveys, preparing to write, 125–26;
    surveys, structuring, 126–32, *127*, *128*, *130*,
    131, *133*; target population, 123; terms, key,
    141; topics and questions, listing, 124; trend
    studies, 140; variables, operationalizing, 125
quantitative research: defined, 4; qualitative
    research *versus*, 106, 108
quantitative research design and considerations,
    105–21; about, 105–6; academic research,
    119–20; benefits, 107–8; best practices
    and key takeaways, 120; confidence level,
    116–19, *118*; error, 116; limitations, 108–9;
    margin of error, 116–19, *118*; principles and
    characteristics, 109–10; reasons for doing
    quantitative research, 106–7; reliability, 120;
    sampling and samples, 111–16, *113*, *114*;
    scales, replication and confirmation of, 120;
    standardization, 107, 110; terms, key, 121;
    validity, 119–20
Quarterly Services Survey Overview, 34
question-and-answer sessions, 200
questions: baseline, 130; battery, 134–35, *135*;
    benchmarking, 130; clear, 137; clearinghouse,
    68, 79; closed-ended, 134–37, *135–37*;

concise, 137; constant-sum, 135–36, *136*;
demographic, 130–32, *131*, *133*; double-
barreled, 137–38; embarrassing, 138;
leading, 138; listing, 124; matrix, 134–35,
135; multiple-choice, 134; open-ended, 134;
personal, 138; race and ethnicity, 132, *133*;
randomizing, 129; rank order, 135; relevant,
138; responses, writing, 139–40; rotating, 129;
softball, 68, 75, 129; tracking, 130; writing,
137–39; yes/no, 134. *See also* research
questions
quotes, qualitative, *190*, 190–91

race and ethnicity questions, 132, *133*
random error, 116
randomizing questions, 129
rank order questions, 135
rating sliders, 135, *136*
raw data, 147
reactivity, 55
readability, 184, *185*
reading the room, 199–200
reasoning: deductive, 156; inductive, 98
recommendations, 163, 166–67, *167*, 171
recordings, 62, 70–71, 75, 80
recruiting, 5, 22–23
redundancy, 97
reflexivity, 53–54
relationships, building, 76
relevant questions, 138
reliability, 120
Relief Ryan (debrief role), 99
removing difficult participants from group, 78–79
reporting. *See* qualitative data analysis and
reporting; quantitative data analysis and
reporting; report writing
report writing: about, 161–62; audience for, 163;
best practices and key takeaways, 173; cover
slide/header, 170; decks, PowerPoint, 102,
165, 172, 181–82; elevator pitch, 163–64;
executive summaries, 171; findings, 171;
formats, 171–72; goal and purpose, 162–63;
long-form reports, 172; memos, 172; methods,
165, 170–71; outline, 164–65; quantitative
research, 157–58; recommendations, 163,
166–67, *167*, 171; report sections, 170–71;
research objective/research questions, 170;
signposts, 166; story, telling, 163, 167–70,
168–69; terms, key, 174; themes, *165*, 171;
thoughts, organizing, 164–67; transitions, 166;
white papers, 172, *172*

requests for proposals (RFPs), 16–18, *17*
research: about, 2–3; cross-sectional, 140; defined,
2; primary, 27; proprietary, 4; public, 4; as
purposeful, 41. *See also* qualitative research;
quantitative research; secondary research
research design, planning for, 5–7. *See also*
qualitative research design and considerations;
quantitative research design and considerations
researchers: ethics and, 42; as experts, 196–97;
influence of, 55; kitchen-sink, 21, 138, 170
research ethics. *See* ethics
research objectives, 6, 16, 20, 21, 170
research questions (RQs): developing, 20–22;
examples, 21–22; in guide, 66; hypotheses
versus, 110; importance of, 144; keeping in
mind, 63; planning for research design, 6; in
report, 170; in RFP, 16
research teams, 7–8, 42, 63
resources: academic, 30–31; government, 33–35;
nonpublic, 29, 30–32; proprietary, 31; publicly
available, 35–36; sharing, 169; vetting, 29–30.
See also public sources
respect, 43, 76
respondents, deleting, 148
responses, writing, 139–40
results: extrapolating, 107; overstated, 109;
summarizing, 107
RFPs. *See* requests for proposals
rigor, 55, 62–63
rotating questions, 129
RQs. *See* research questions

sample size, 108, 117–19, *118*
sampling: about, 111; cluster, 114; convenience,
115; disproportionate stratified, 113;
nonprobability, 114–16; probability, 112–14,
113, *114*; proportionate stratified, 113, *114*;
simple random, 112–13; snowball, 115–16;
stratified random, 113, *113*; volunteer, 115
sampling error, 116
sampling frame, 112
Saturday Night Live, 60
scales: defined, 120; even-numbered, 139; Likert,
134–35, *135*; maximum-difference, 150; odd-
numbered, 139; replication/confirmation of,
120; semantic differential, 136–37, *137*
scents, 72
screeners, 5, 126–28, *127*, *128*
scripts, 198
secondary research: about, 27; academic
resources, 30–31; amount needed, 28;

audience/market analytics, 32; best practices and key takeaways, 37; centralized information and data, 31; conducting, 28–29; defined, 27; government resources, 33–35; importance of, 15, 19; internal client materials, 30; media coverage and content, 36–37; nonpublic sources, 29, 30–32; proprietary resources, 31; public sources, 29, 32–37; questions, defining, 28–29; sources, 29–37; terms, key, 38; trend analysis, 32; vetting sources, 29–30

semantic differential scales, 136–37, *137*
shoes, 15
shop-alongs, 58
shortcuts, avoiding, 63
signposts, 166, *178*, 178–79
silence, 76
Silver, Nate, 36
simple random sampling, 112–13
skip patterns, 129
slang, 138
SMART business objectives, 20
snowball sampling, 115–16
softball questions, 68, 75, 129
sources. *See* resources
standardization, 107, 110
standing behind difficult participants, 78
starting work: budgets, 22–23, *24*; business objectives, 20; needs, understanding and assessing, 19–20; pitching new business, 18–19; research objectives, 20; research questions, 20–22; RFPs, 16–18, *17*
statistical models: cluster analysis, 152–53; conjoint analysis, 149–50; discrete choice modeling, 150–51; factor analysis, 151–52; maximum-difference scaling, 150
story, telling: as creative exercise, 88–89; data, sharing strategically, 169; deliverables, 176–78, *177*; flow, focusing on, 169–70; focused, staying, 170; quantitative data analysis and reporting, 156–57, *158*; report writing, 163, 167–70, *168–69*
storyteller role, 102
stratified random sample, 113, *113*
stratum, defined, 113
students: community college, 83, *84*; international, 50
Stylus, 32
summarizing results, 107
Survey Monkey, 138, 192

surveys: about, 106; body of, 128–30, *130*; brainstorming, 125–26; brand information, 130; as budget component, 23; category information, 129–30; competitor information, 130; demographic questions, 130–32, *131*, *133*; editing, 133; ethics and, 126, 131; preparing to write, 125–26; race and ethnicity questions, 132, *133*; screeners, 126–28, *127*, *128*; softball questions, 129; structuring, 126–32; values, perceptions, and behaviors, 129

tables, custom, 153, 155, *155*
talent, additional, 23
"talk to the hand," 78
target audience, 5–6
target population, 123
tattoos, 14
teams, research, 7–8, 42, 63
technology issues, 79–80
television channel viewership survey, *128*, *130*
"tells," 15
text-based programs, 176–77, *177*
themes, 102, 165, 171
through line, 101
tics, nervous, 15
time constraints, 56, 76, 199
timetables, 6, 16, 22, 66, *67*
topics, listing, 124
topline presentations, 16, 18, 98, 101–3, 157
tracking questions, 130
transitions, 69, 166
travel, as budget component, 22
trend analysis, 32
trend studies, 140
Trendwatching, 32
triangulating methods, 62
trust, 63
typos, 162

U.S. Census, 33–34, 111, 132, *133*
UNICEF, 35
users of consumer insights research, 1

validity, 119–20
values, 129
variables: behavioral, 5; coding/recoding, 148; defined, 5; lifestyle, 5; operationalizing, 125; relationships among, 107. *See also* demographics; psychographics
verbal notice, to difficult participants, 78

verbatims, 190
vetting secondary research sources, 29–30
video recordings, 75
visual decks, 19, 102, *165*, 172, 181–82
volunteer samples, 115
WARC, 31, *32*
weighting, 147, 153, *154*
white papers, 172, *172*
white space, 184, *185*

women's football fan clothing, 163–64, 165
Word, 176, *177*
words: action, 22; biased, 138
World Bank, 35
World Factbook, 34
World Health Organization, 35
Wunderman Thompson Intelligence, 32

yes/no questions, 134

About the Author

Danielle Sarver Coombs, PhD, is a professor in the School of Media and Journalism at Kent State University. She is an author, media commentator, and consultant on areas related to sports, politics, and politics of sport. Prior to joining Kent State, Danielle was a consumer insights researcher and brand consultant in New York and Cleveland, working on a wide range of high-profile brands in media, fashion, consumer packaged goods, and nonprofits/public service.